COFFIN BOUND™

Volume 1

HAPPY ASHES

image®

ARTIST
DANI

WRITER
Dan **WATTERS**

COLORIST
Brad **SIMPSON**

LETTERER
Aditya **BIDIKAR**

GRAPHIC DESIGNER
Emma **PRICE**

DON'T MISS IT!
JUST 500ft

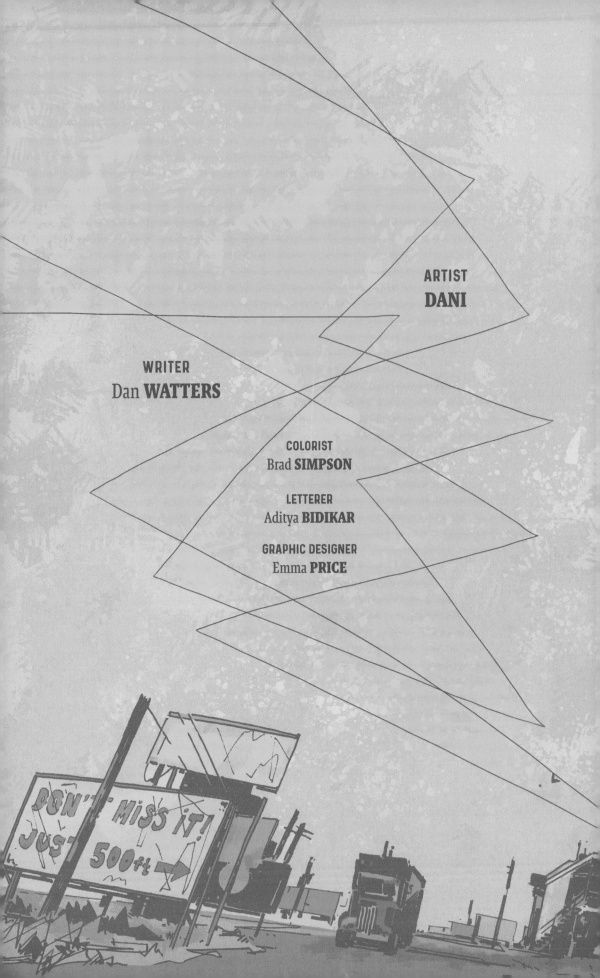

"INDISTINCT,
the shape of us."

I remember reading an early draft of the first issue of *Coffin Bound*. There was no art for it yet. Dani hadn't inked magic on to paper. It was words, in courier—descriptions, characters, dialogue. I remember telling Dan I thought it was good. It was very good, but I couldn't quite get a grip on what he was aiming for.

I've just finished re-reading the first volume before I sat down to write this and I'm grinning, amused at my own short-sightedness and in admiration of Dan's brilliance. It's there, a bigger picture, a beastly shape that lumbers behind the pages, panels and scenes of this book– one that reveals its flesh as we peel back layers of skin.

"Do you think we exist as a sum of our parts? Or in reducing ourselves, you and I, do we change critically?"

Coffin Bound is about shedding. Its central aesthetic is all over the pages of course. A protagonist discarding her life, a cult shedding the imperfect, replacing it with the "better". Strippers showing flesh and a particularly brilliant character, obsessed with the obliteration of surface—all discoveries to be made in the reading. But *Coffin Bound*'s aesthetic perforates its boundaries. It seeps out from the story, into the form, into the art. The dialogue sheds all things superfluous. There is no stuttering. No inconsequential small-talk. Every word and line is ripe with meaning and flavor. Each sentence, brimming with character. And, even with the dramatic settings and locations, there is almost a sense of watching a play in a small and intimate theatre. The actors fill the space with their character. Your experience of their performance is visceral. And by the end, the story sheds its characters until all that remain are the consequences.

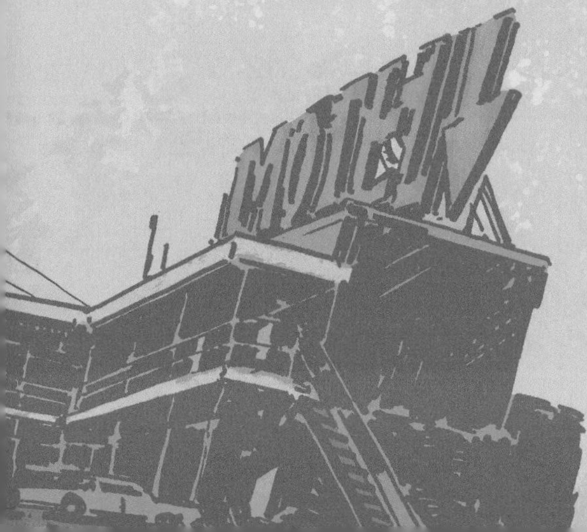

Dani's art imbibes this aesthetic in interesting ways. Her work is detailed. From the mess on Izzy's floor to the detail of the possessions in the backseat of her car. It's all there but look closer. Smoke is a tangle of marks. A face in the dark is not drawn with lines but insinuated through their absence. And where we need to see only a shape, the ink and the art give way. The edges of panels themselves morph to silhouettes in negative space. The stark reality of this high-contrast world is made by shedding the unnecessary, by having no need for greys where black and white will do.

"What if we had it all wrong? What if the sums of our parts—all our surfaces and objects—are just a part of the tangle of us?"

For me, the drive to create art comes from the need to express something that is, at least in part, abstract. Something human that is conveyed not by a singular object, but by a tangle. Comics has had a difficult time contending with its own existence as an artform. It is lazily dismissed as juvenile or pulp or genre. It can, on occasion, be all these things. Certainly, there are these elements in *Coffin Bound*, but when you have arrived at its last page, the artistic merit of this comic is unquestionable. The complex and nuanced exploration of its own artistic tangle is enthralling. Through the guns, bullets, dead-vultures and earth-eaters, it has something to say in abstraction. A commentary about who we are, what we are made of, what we will leave behind and what we mean to those around us.

"GLUB GLUB"

—**Ram V**, London

" My last request:
Everything I leave behind me ...
to be **BURNED UNREAD."**
— FRANZ KAFKA

$3.99 US • Issue ONE • $3.99 US • Issue ONE • $3.99 US • Issue ONE

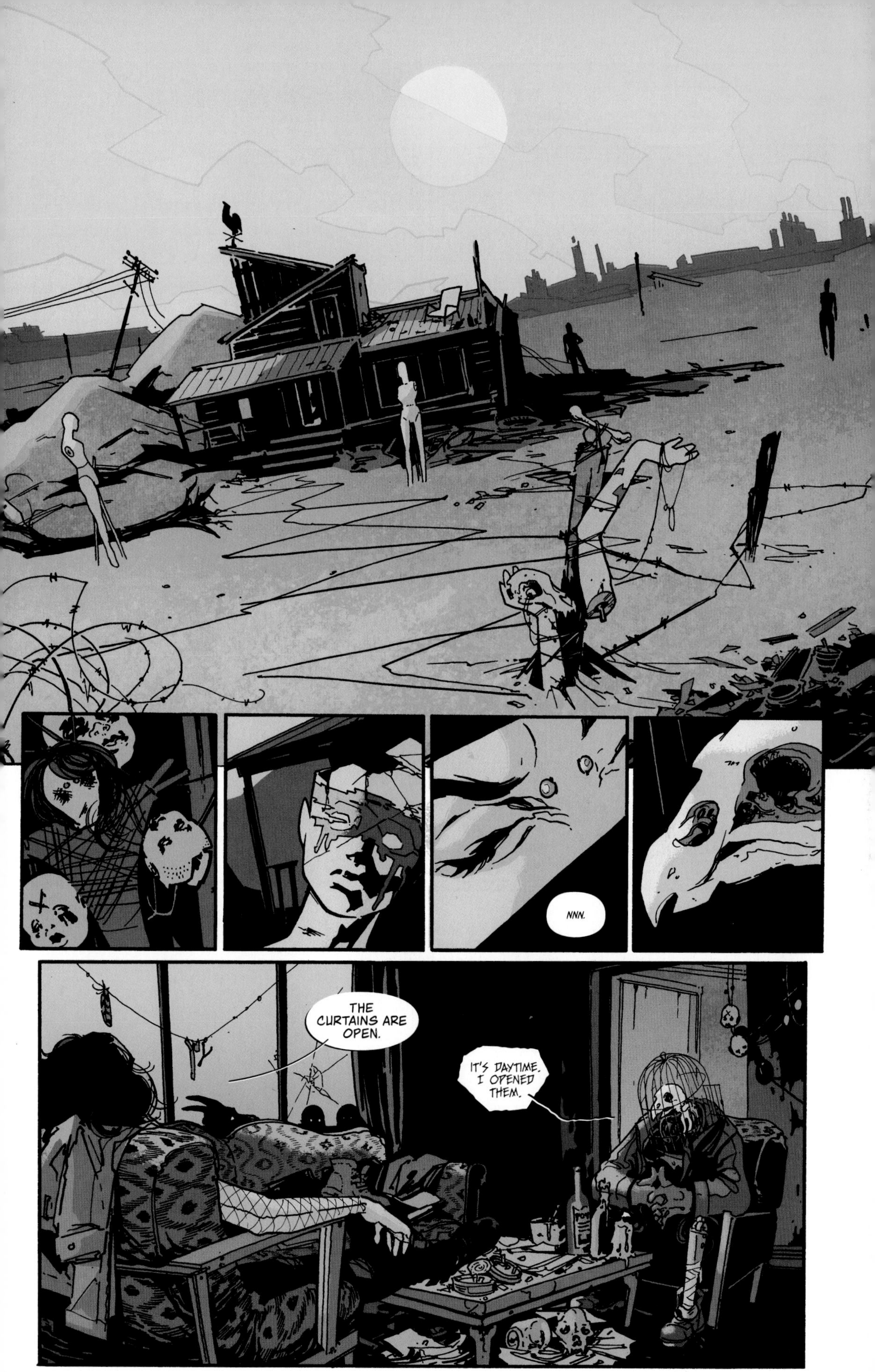
NNN.
THE CURTAINS ARE OPEN.
IT'S DAYTIME. I OPENED THEM.

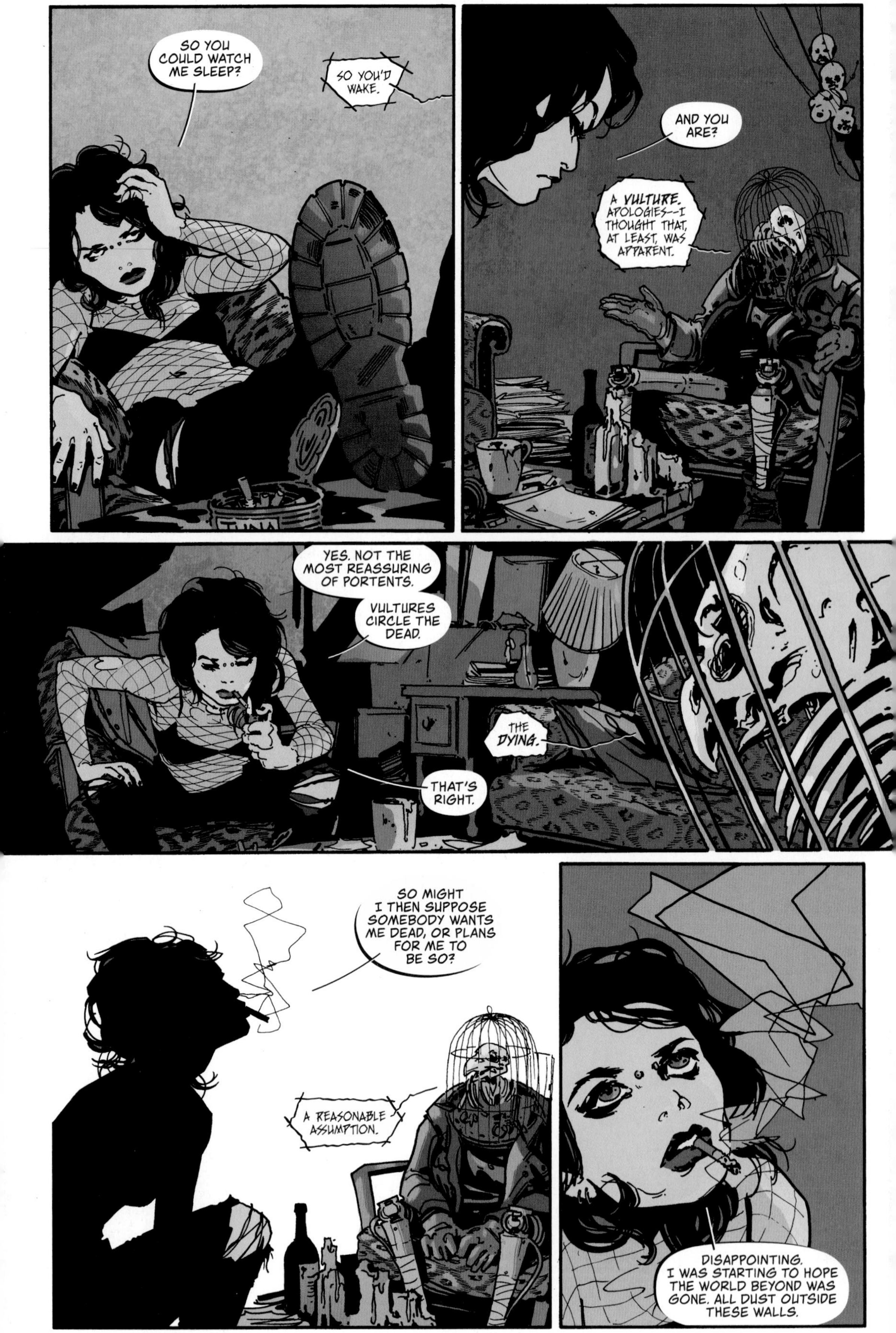
SO YOU COULD WATCH ME SLEEP?
SO YOU'D WAKE.
AND YOU ARE?
A VULTURE. APOLOGIES--I THOUGHT THAT, AT LEAST, WAS APPARENT.
YES. NOT THE MOST REASSURING OF PORTENTS.
VULTURES CIRCLE THE DEAD.
THE DYING.
THAT'S RIGHT.
SO MIGHT I THEN SUPPOSE SOMEBODY WANTS ME DEAD, OR PLANS FOR ME TO BE SO?
A REASONABLE ASSUMPTION.
DISAPPOINTING. I WAS STARTING TO HOPE THE WORLD BEYOND WAS GONE. ALL DUST OUTSIDE THESE WALLS.

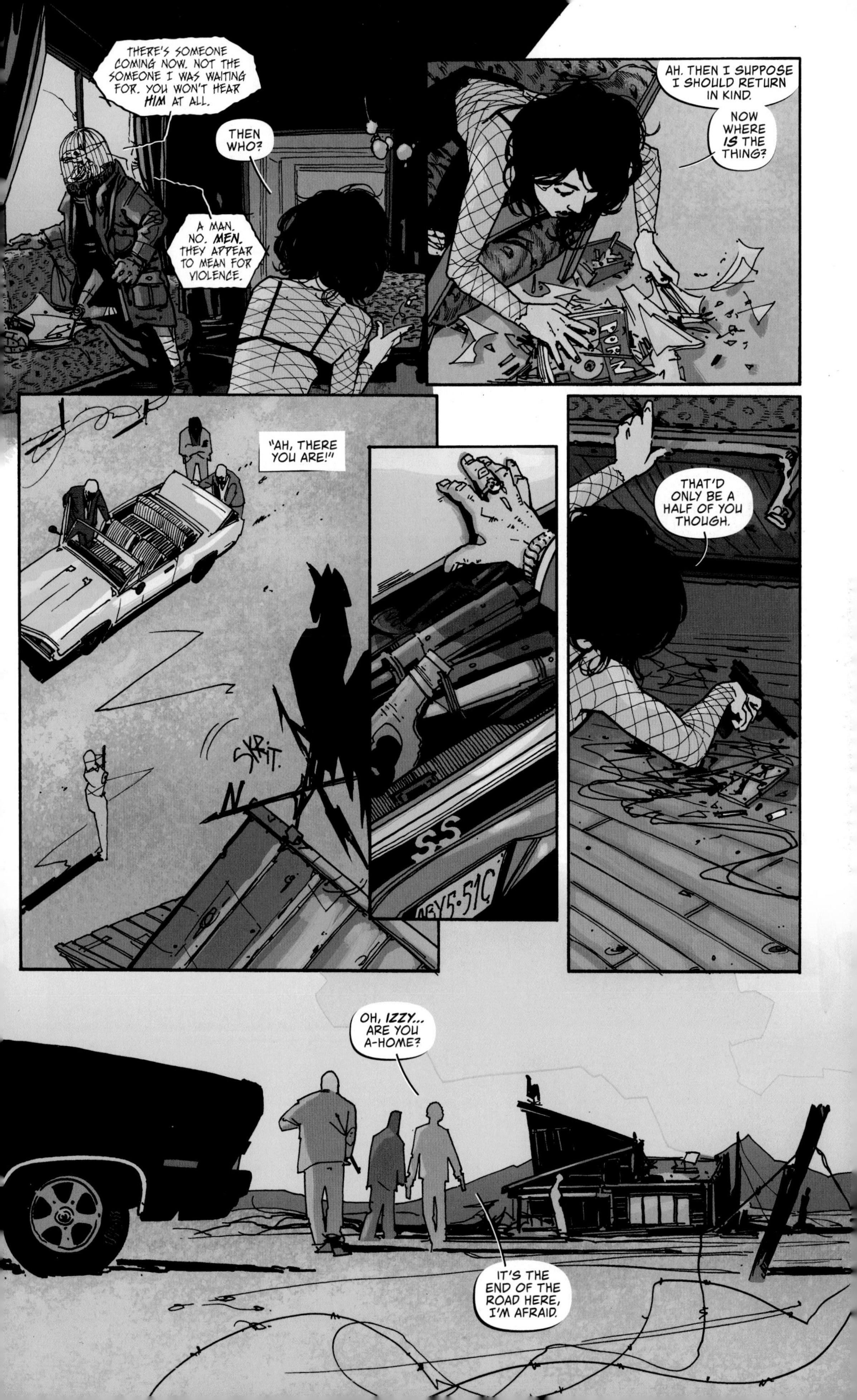
THERE'S SOMEONE COMING NOW. NOT THE SOMEONE I WAS WAITING FOR. YOU WON'T HEAR HIM AT ALL.
THEN WHO?
A MAN. NO. MEN. THEY APPEAR TO MEAN FOR VIOLENCE.
AH. THEN I SUPPOSE I SHOULD RETURN IN KIND.
NOW WHERE IS THE THING?
PORN
"AH, THERE YOU ARE!"
SKRIT.
THAT'D ONLY BE A HALF OF YOU THOUGH.
OH, IZZY... ARE YOU A-HOME?
IT'S THE END OF THE ROAD HERE, I'M AFRAID.

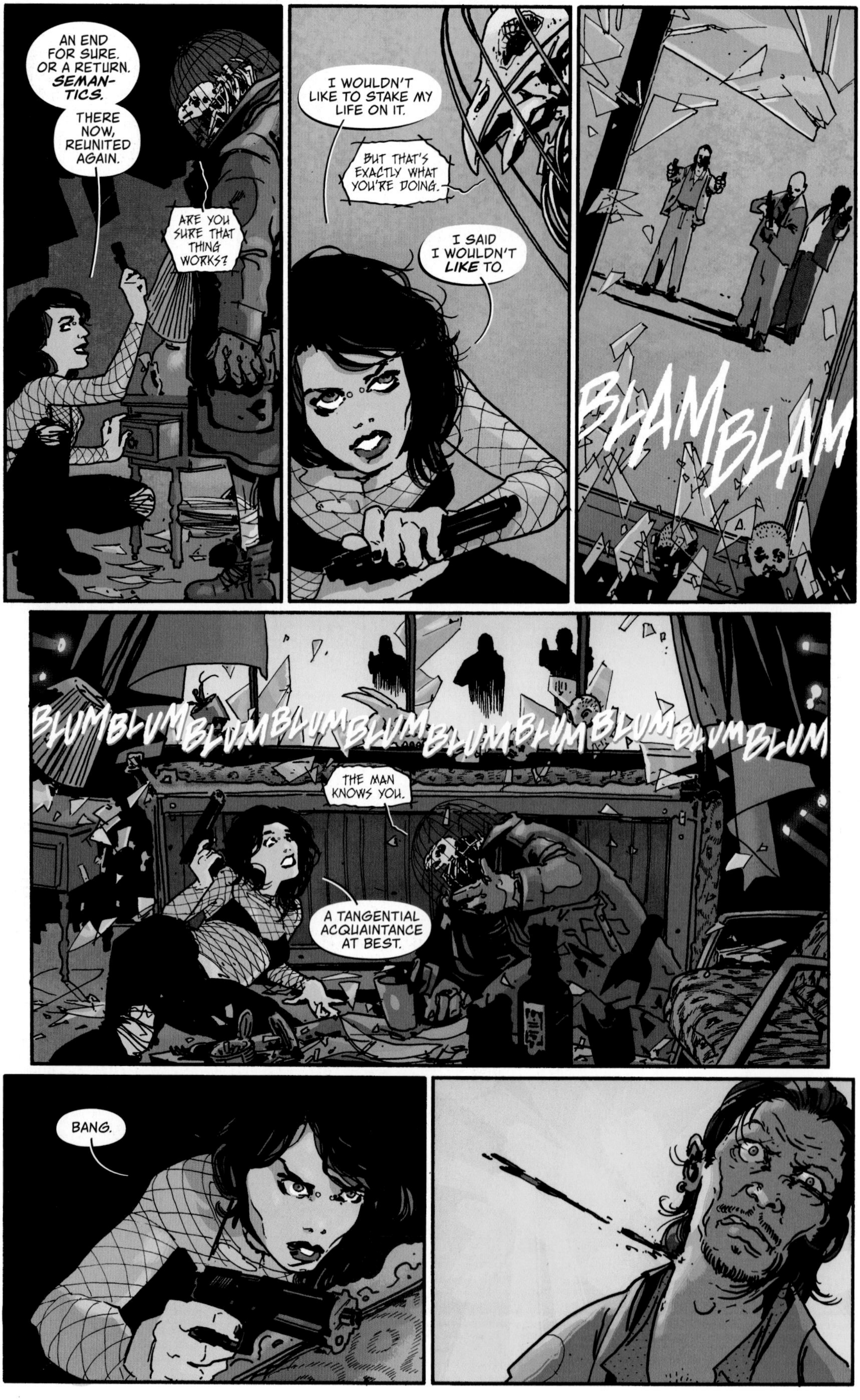
AN END FOR SURE. OR A RETURN. SEMANTICS.
THERE NOW, REUNITED AGAIN.
ARE YOU SURE THAT THING WORKS?
I WOULDN'T LIKE TO STAKE MY LIFE ON IT.
BUT THAT'S EXACTLY WHAT YOU'RE DOING.
I SAID I WOULDN'T LIKE TO.
BLAM BLAM
BLUM BLUM BLUM BLUM BLUM BLUM BLUM BLUM BLUM BLUM
THE MAN KNOWS YOU.
A TANGENTIAL ACQUAINTANCE AT BEST.
BANG.

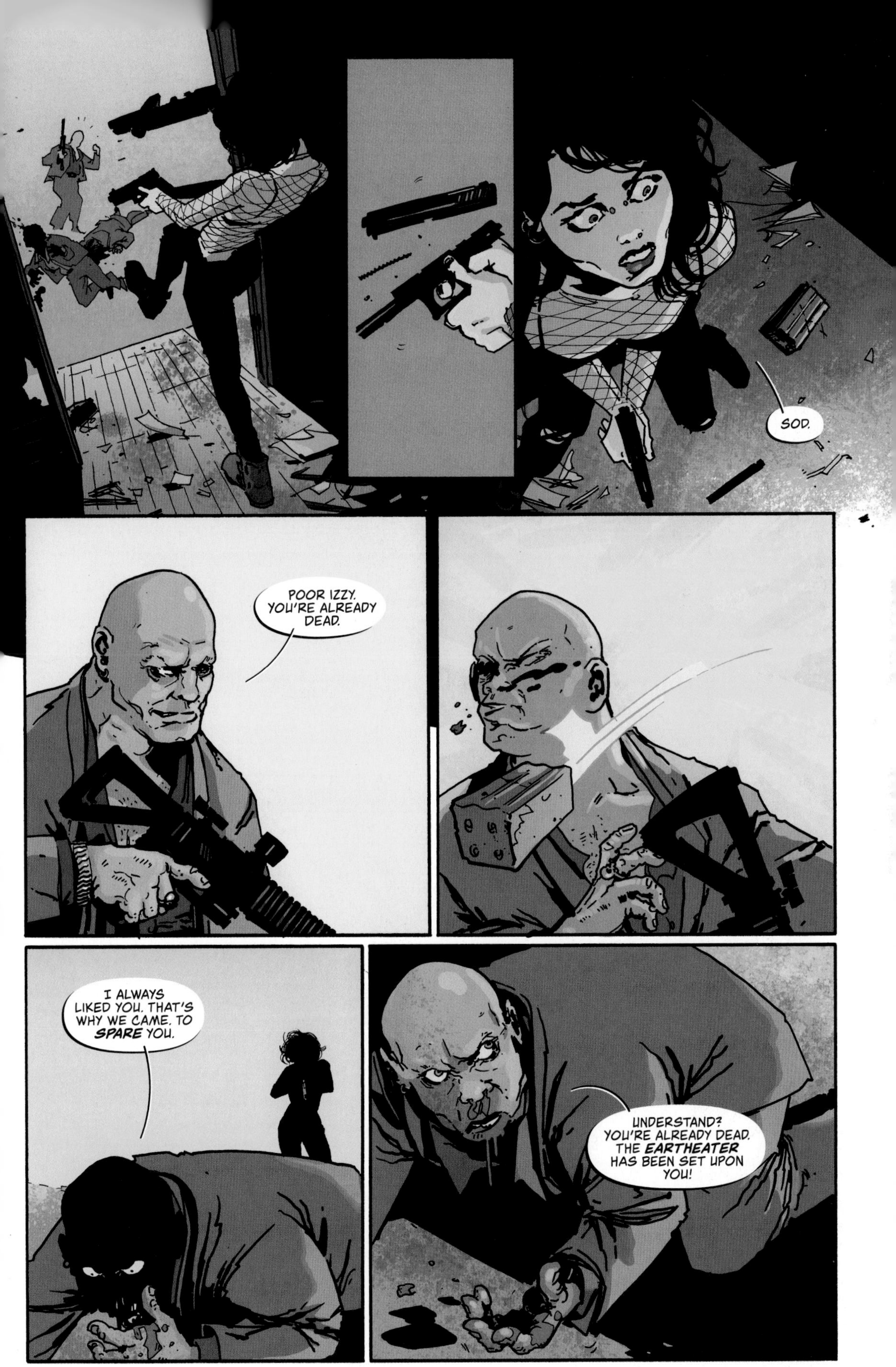
SOD.
POOR IZZY. YOU'RE ALREADY DEAD.
I ALWAYS LIKED YOU. THAT'S WHY WE CAME. TO SPARE YOU.
UNDERSTAND? YOU'RE ALREADY DEAD. THE EARTHEATER HAS BEEN SET UPON YOU!

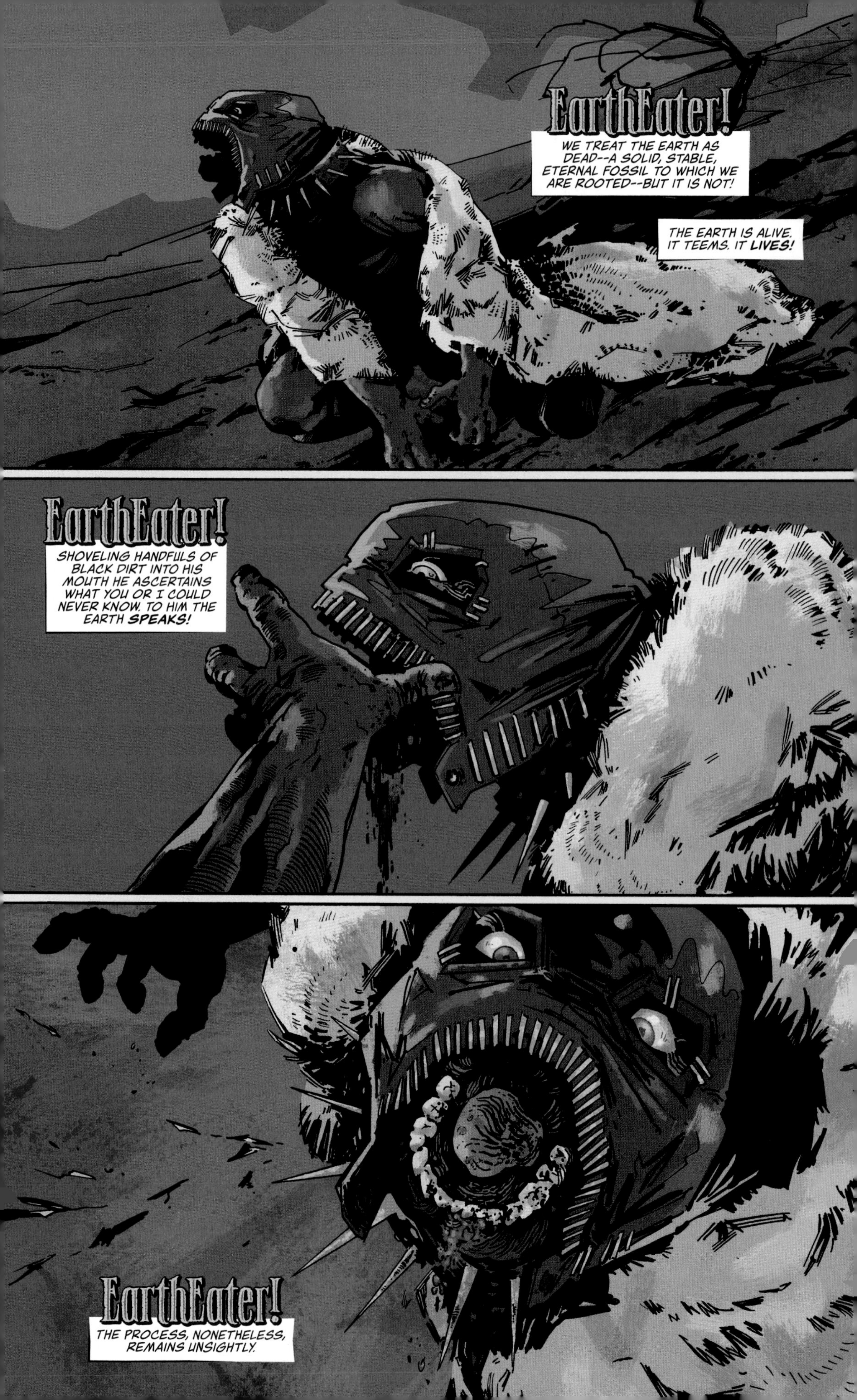
EarthEater!
WE TREAT THE EARTH AS DEAD--A SOLID, STABLE, ETERNAL FOSSIL TO WHICH WE ARE ROOTED--BUT IT IS NOT!
THE EARTH IS ALIVE. IT TEEMS. IT LIVES!
EarthEater!
SHOVELING HANDFULS OF BLACK DIRT INTO HIS MOUTH HE ASCERTAINS WHAT YOU OR I COULD NEVER KNOW. TO HIM THE EARTH SPEAKS!
EarthEater!
THE PROCESS, NONETHELESS, REMAINS UNSIGHTLY.

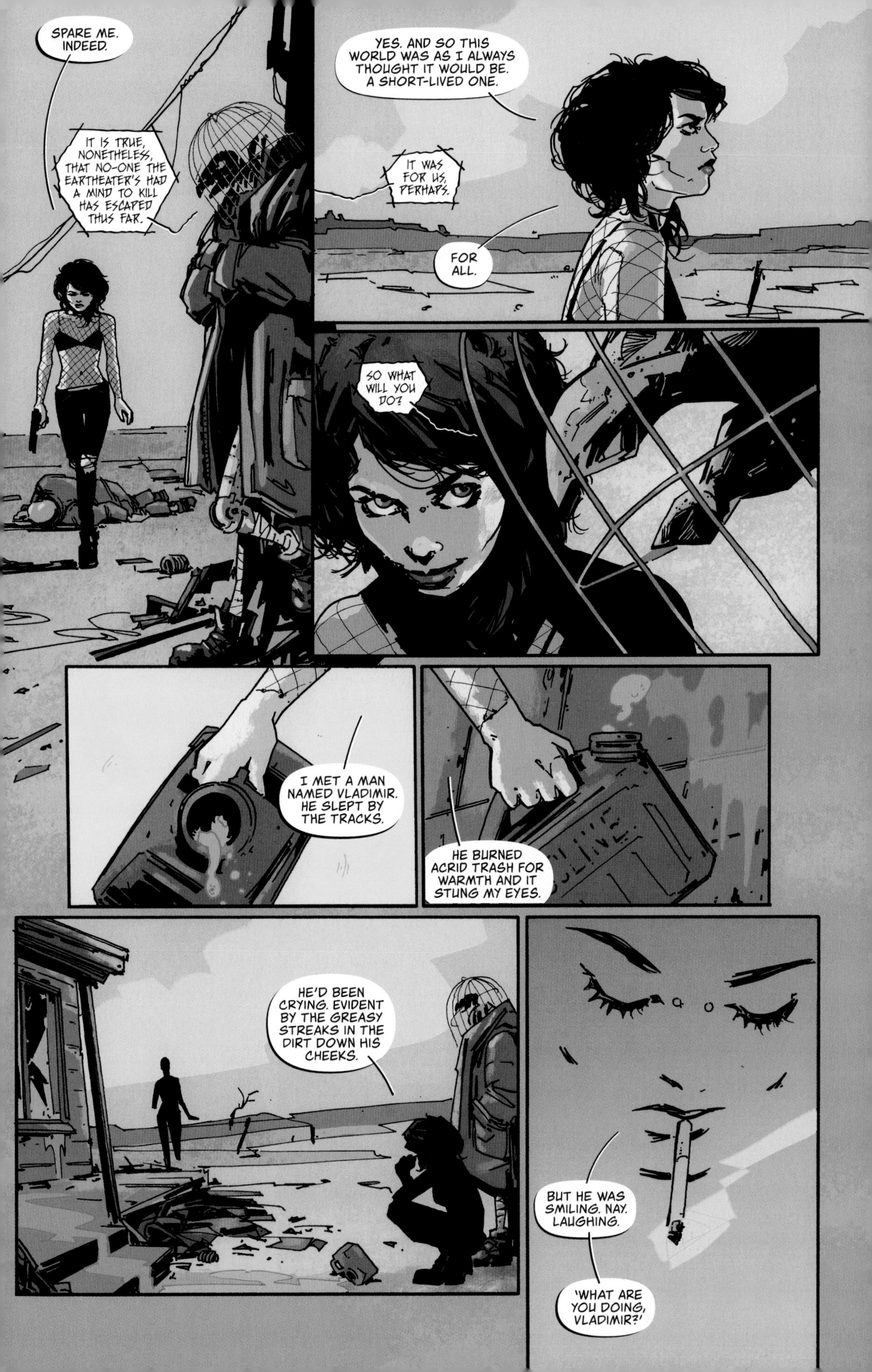
SPARE ME. INDEED.
IT IS TRUE, NONETHELESS, THAT NO-ONE THE EARTHEATER'S HAD A MIND TO KILL HAS ESCAPED THUS FAR.
YES. AND SO THIS WORLD WAS AS I ALWAYS THOUGHT IT WOULD BE. A SHORT-LIVED ONE.
IT WAS FOR US, PERHAPS.
FOR ALL.
SO WHAT WILL YOU DO?
I MET A MAN NAMED VLADIMIR. HE SLEPT BY THE TRACKS.
HE BURNED ACRID TRASH FOR WARMTH AND IT STUNG MY EYES.
HE'D BEEN CRYING. EVIDENT BY THE GREASY STREAKS IN THE DIRT DOWN HIS CHEEKS.
BUT HE WAS SMILING. NAY. LAUGHING.
'WHAT ARE YOU DOING, VLADIMIR?'

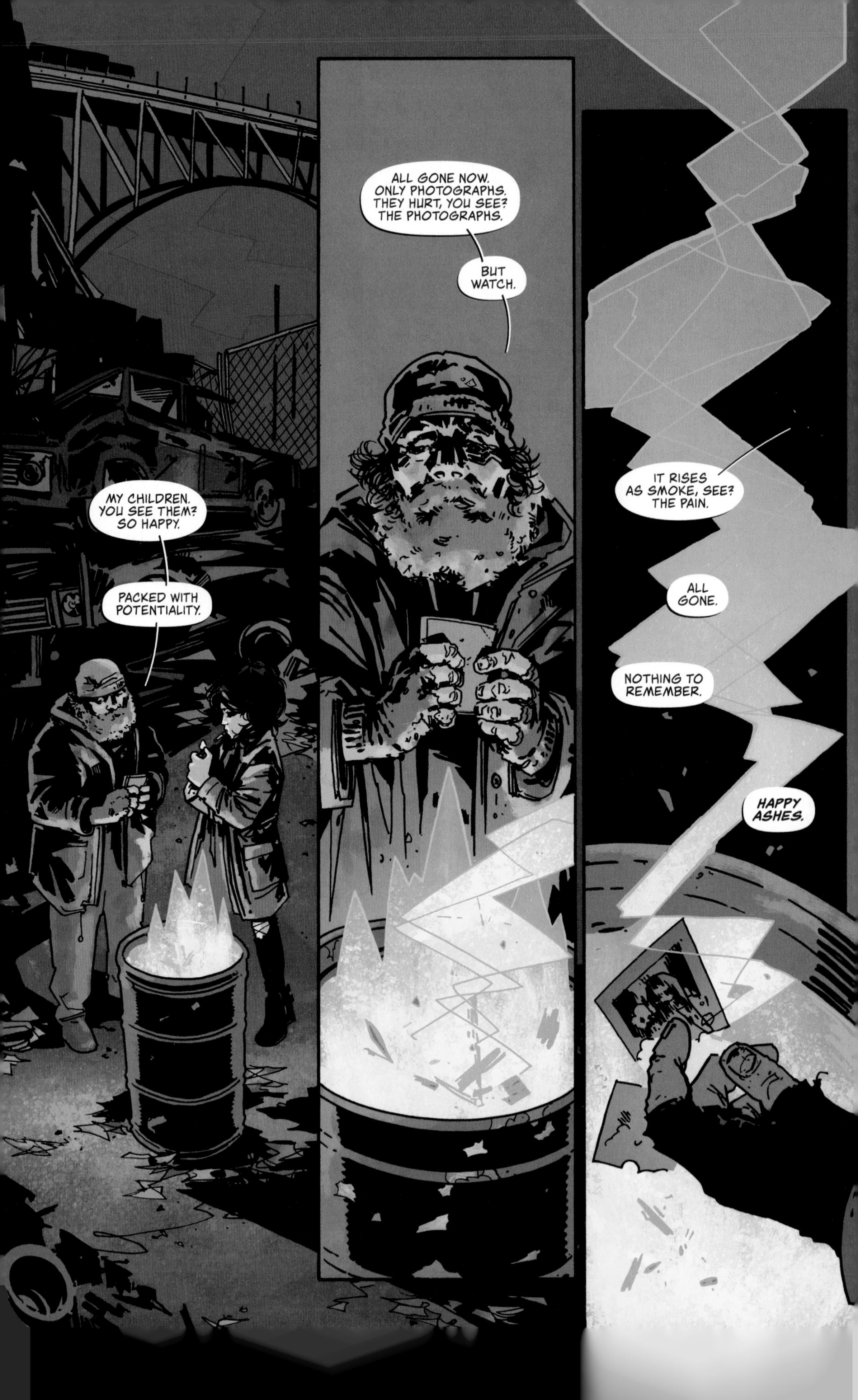

MY CHILDREN. YOU SEE THEM? SO HAPPY.
PACKED WITH POTENTIALITY.
ALL GONE NOW. ONLY PHOTOGRAPHS. THEY HURT, YOU SEE? THE PHOTOGRAPHS.
BUT WATCH.
IT RISES AS SMOKE, SEE? THE PAIN.
ALL GONE.
NOTHING TO REMEMBER.
HAPPY ASHES.

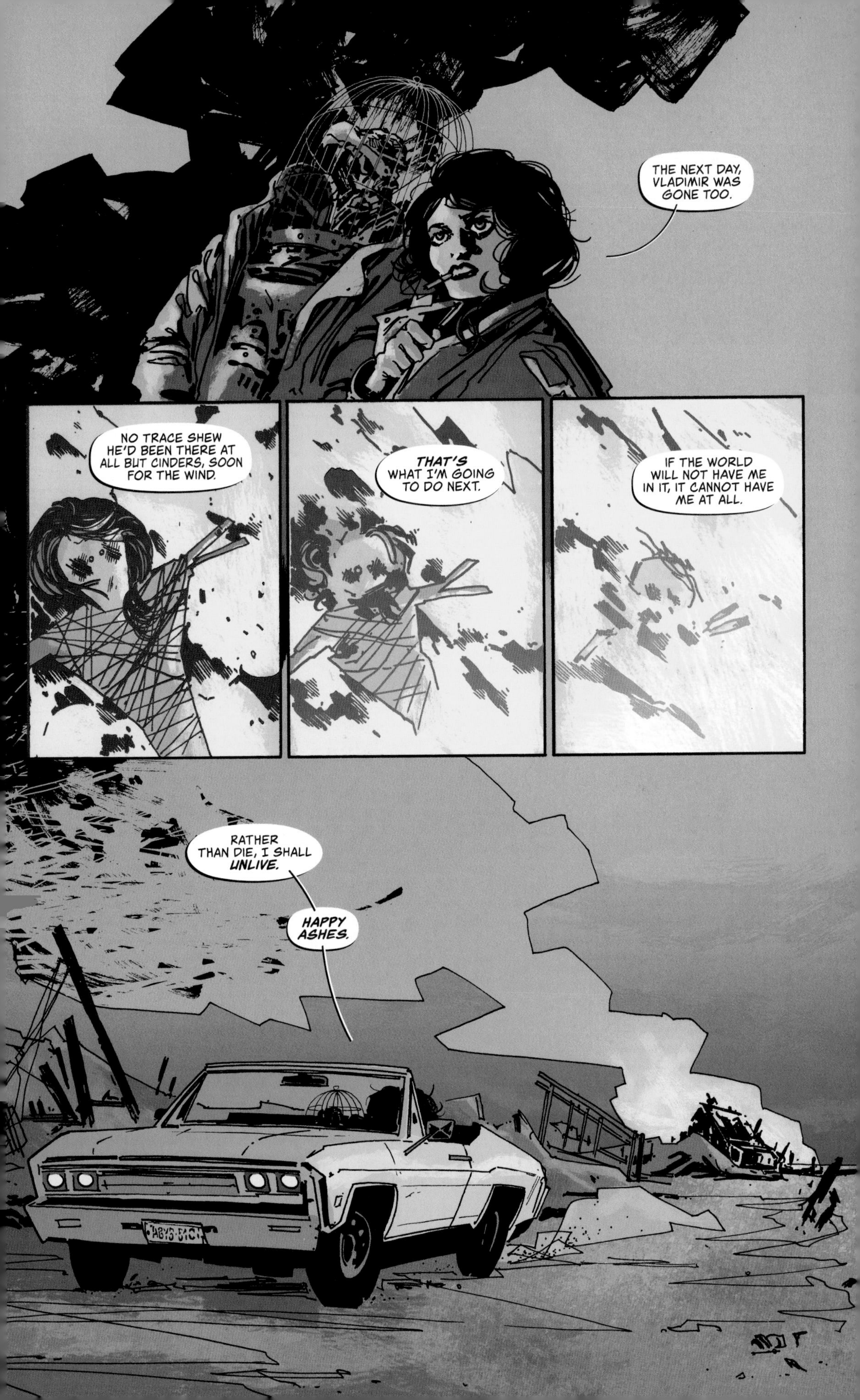
THE NEXT DAY, VLADIMIR WAS GONE TOO.
NO TRACE SHEW HE'D BEEN THERE AT ALL BUT CINDERS, SOON FOR THE WIND.
THAT'S WHAT I'M GOING TO DO NEXT.
IF THE WORLD WILL NOT HAVE ME IN IT, IT CANNOT HAVE ME AT ALL.
RATHER THAN DIE, I SHALL UNLIVE.
HAPPY ASHES.

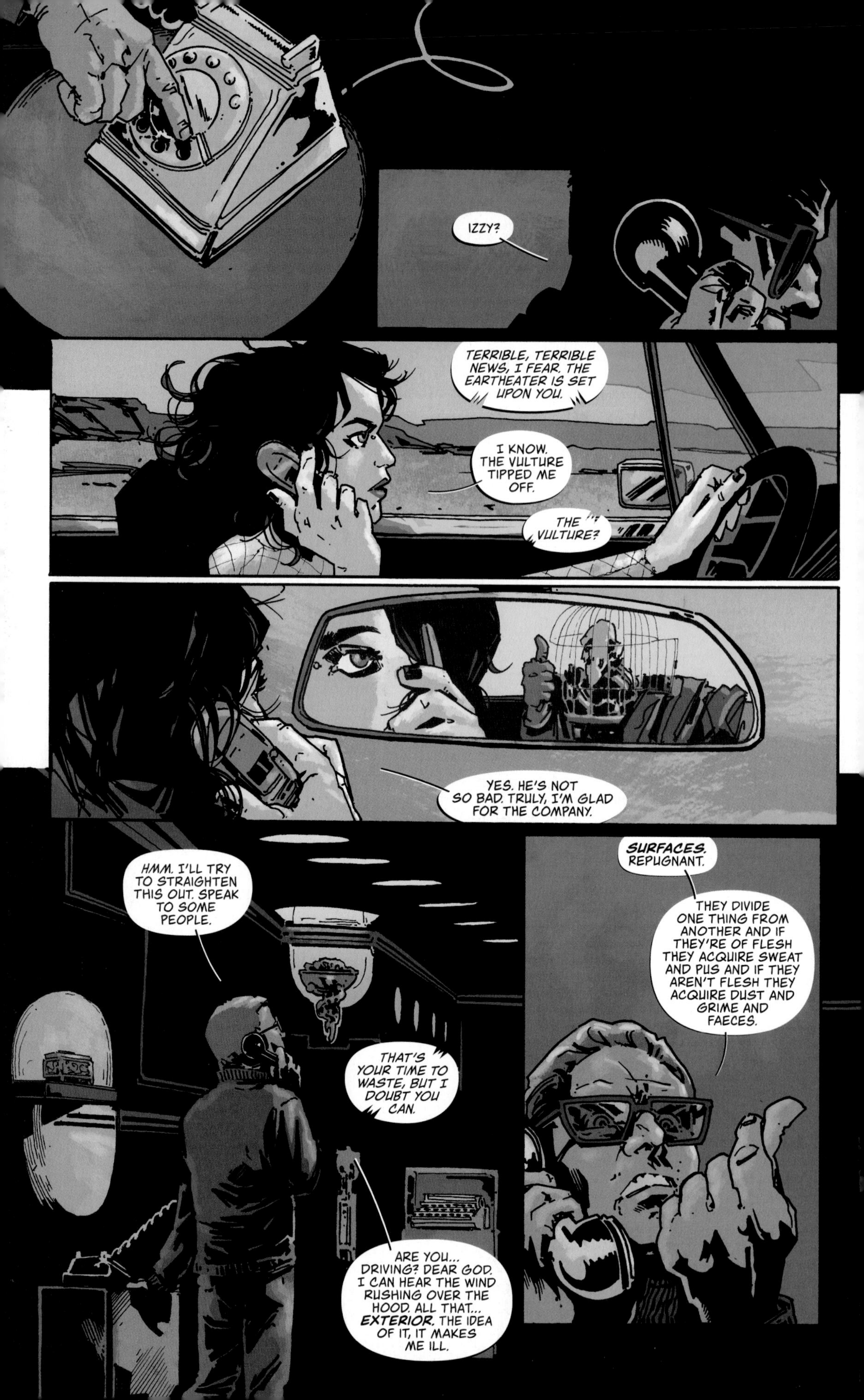
IZZY?
TERRIBLE, TERRIBLE NEWS, I FEAR. THE EARTHEATER IS SET UPON YOU.
I KNOW. THE VULTURE TIPPED ME OFF.
THE VULTURE?
YES. HE'S NOT SO BAD. TRULY, I'M GLAD FOR THE COMPANY.
HMM. I'LL TRY TO STRAIGHTEN THIS OUT. SPEAK TO SOME PEOPLE.
THAT'S YOUR TIME TO WASTE, BUT I DOUBT YOU CAN.
ARE YOU... DRIVING? DEAR GOD. I CAN HEAR THE WIND RUSHING OVER THE HOOD. ALL THAT... EXTERIOR. THE IDEA OF IT, IT MAKES ME ILL.
SURFACES. REPUGNANT.
THEY DIVIDE ONE THING FROM ANOTHER AND IF THEY'RE OF FLESH THEY ACQUIRE SWEAT AND PUS AND IF THEY AREN'T FLESH THEY ACQUIRE DUST AND GRIME AND FAECES.

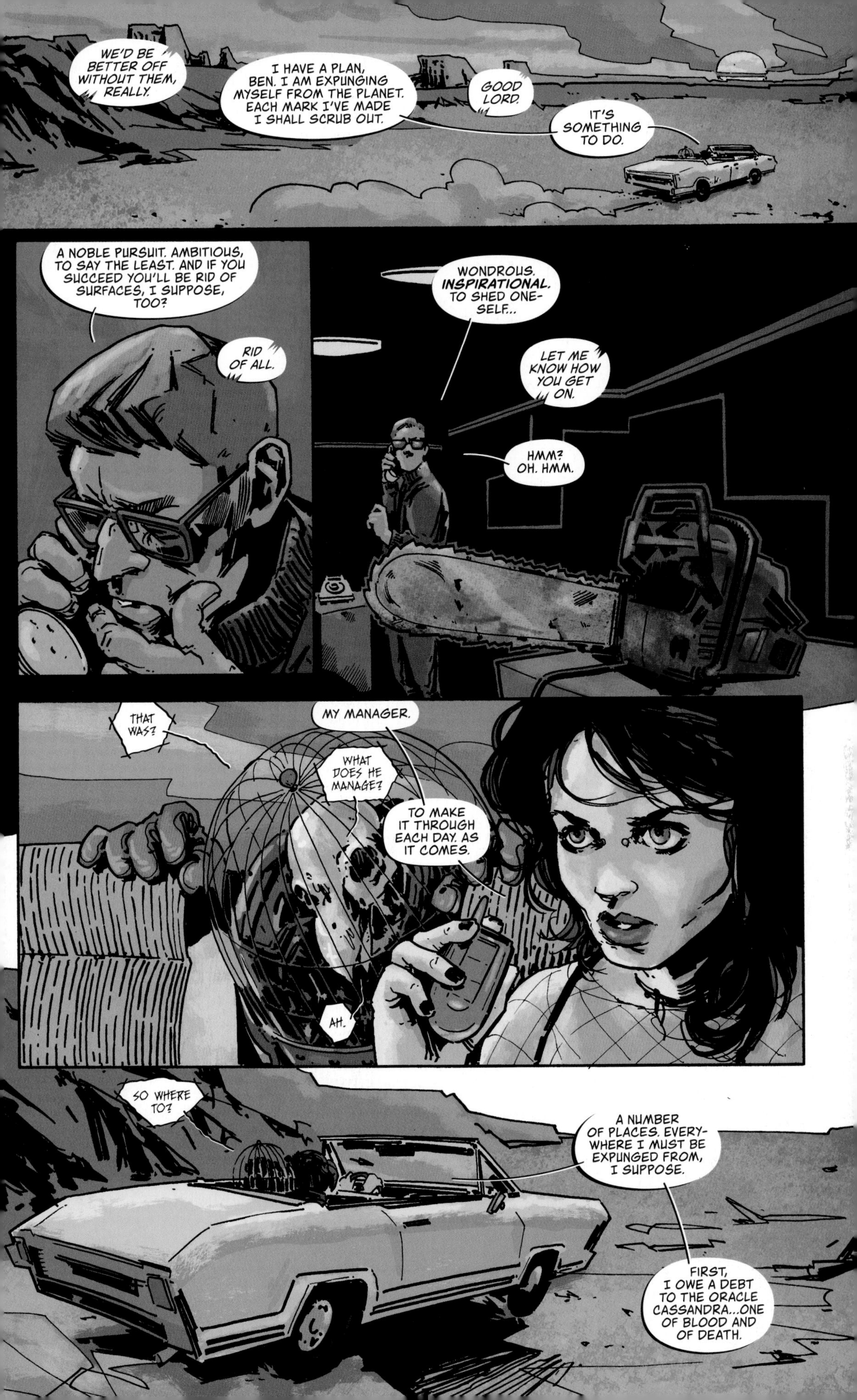
WE'D BE BETTER OFF WITHOUT THEM, REALLY.
I HAVE A PLAN, BEN. I AM EXPUNGING MYSELF FROM THE PLANET. EACH MARK I'VE MADE I SHALL SCRUB OUT.
GOOD LORD.
IT'S SOMETHING TO DO.
A NOBLE PURSUIT. AMBITIOUS, TO SAY THE LEAST. AND IF YOU SUCCEED YOU'LL BE RID OF SURFACES, I SUPPOSE, TOO?
RID OF ALL.
WONDROUS. **INSPIRATIONAL.** TO SHED ONE-SELF...
LET ME KNOW HOW YOU GET ON.
HMM? OH. HMM.
THAT WAS?
MY MANAGER.
WHAT DOES HE MANAGE?
TO MAKE IT THROUGH EACH DAY. AS IT COMES.
AH.
SO WHERE TO?
A NUMBER OF PLACES. EVERY-WHERE I MUST BE EXPUNGED FROM, I SUPPOSE.
FIRST, I OWE A DEBT TO THE ORACLE CASSANDRA...ONE OF BLOOD AND OF DEATH.

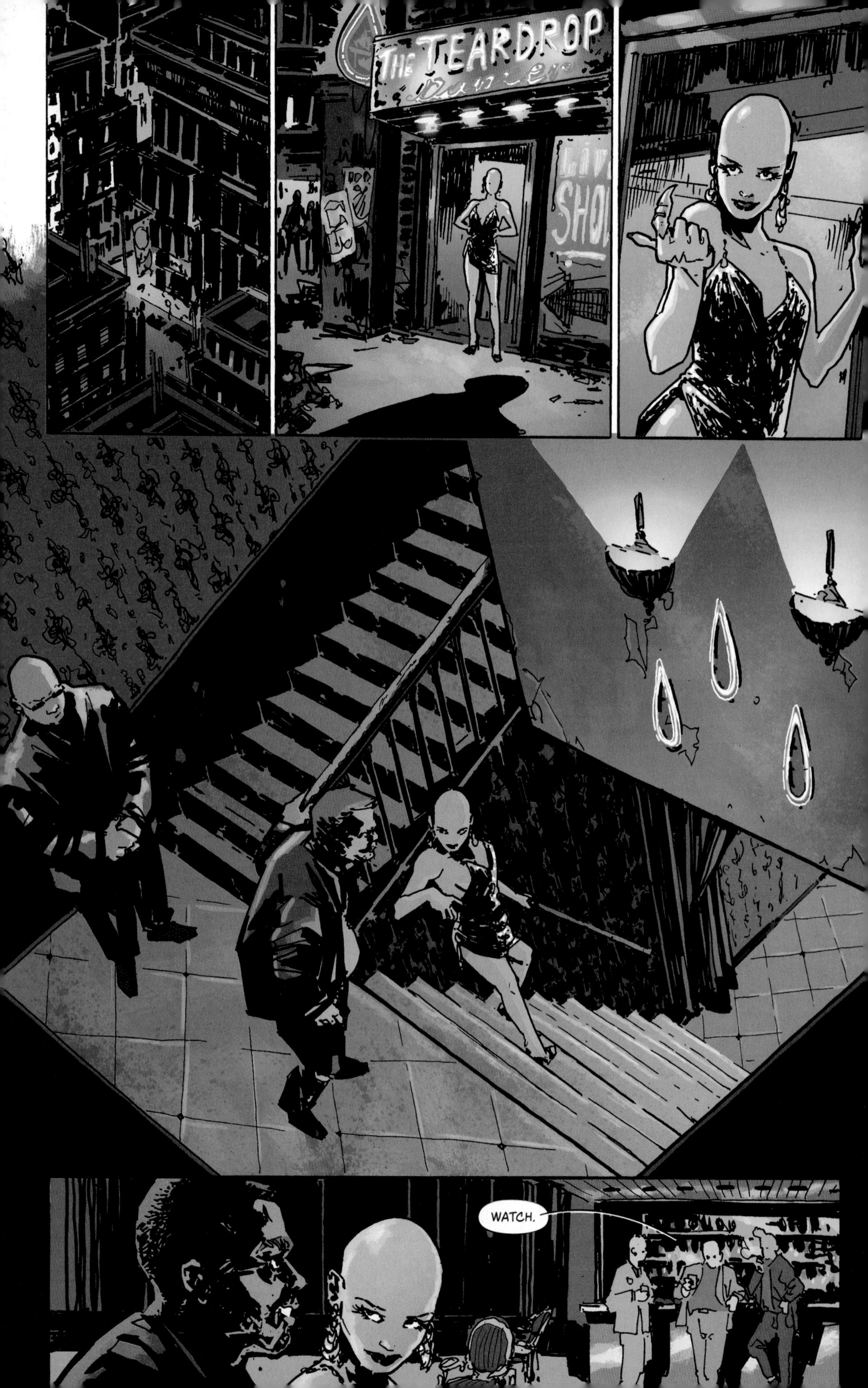
HOTEL
THE TEARDROP
LOVE SHOW
WATCH.

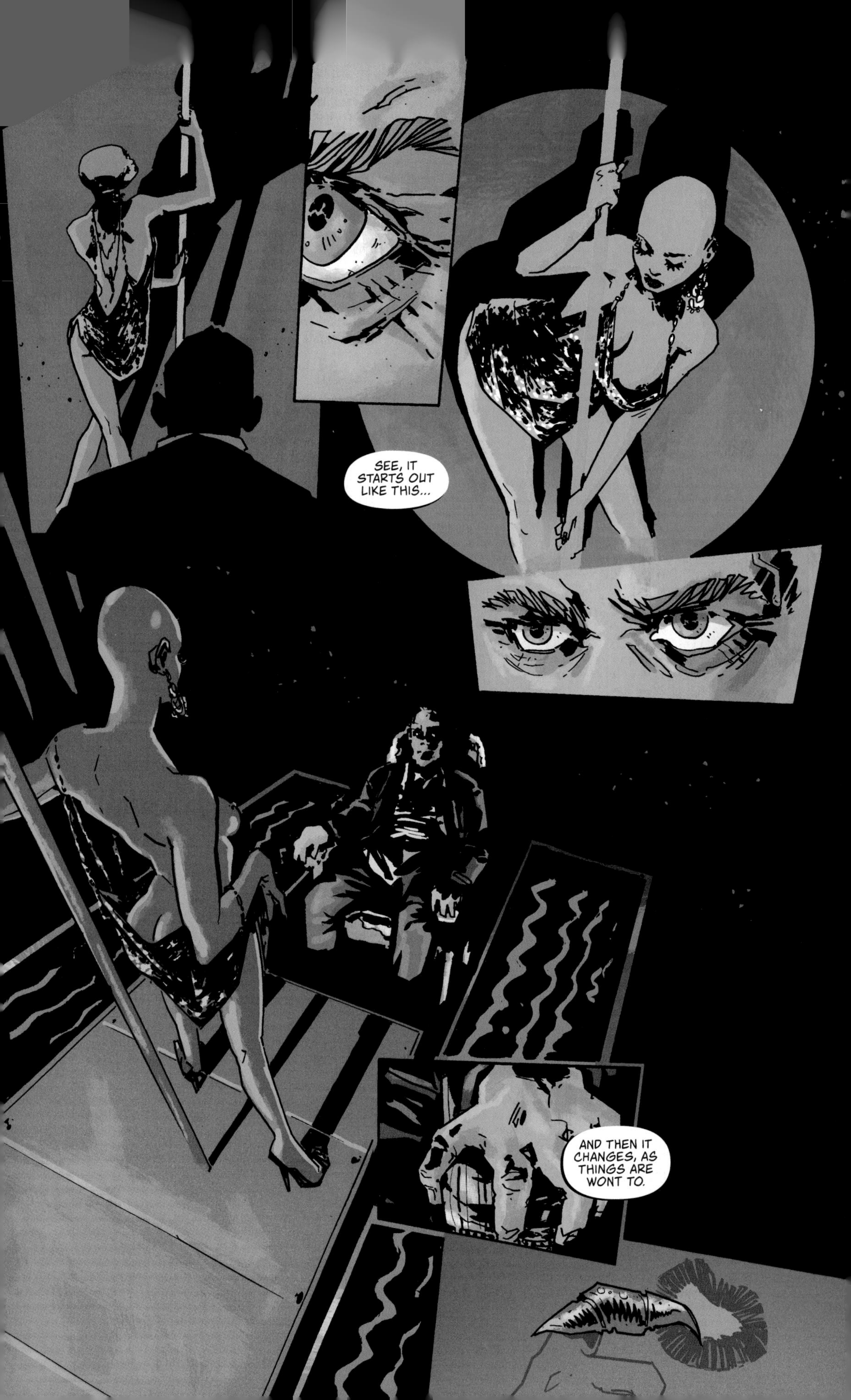
SEE, IT STARTS OUT LIKE THIS...
AND THEN IT CHANGES, AS THINGS ARE WONT TO.

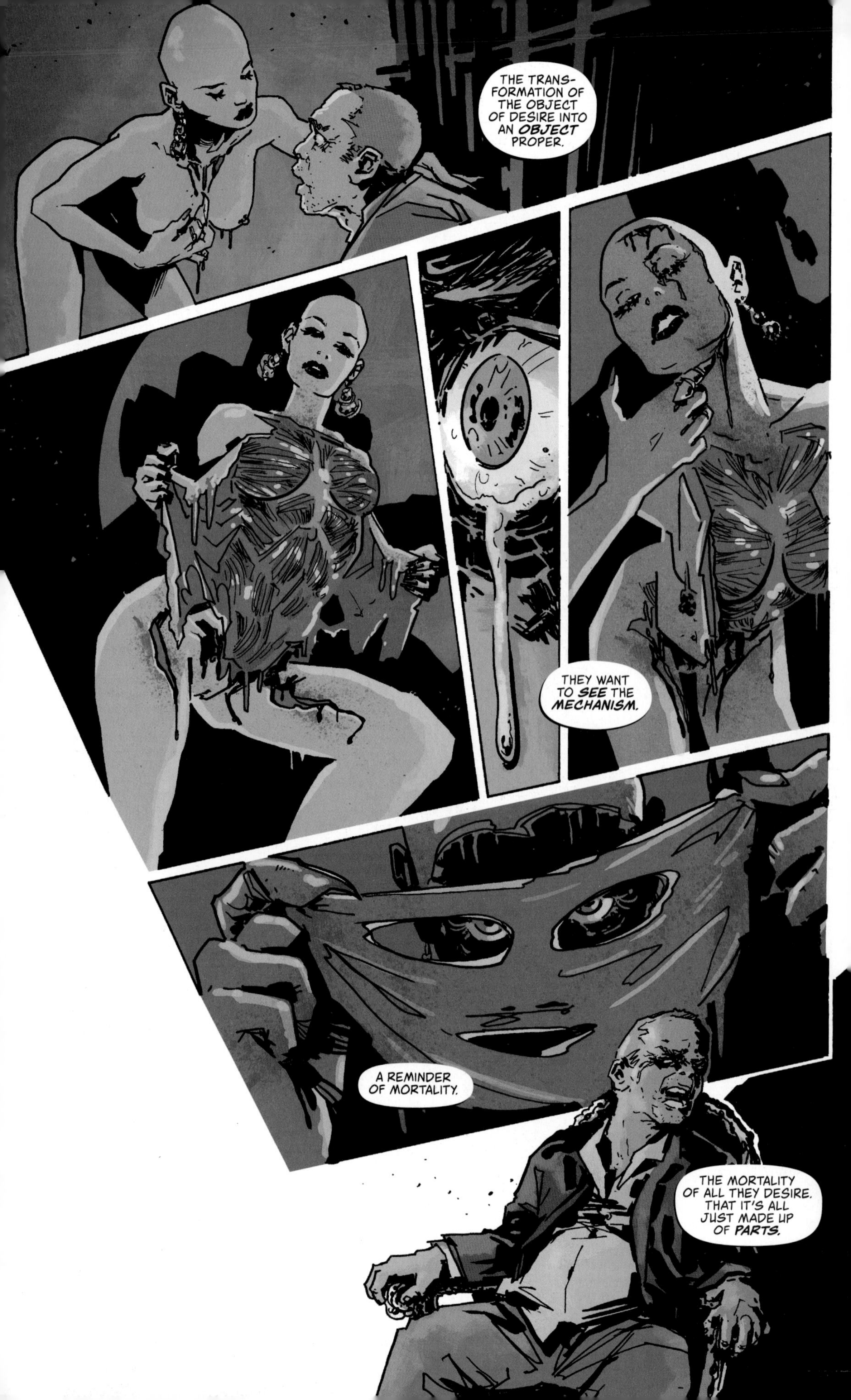
THE TRANS-
FORMATION OF
THE OBJECT
OF DESIRE INTO
AN *OBJECT*
PROPER.
THEY WANT
TO *SEE* THE
MECHANISM.
A REMINDER
OF MORTALITY.
THE MORTALITY
OF ALL THEY DESIRE.
THAT IT'S ALL
JUST MADE UP
OF *PARTS.*

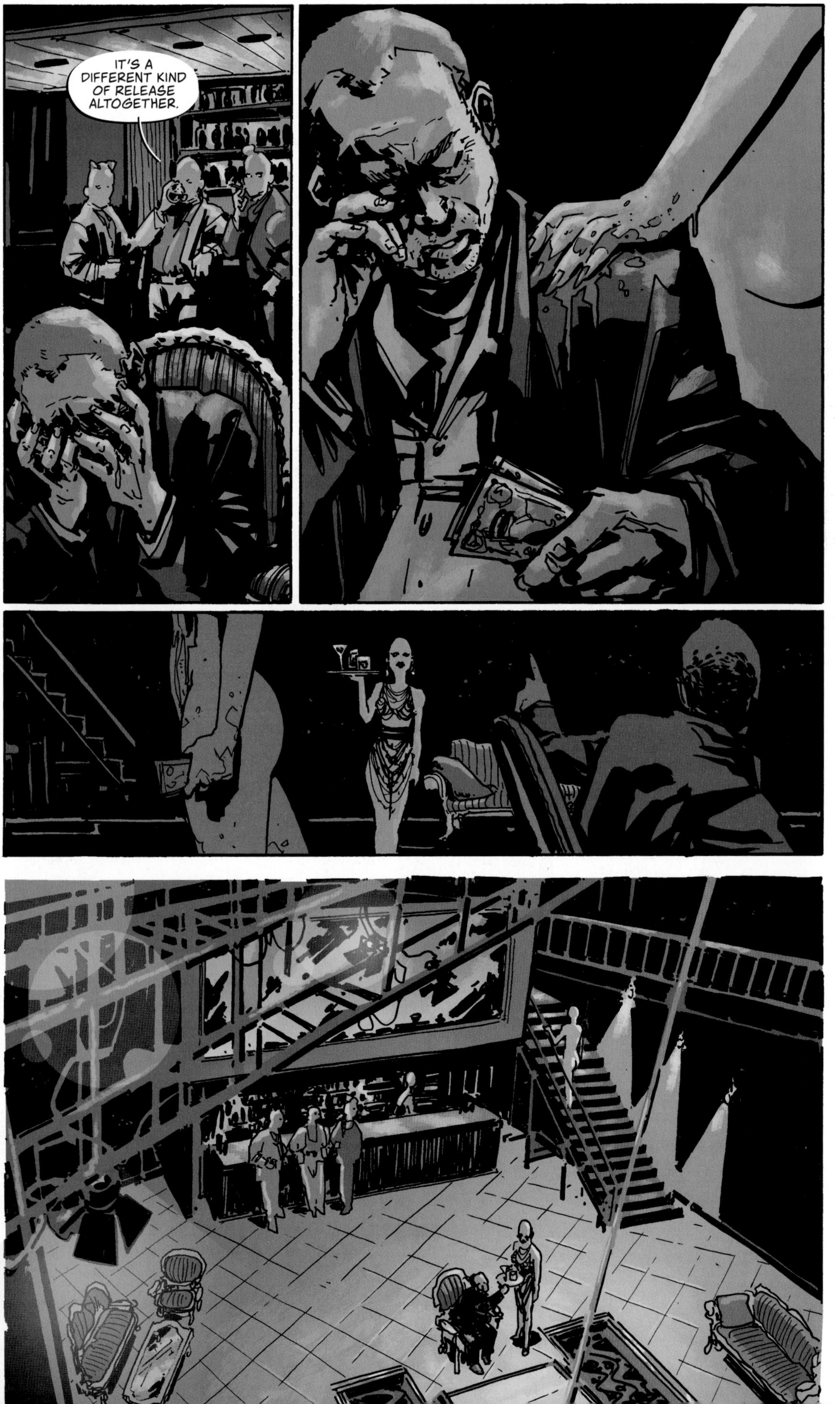
IT'S A DIFFERENT KIND OF RELEASE ALTOGETHER.

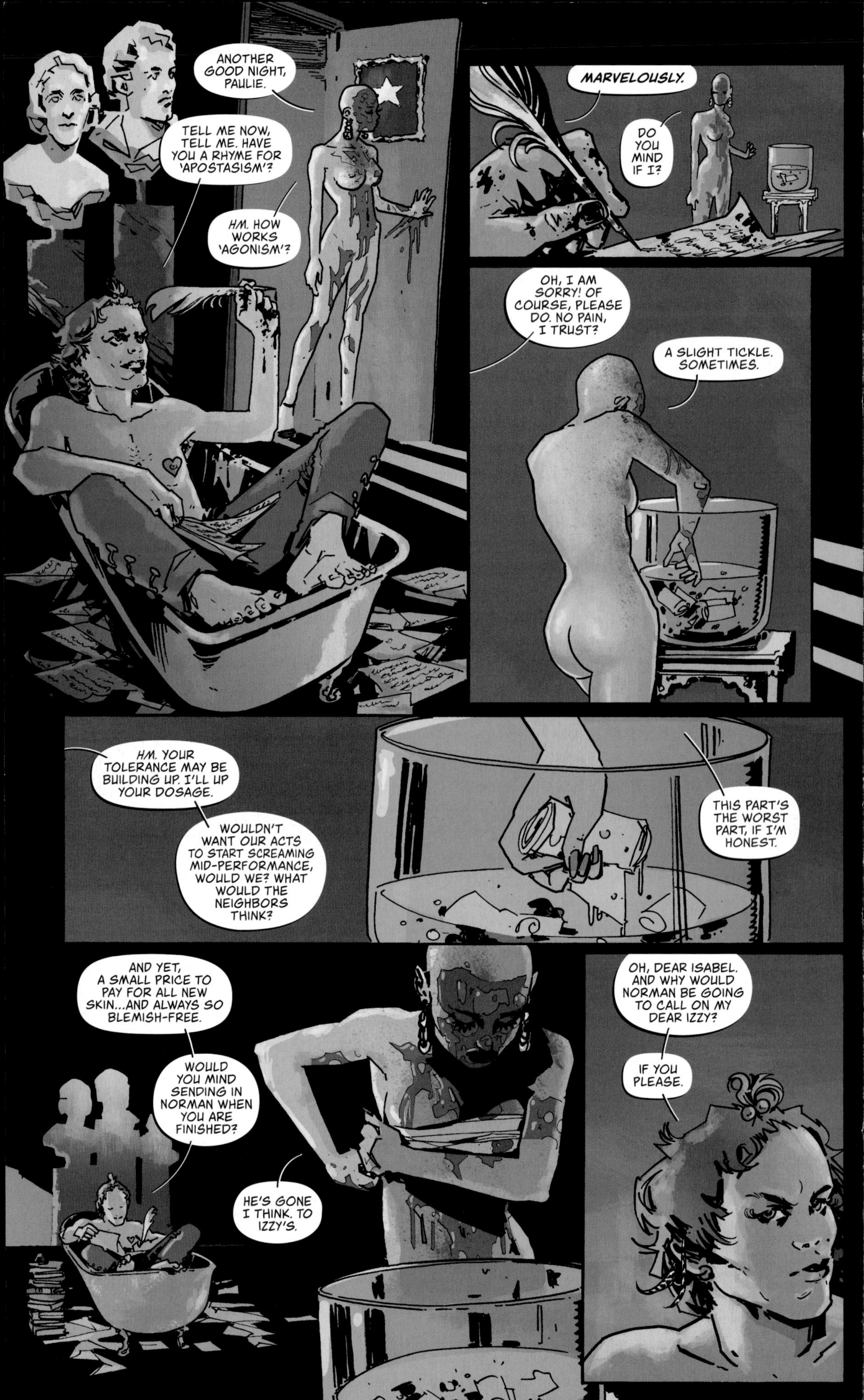
ANOTHER GOOD NIGHT, PAULIE.
TELL ME NOW, TELL ME. HAVE YOU A RHYME FOR 'APOSTASISM'?
HM. HOW WORKS 'AGONISM'?
MARVELOUSLY.
DO YOU MIND IF I?
OH, I AM SORRY! OF COURSE, PLEASE DO. NO PAIN, I TRUST?
A SLIGHT TICKLE. SOMETIMES.
HM. YOUR TOLERANCE MAY BE BUILDING UP. I'LL UP YOUR DOSAGE.
WOULDN'T WANT OUR ACTS TO START SCREAMING MID-PERFORMANCE, WOULD WE? WHAT WOULD THE NEIGHBORS THINK?
THIS PART'S THE WORST PART, IF I'M HONEST.
AND YET, A SMALL PRICE TO PAY FOR ALL NEW SKIN...AND ALWAYS SO BLEMISH-FREE.
WOULD YOU MIND SENDING IN NORMAN WHEN YOU ARE FINISHED?
HE'S GONE I THINK. TO IZZY'S.
OH, DEAR ISABEL. AND WHY WOULD NORMAN BE GOING TO CALL ON MY DEAR IZZY?
IF YOU PLEASE.

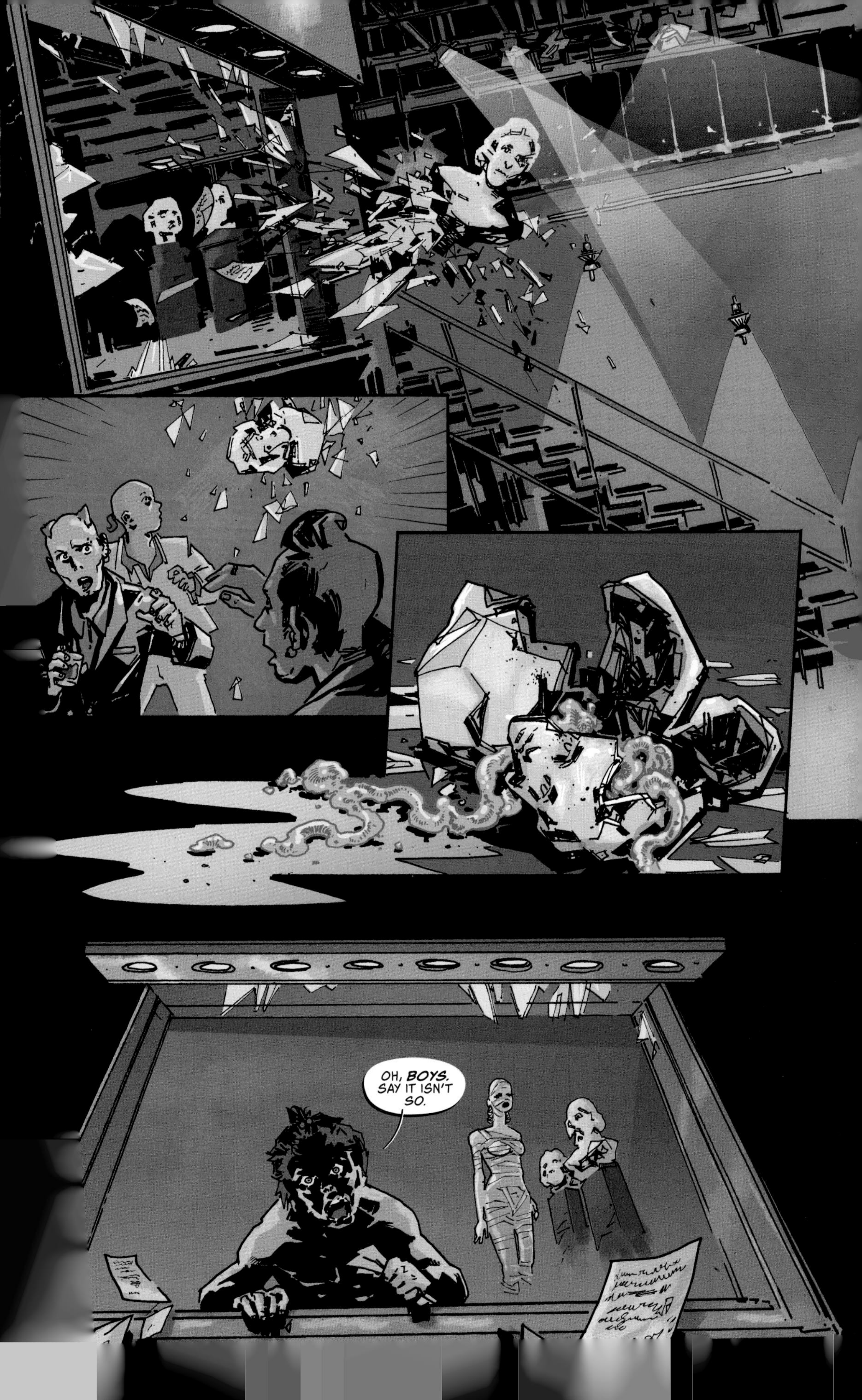
OH, BOYS. SAY IT ISN'T SO.

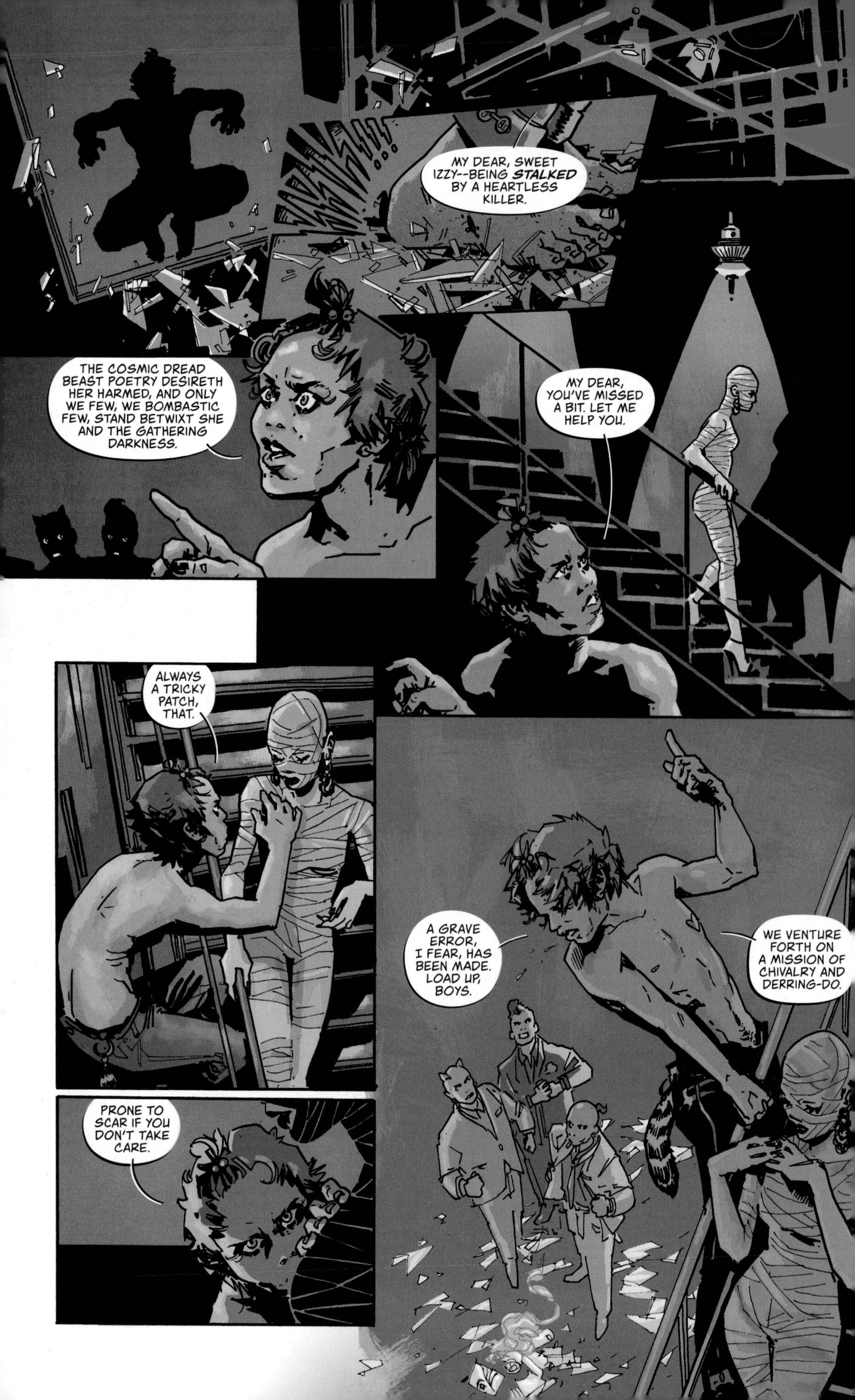

MY DEAR, SWEET IZZY--BEING *STALKED* BY A HEARTLESS KILLER.
THE COSMIC DREAD BEAST POETRY DESIRETH HER HARMED, AND ONLY WE FEW, WE BOMBASTIC FEW, STAND BETWIXT SHE AND THE GATHERING DARKNESS.
MY DEAR, YOU'VE MISSED A BIT. LET ME HELP YOU.
ALWAYS A TRICKY PATCH, THAT.
PRONE TO SCAR IF YOU DON'T TAKE CARE.
A GRAVE ERROR, I FEAR, HAS BEEN MADE. LOAD UP, BOYS.
WE VENTURE FORTH ON A MISSION OF CHIVALRY AND DERRING-DO.

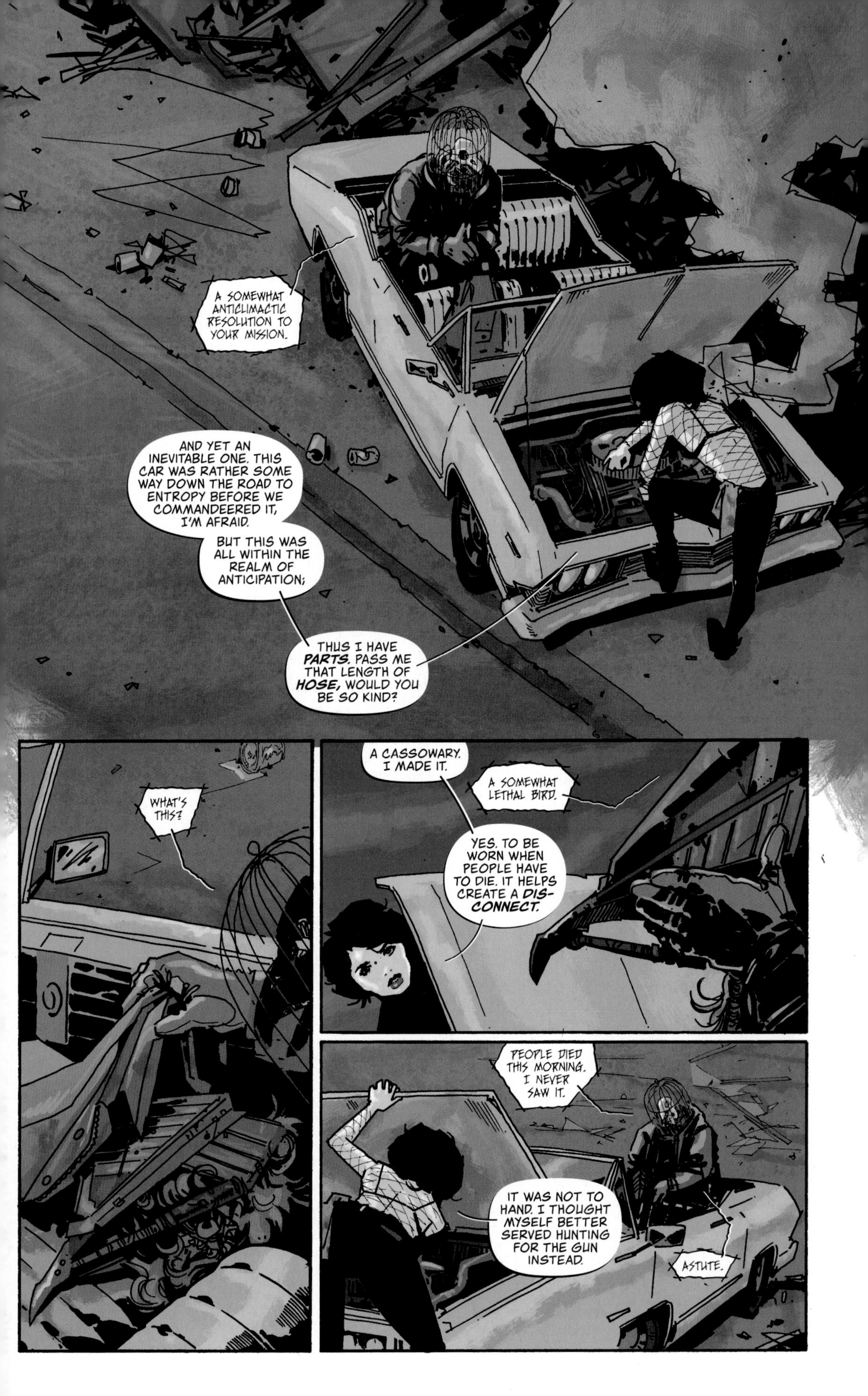
A SOMEWHAT ANTICLIMACTIC RESOLUTION TO YOUR MISSION.
AND YET AN INEVITABLE ONE. THIS CAR WAS RATHER SOME WAY DOWN THE ROAD TO ENTROPY BEFORE WE COMMANDEERED IT, I'M AFRAID.
BUT THIS WAS ALL WITHIN THE REALM OF ANTICIPATION;
THUS I HAVE PARTS. PASS ME THAT LENGTH OF HOSE, WOULD YOU BE SO KIND?
WHAT'S THIS?
A CASSOWARY. I MADE IT.
A SOMEWHAT LETHAL BIRD.
YES. TO BE WORN WHEN PEOPLE HAVE TO DIE. IT HELPS CREATE A DISCONNECT.
PEOPLE DIED THIS MORNING. I NEVER SAW IT.
IT WAS NOT TO HAND. I THOUGHT MYSELF BETTER SERVED HUNTING FOR THE GUN INSTEAD.
ASTUTE.

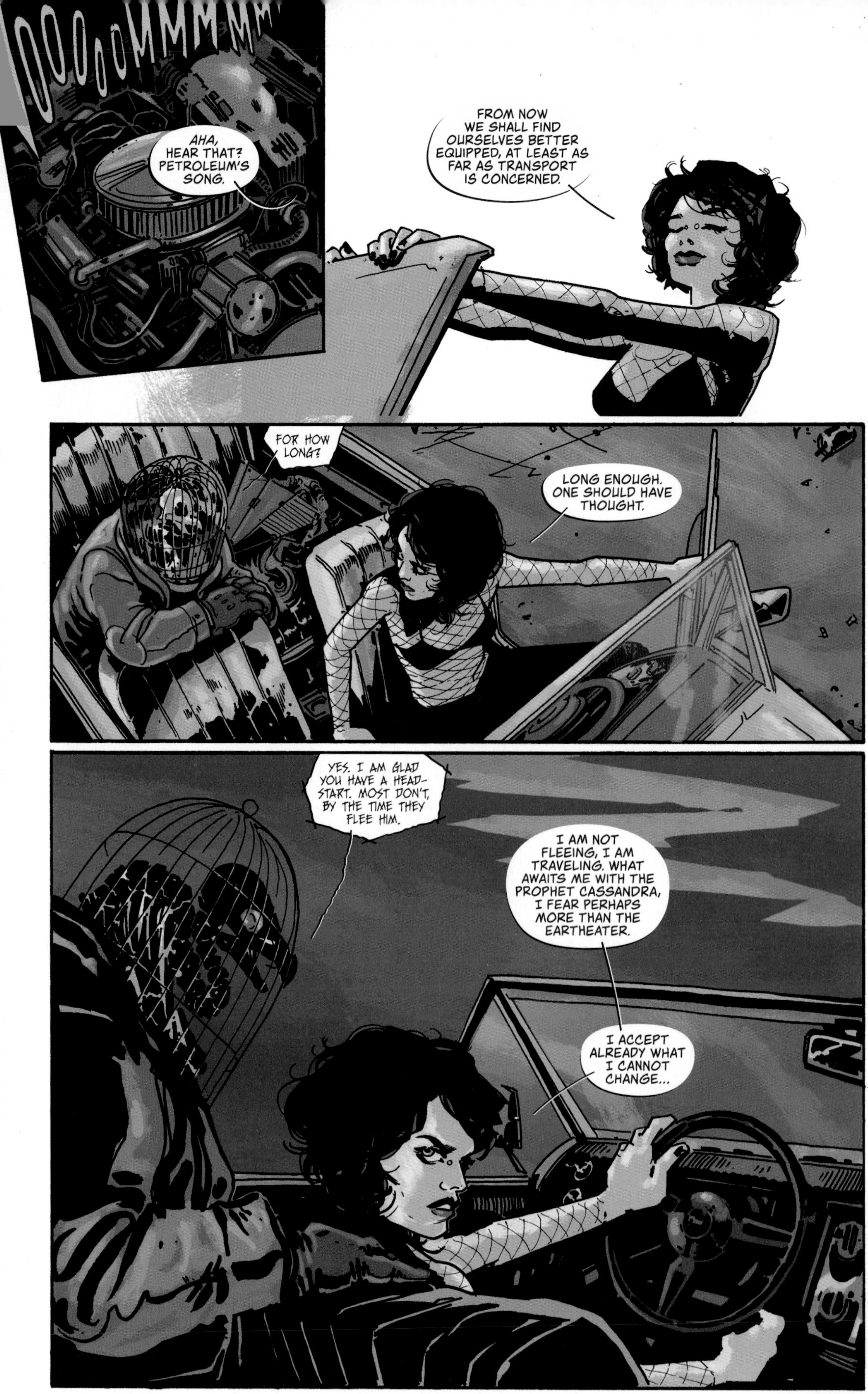
OOOOOMMMMM
AHA, HEAR THAT? PETROLEUM'S SONG.
FROM NOW WE SHALL FIND OURSELVES BETTER EQUIPPED, AT LEAST AS FAR AS TRANSPORT IS CONCERNED.
FOR HOW LONG?
LONG ENOUGH. ONE SHOULD HAVE THOUGHT.
YES. I AM GLAD YOU HAVE A HEAD-START. MOST DON'T, BY THE TIME THEY FLEE HIM.
I AM NOT FLEEING, I AM TRAVELING. WHAT AWAITS ME WITH THE PROPHET CASSANDRA, I FEAR PERHAPS MORE THAN THE EARTHEATER.
I ACCEPT ALREADY WHAT I CANNOT CHANGE...

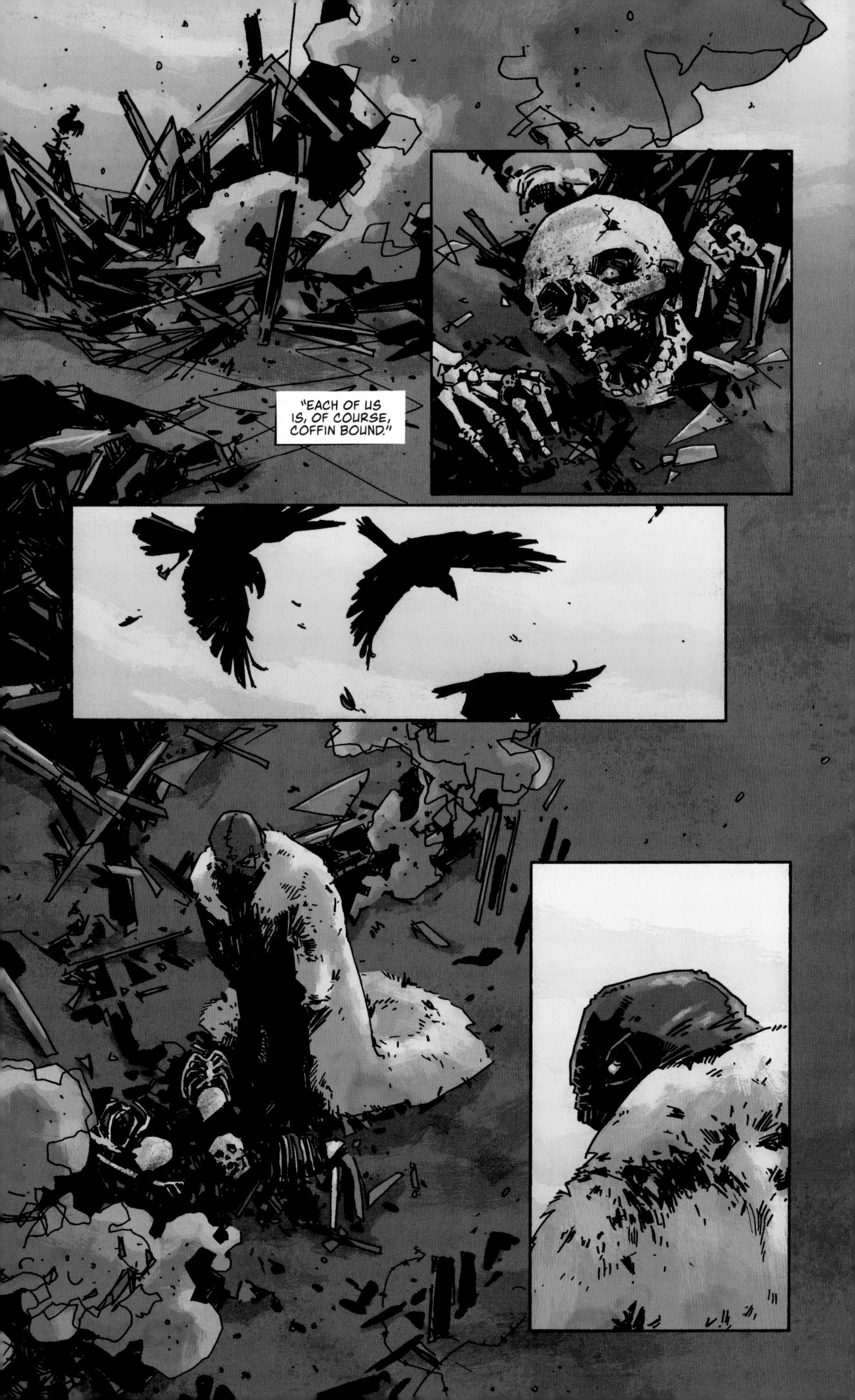
"EACH OF US IS, OF COURSE, COFFIN BOUND."

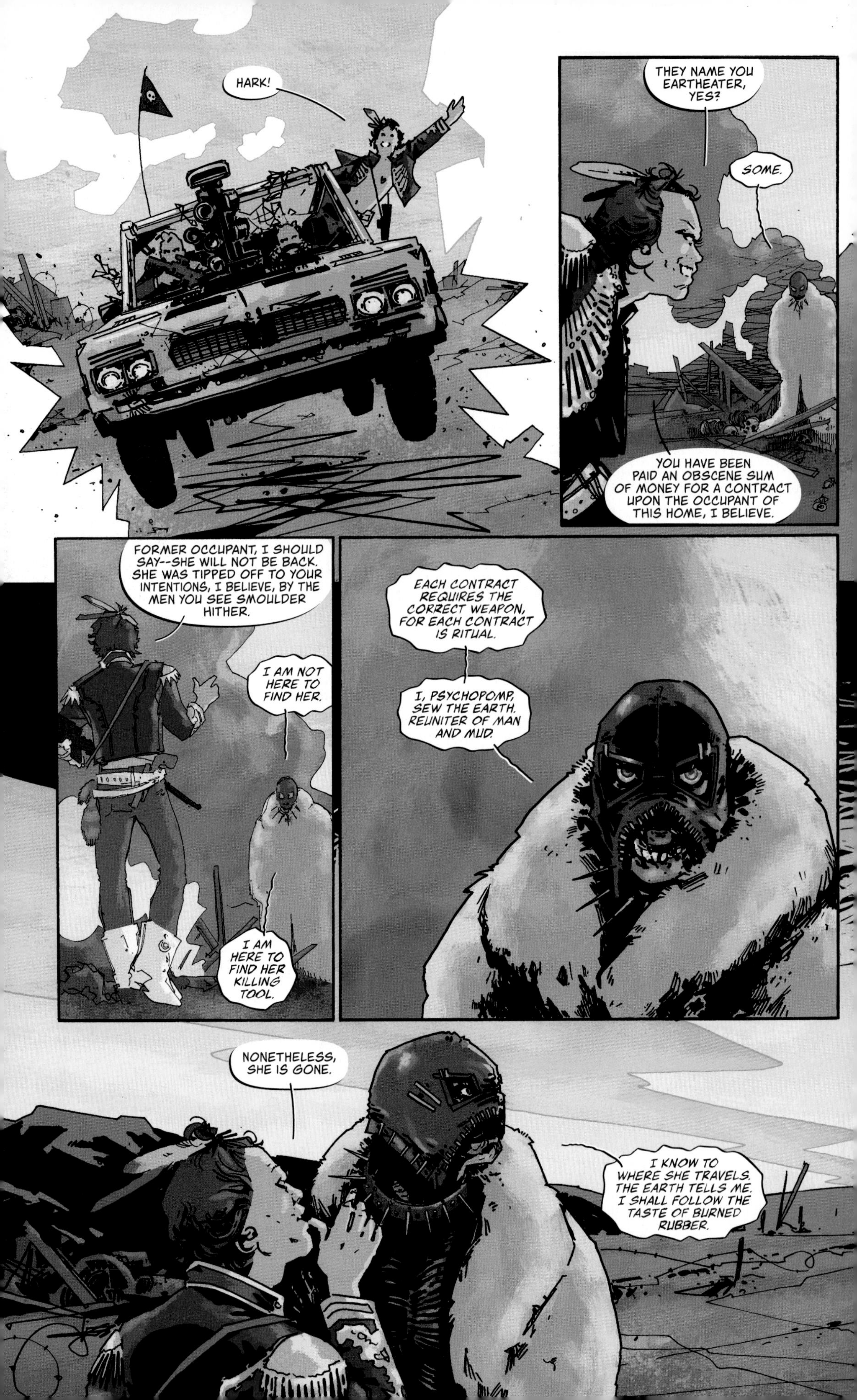
HARK!
THEY NAME YOU EARTHEATER, YES?
SOME.
YOU HAVE BEEN PAID AN OBSCENE SUM OF MONEY FOR A CONTRACT UPON THE OCCUPANT OF THIS HOME, I BELIEVE.
FORMER OCCUPANT, I SHOULD SAY--SHE WILL NOT BE BACK. SHE WAS TIPPED OFF TO YOUR INTENTIONS, I BELIEVE, BY THE MEN YOU SEE SMOULDER HITHER.
I AM NOT HERE TO FIND HER.
I AM HERE TO FIND HER KILLING TOOL.
EACH CONTRACT REQUIRES THE CORRECT WEAPON, FOR EACH CONTRACT IS RITUAL.
I, PSYCHOPOMP, SEW THE EARTH. REUNITER OF MAN AND MUD.
NONETHELESS, SHE IS GONE.
I KNOW TO WHERE SHE TRAVELS. THE EARTH TELLS ME. I SHALL FOLLOW THE TASTE OF BURNED RUBBER.

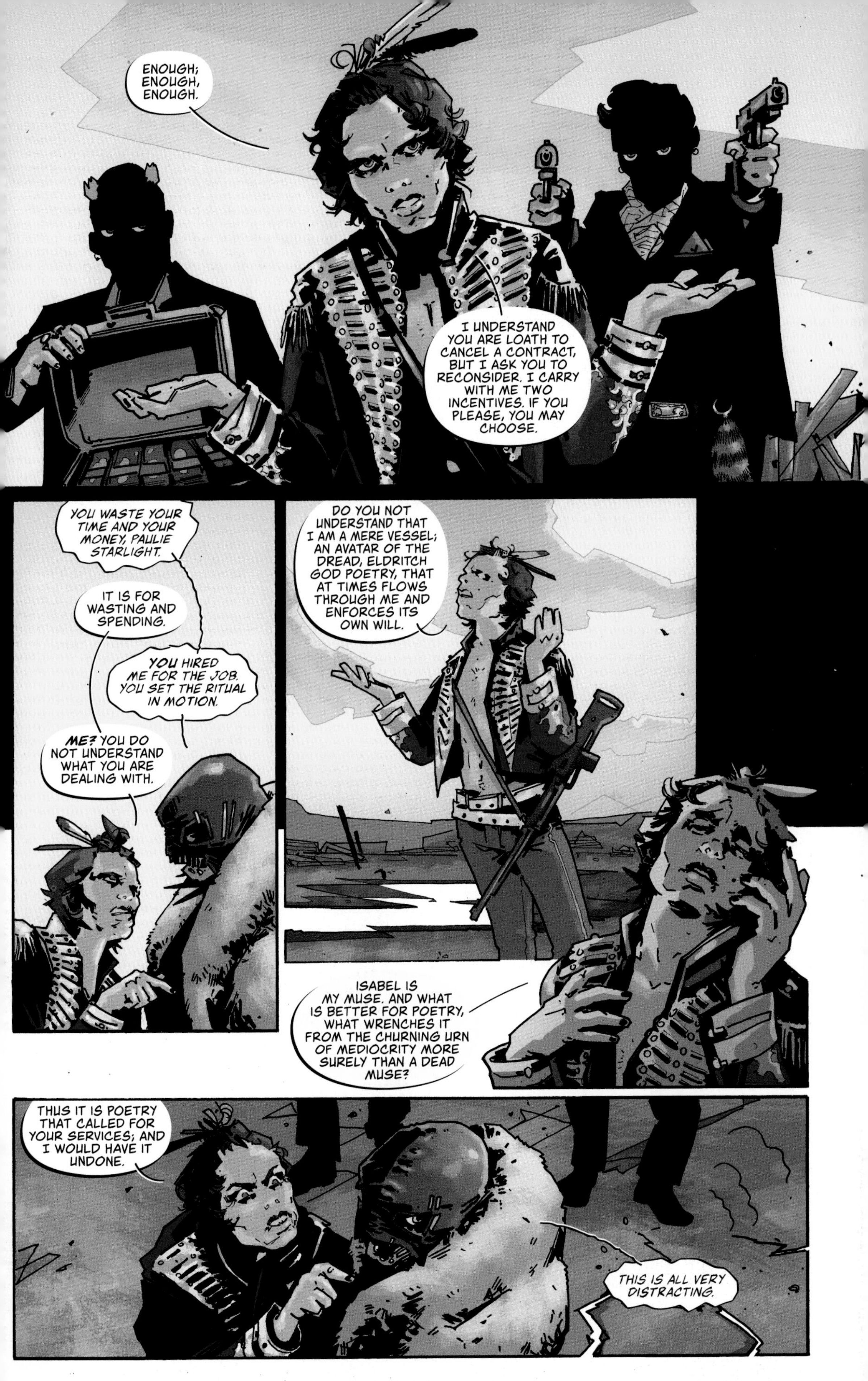
ENOUGH; ENOUGH, ENOUGH.
I UNDERSTAND YOU ARE LOATH TO CANCEL A CONTRACT, BUT I ASK YOU TO RECONSIDER. I CARRY WITH ME TWO INCENTIVES. IF YOU PLEASE, YOU MAY CHOOSE.
YOU WASTE YOUR TIME AND YOUR MONEY, PAULIE STARLIGHT.
IT IS FOR WASTING AND SPENDING.
YOU HIRED ME FOR THE JOB. YOU SET THE RITUAL IN MOTION.
ME? YOU DO NOT UNDERSTAND WHAT YOU ARE DEALING WITH.
DO YOU NOT UNDERSTAND THAT I AM A MERE VESSEL; AN AVATAR OF THE DREAD, ELDRITCH GOD POETRY, THAT AT TIMES FLOWS THROUGH ME AND ENFORCES ITS OWN WILL.
ISABEL IS MY MUSE. AND WHAT IS BETTER FOR POETRY, WHAT WRENCHES IT FROM THE CHURNING URN OF MEDIOCRITY MORE SURELY THAN A DEAD MUSE?
THUS IT IS POETRY THAT CALLED FOR YOUR SERVICES; AND I WOULD HAVE IT UNDONE.
THIS IS ALL VERY DISTRACTING.

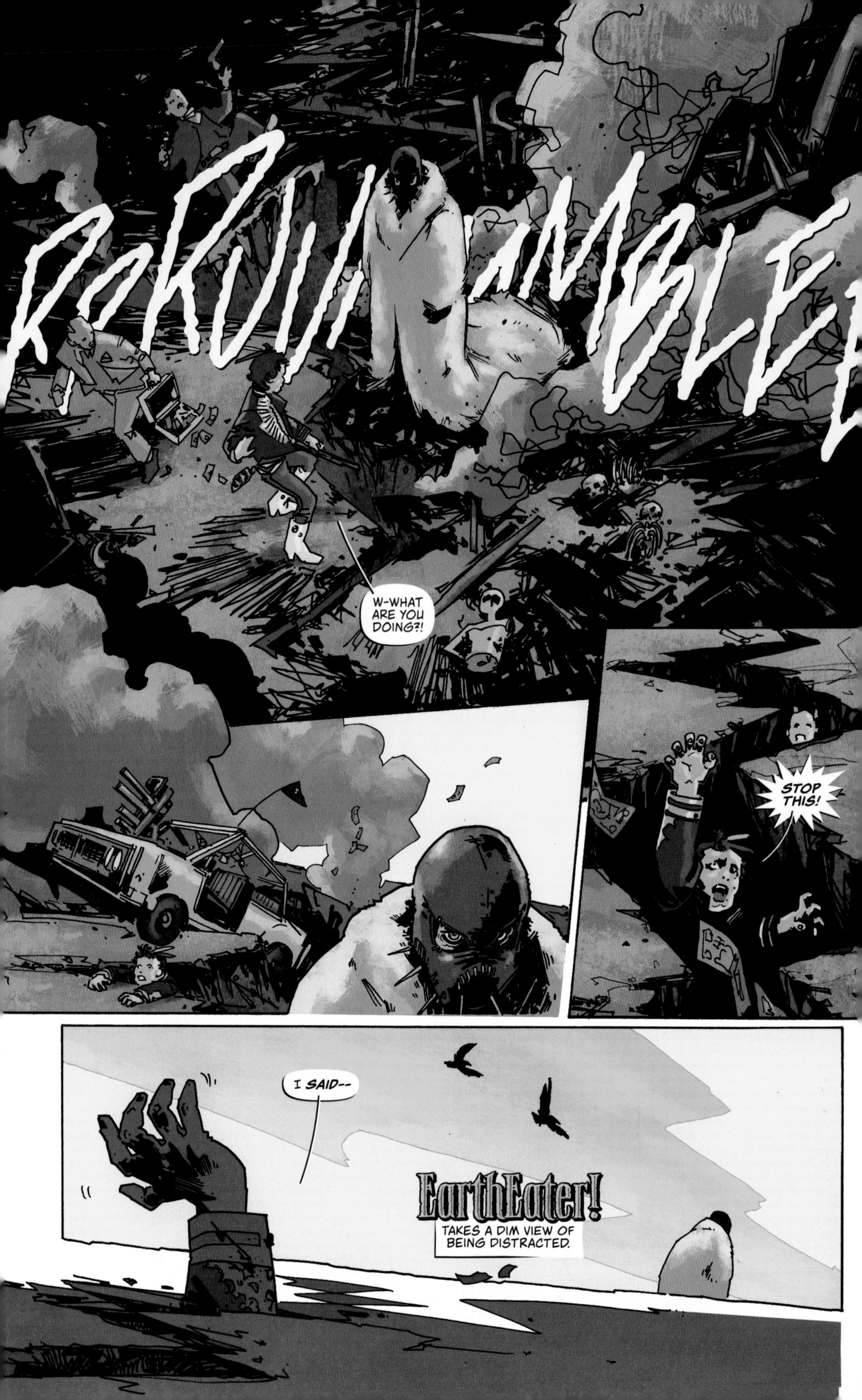
W-WHAT ARE YOU DOING?!
STOP THIS!
I SAID--
EarthEater!
TAKES A DIM VIEW OF BEING DISTRACTED.

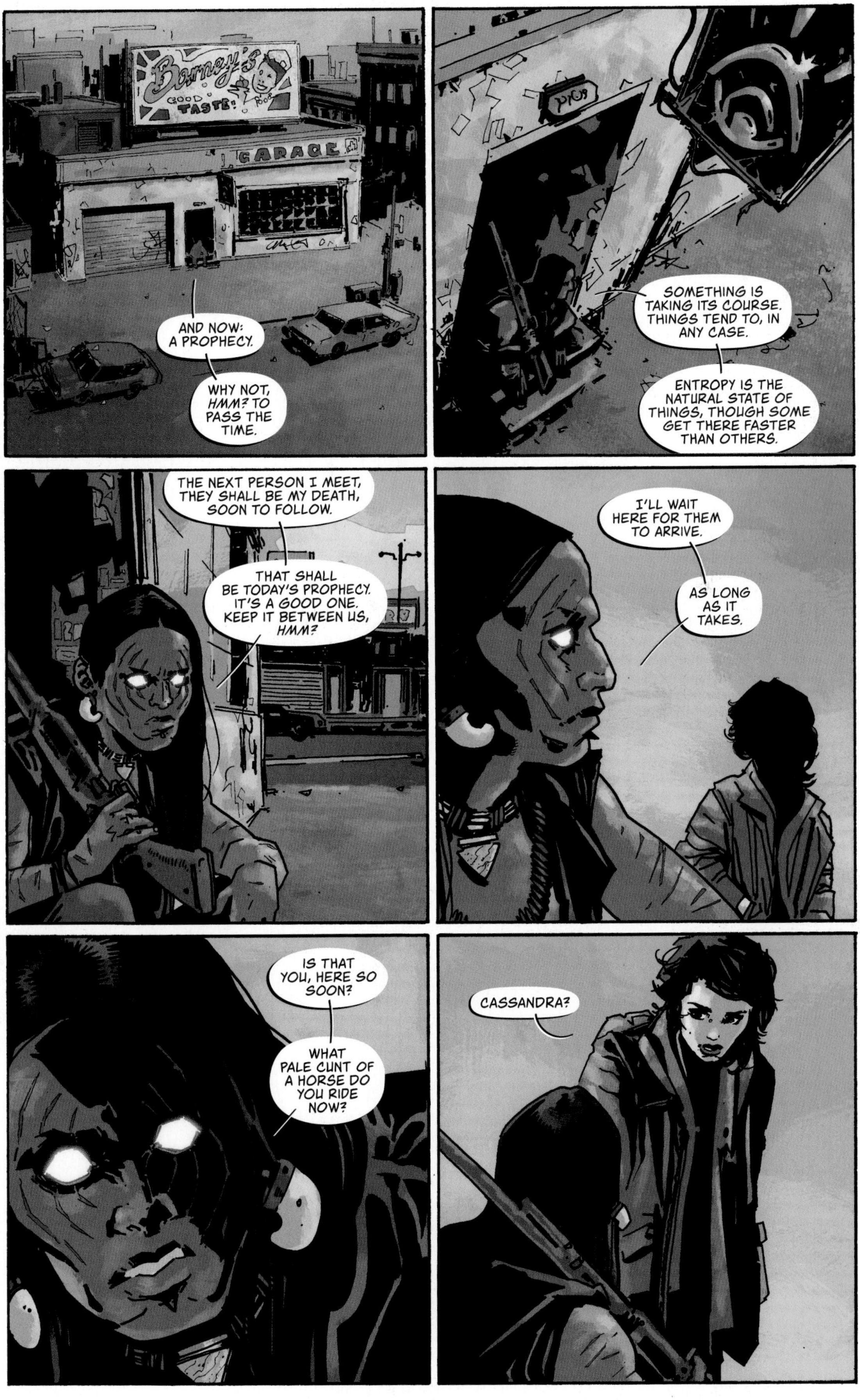
AND NOW: A PROPHECY.
WHY NOT, HMM? TO PASS THE TIME.
SOMETHING IS TAKING ITS COURSE. THINGS TEND TO, IN ANY CASE.
ENTROPY IS THE NATURAL STATE OF THINGS, THOUGH SOME GET THERE FASTER THAN OTHERS.
THE NEXT PERSON I MEET, THEY SHALL BE MY DEATH, SOON TO FOLLOW.
THAT SHALL BE TODAY'S PROPHECY. IT'S A GOOD ONE. KEEP IT BETWEEN US, HMM?
I'LL WAIT HERE FOR THEM TO ARRIVE.
AS LONG AS IT TAKES.
IS THAT YOU, HERE SO SOON?
WHAT PALE CUNT OF A HORSE DO YOU RIDE NOW?
CASSANDRA?

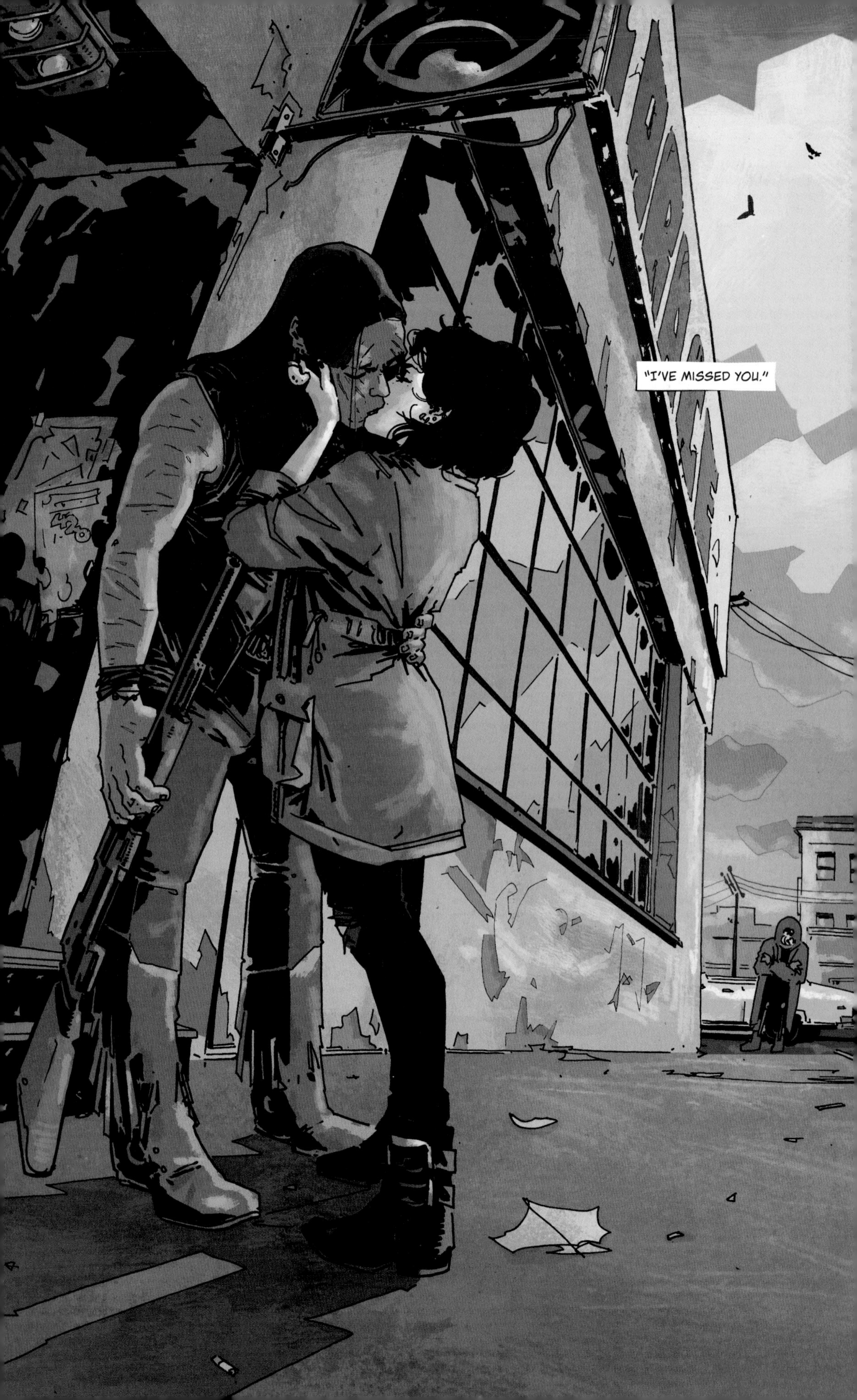
"I'VE MISSED YOU."

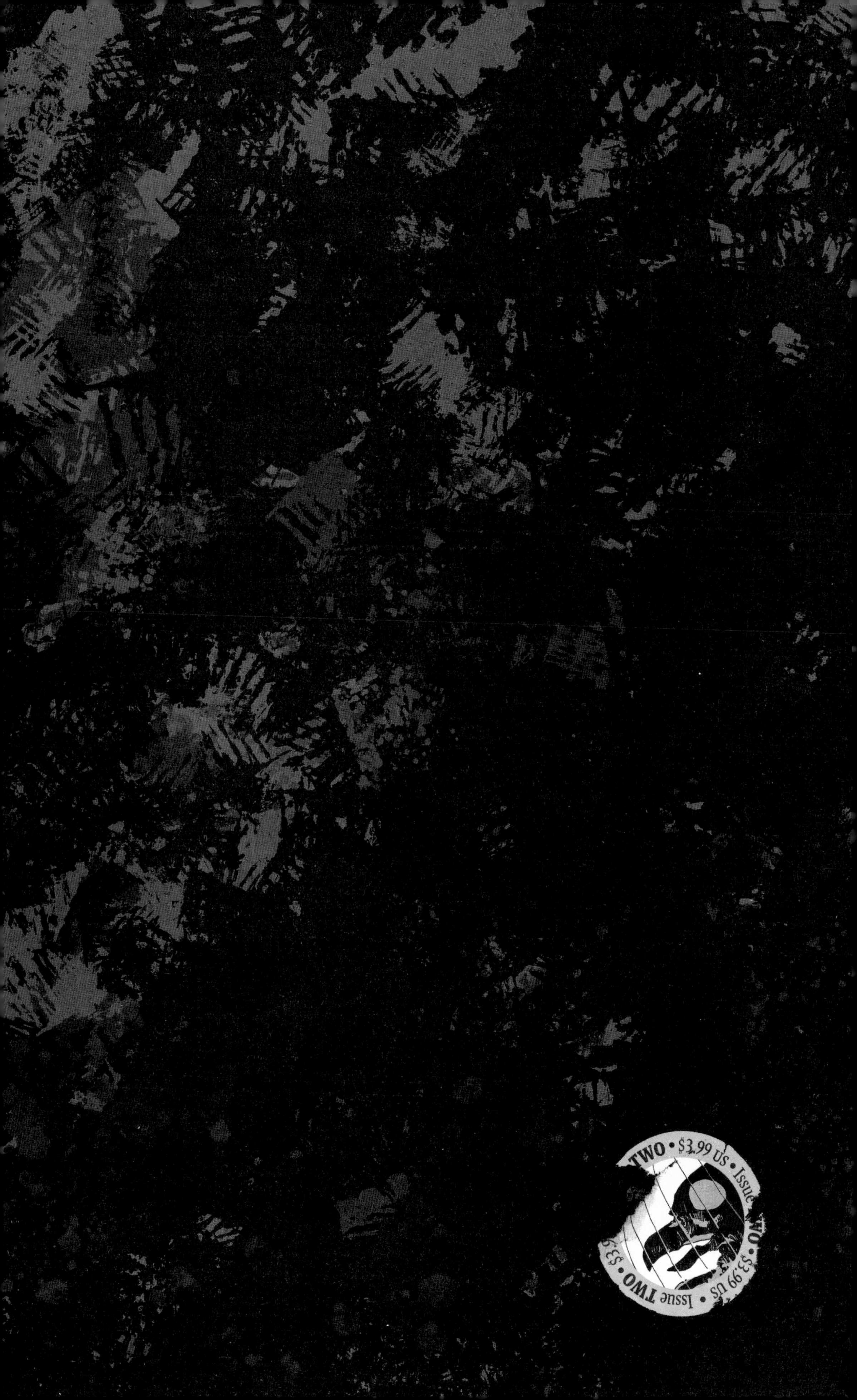

TWO • $3.99 US • Issue TWO • $3.99 US • Issue TWO • $3.99 US

" You've been
SIGNIFICANTLY ASSASSINATED,
SUFFICIENTLY SUICIDED,
to be able now to stand on your own two feet, like a big boy. **"**
— SAMUEL BECKETT, THE UNNAMABLE

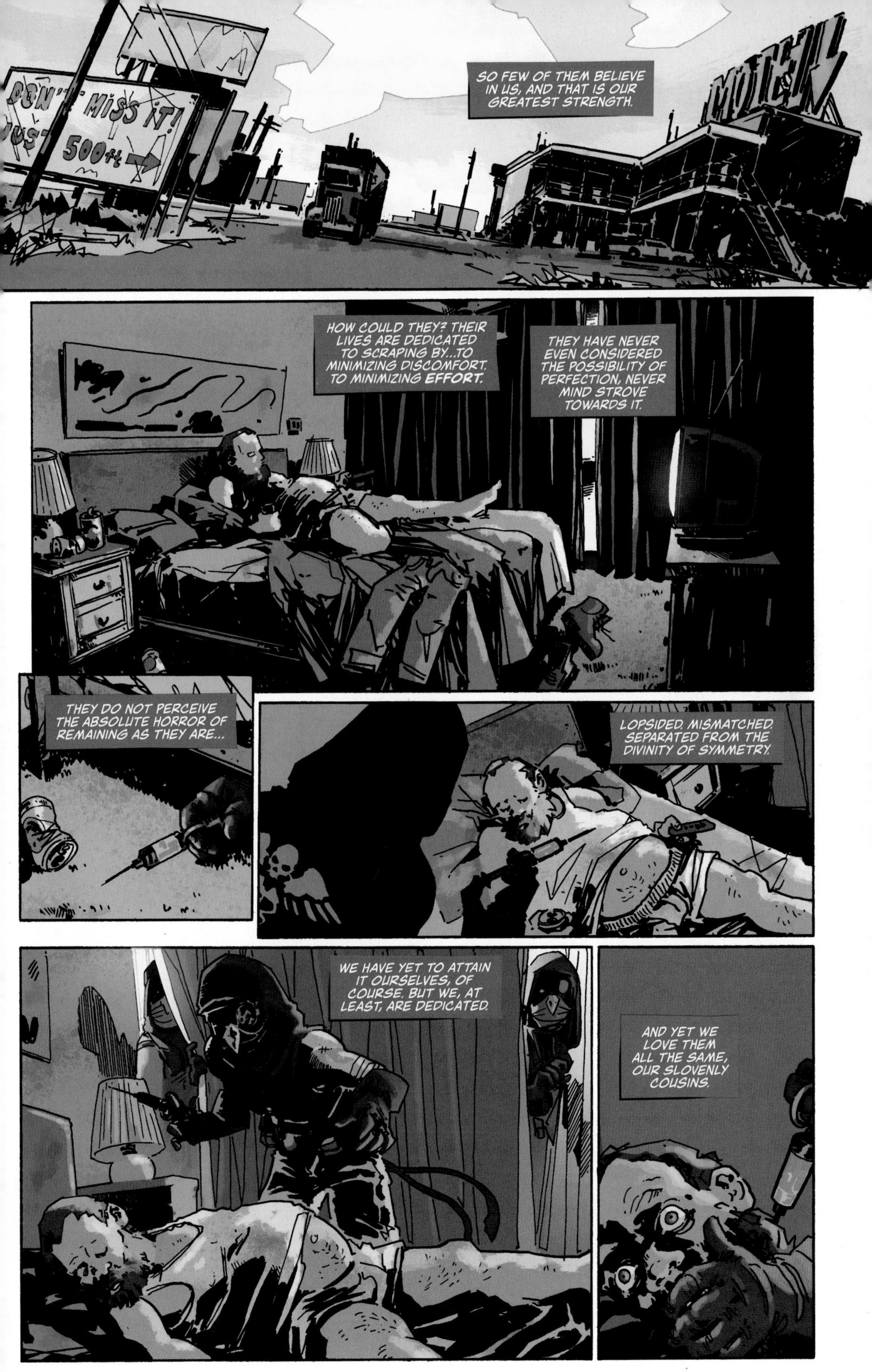
DON'T MISS IT!
JUST 500ft
MOTEL
SO FEW OF THEM BELIEVE IN US, AND THAT IS OUR GREATEST STRENGTH.
HOW COULD THEY? THEIR LIVES ARE DEDICATED TO SCRAPING BY...TO MINIMIZING DISCOMFORT. TO MINIMIZING EFFORT.
THEY HAVE NEVER EVEN CONSIDERED THE POSSIBILITY OF PERFECTION, NEVER MIND STROVE TOWARDS IT.
THEY DO NOT PERCEIVE THE ABSOLUTE HORROR OF REMAINING AS THEY ARE...
LOPSIDED. MISMATCHED. SEPARATED FROM THE DIVINITY OF SYMMETRY.
WE HAVE YET TO ATTAIN IT OURSELVES, OF COURSE. BUT WE, AT LEAST, ARE DEDICATED.
AND YET WE LOVE THEM ALL THE SAME, OUR SLOVENLY COUSINS.

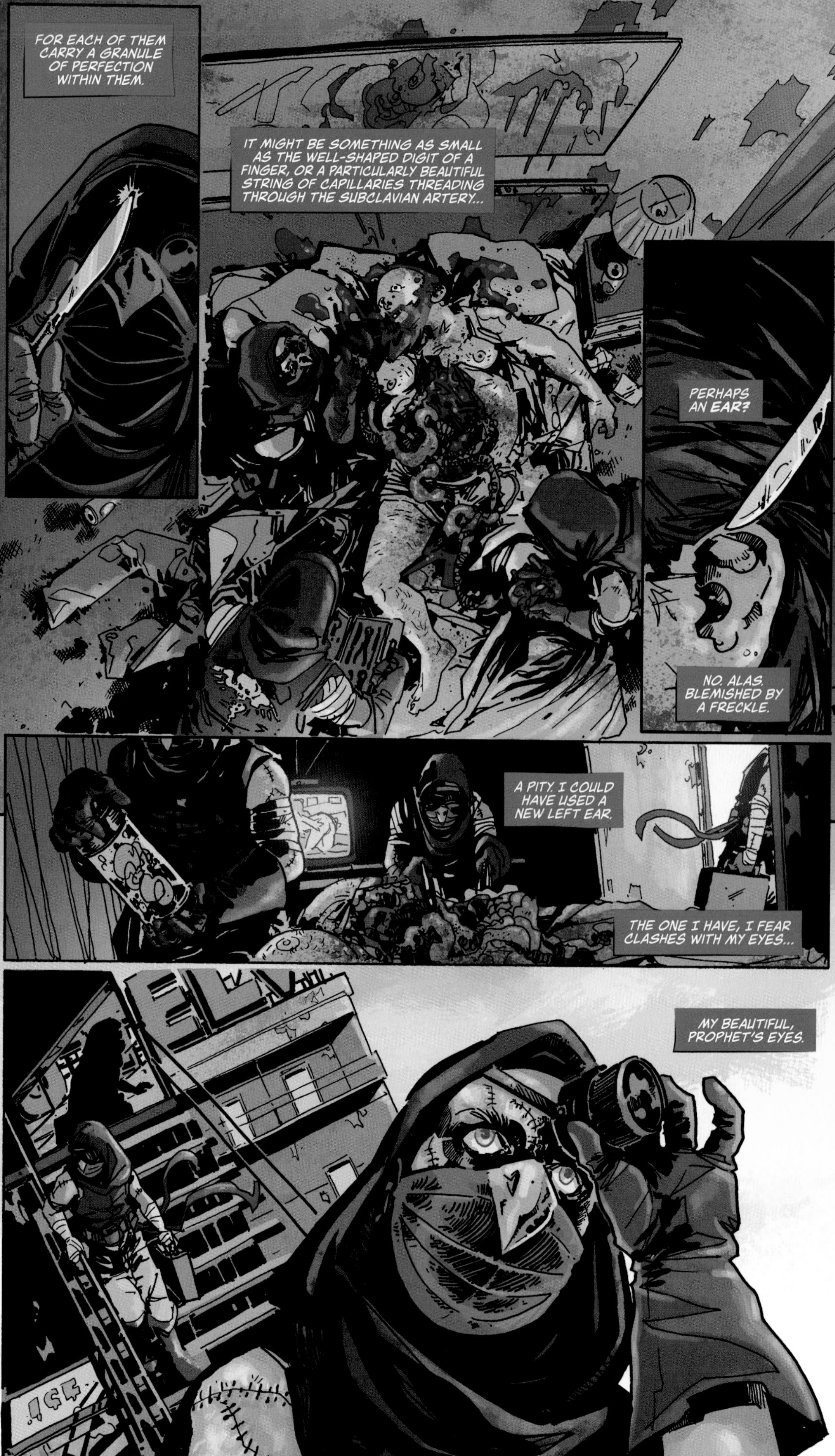
FOR EACH OF THEM CARRY A GRANULE OF PERFECTION WITHIN THEM.
IT MIGHT BE SOMETHING AS SMALL AS THE WELL-SHAPED DIGIT OF A FINGER, OR A PARTICULARLY BEAUTIFUL STRING OF CAPILLARIES THREADING THROUGH THE SUBCLAVIAN ARTERY...
PERHAPS AN EAR?
NO. ALAS. BLEMISHED BY A FRECKLE.
A PITY. I COULD HAVE USED A NEW LEFT EAR.
THE ONE I HAVE, I FEAR CLASHES WITH MY EYES...
MY BEAUTIFUL, PROPHET'S EYES.

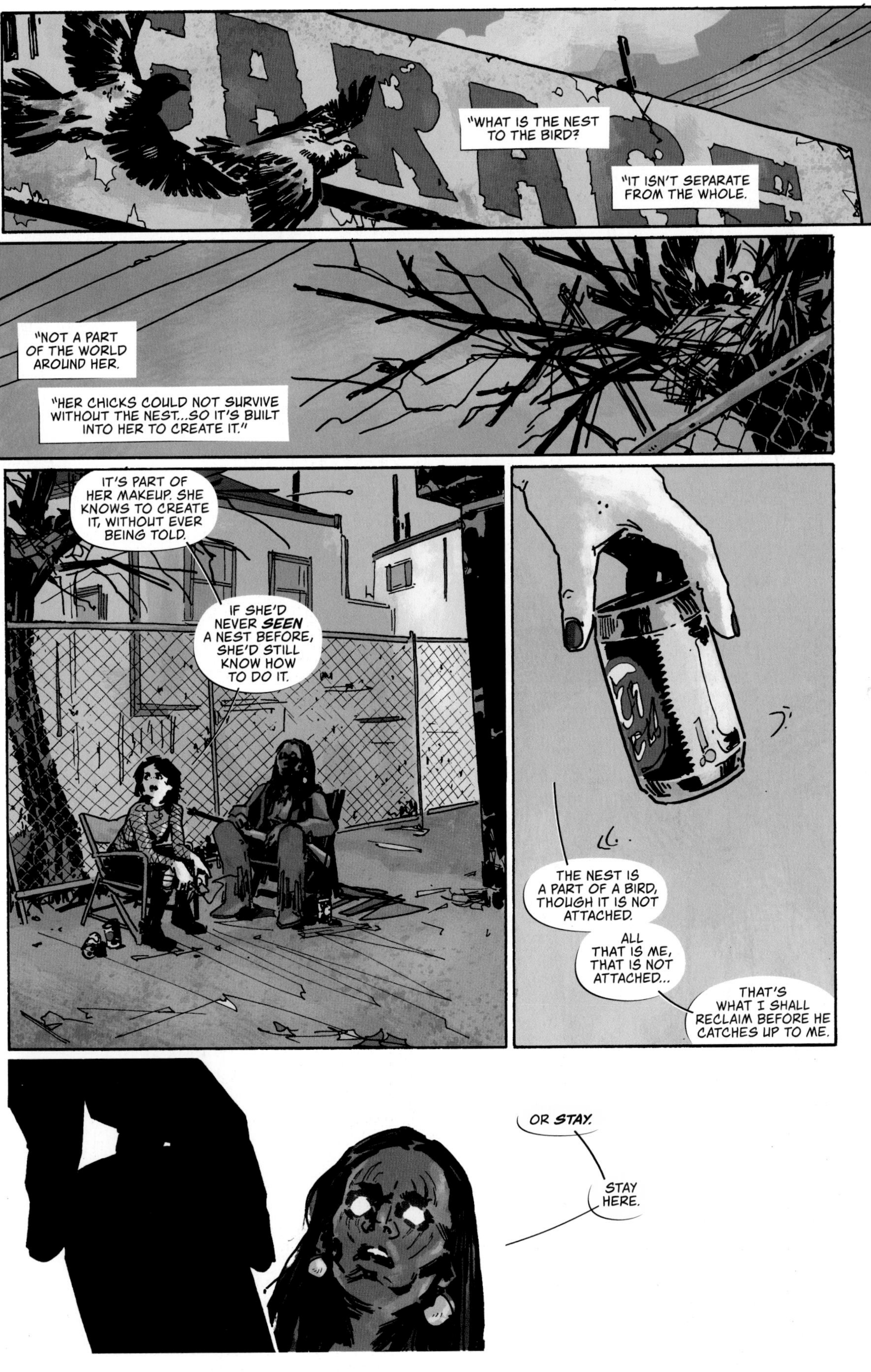
"WHAT IS THE NEST TO THE BIRD?
"IT ISN'T SEPARATE FROM THE WHOLE.
"NOT A PART OF THE WORLD AROUND HER.
"HER CHICKS COULD NOT SURVIVE WITHOUT THE NEST...SO IT'S BUILT INTO HER TO CREATE IT."
IT'S PART OF HER MAKEUP. SHE KNOWS TO CREATE IT, WITHOUT EVER BEING TOLD.
IF SHE'D NEVER SEEN A NEST BEFORE, SHE'D STILL KNOW HOW TO DO IT.
THE NEST IS A PART OF A BIRD, THOUGH IT IS NOT ATTACHED.
ALL THAT IS ME, THAT IS NOT ATTACHED...
THAT'S WHAT I SHALL RECLAIM BEFORE HE CATCHES UP TO ME.
OR STAY.
STAY HERE.

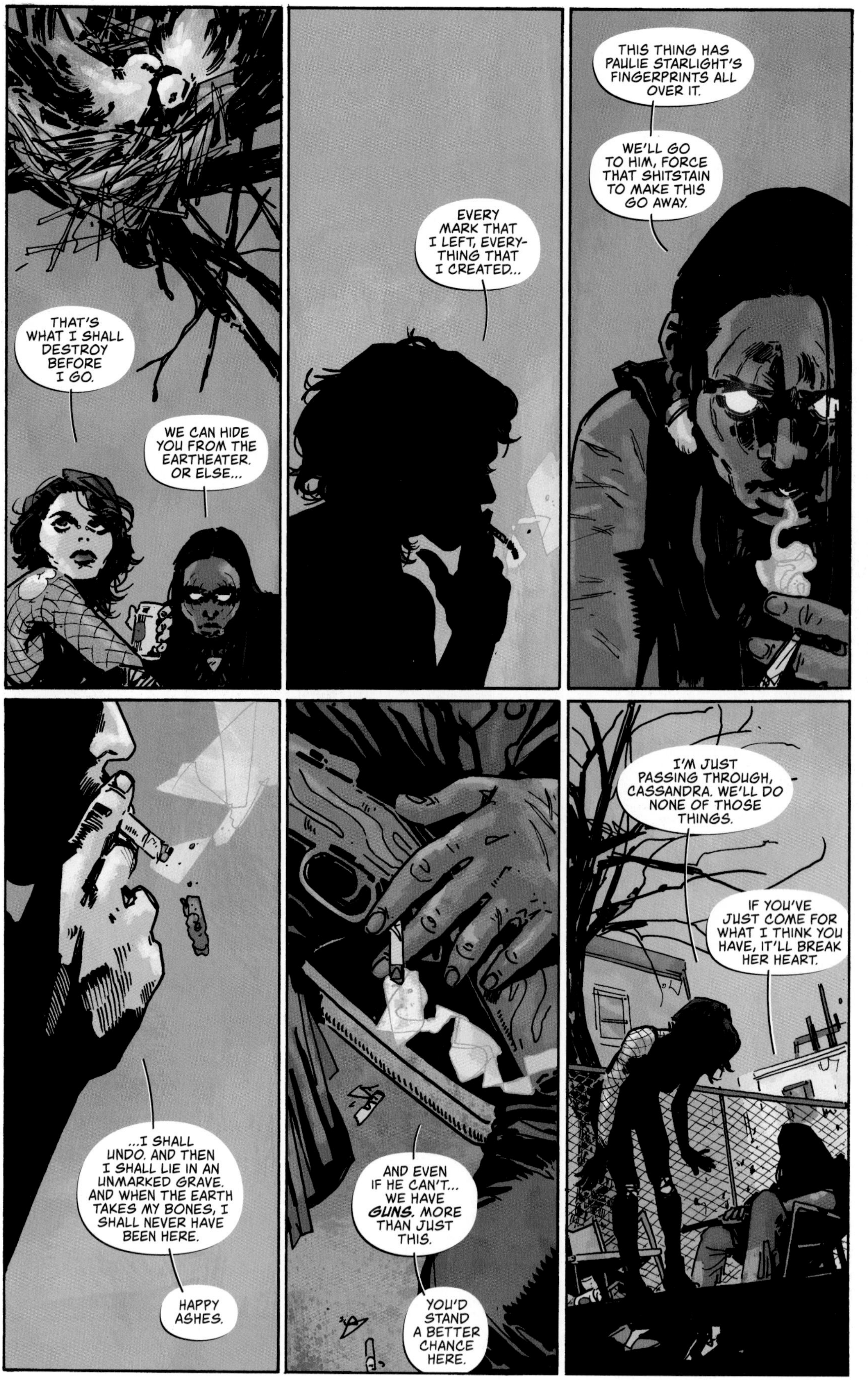
THAT'S WHAT I SHALL DESTROY BEFORE I GO.
WE CAN HIDE YOU FROM THE EARTHEATER. OR ELSE...
EVERY MARK THAT I LEFT, EVERYTHING THAT I CREATED...
THIS THING HAS PAULIE STARLIGHT'S FINGERPRINTS ALL OVER IT.
WE'LL GO TO HIM, FORCE THAT SHITSTAIN TO MAKE THIS GO AWAY.
...I SHALL UNDO. AND THEN I SHALL LIE IN AN UNMARKED GRAVE. AND WHEN THE EARTH TAKES MY BONES, I SHALL NEVER HAVE BEEN HERE.
HAPPY ASHES.
AND EVEN IF HE CAN'T... WE HAVE GUNS. MORE THAN JUST THIS.
YOU'D STAND A BETTER CHANCE HERE.
I'M JUST PASSING THROUGH, CASSANDRA. WE'LL DO NONE OF THOSE THINGS.
IF YOU'VE JUST COME FOR WHAT I THINK YOU HAVE, IT'LL BREAK HER HEART.

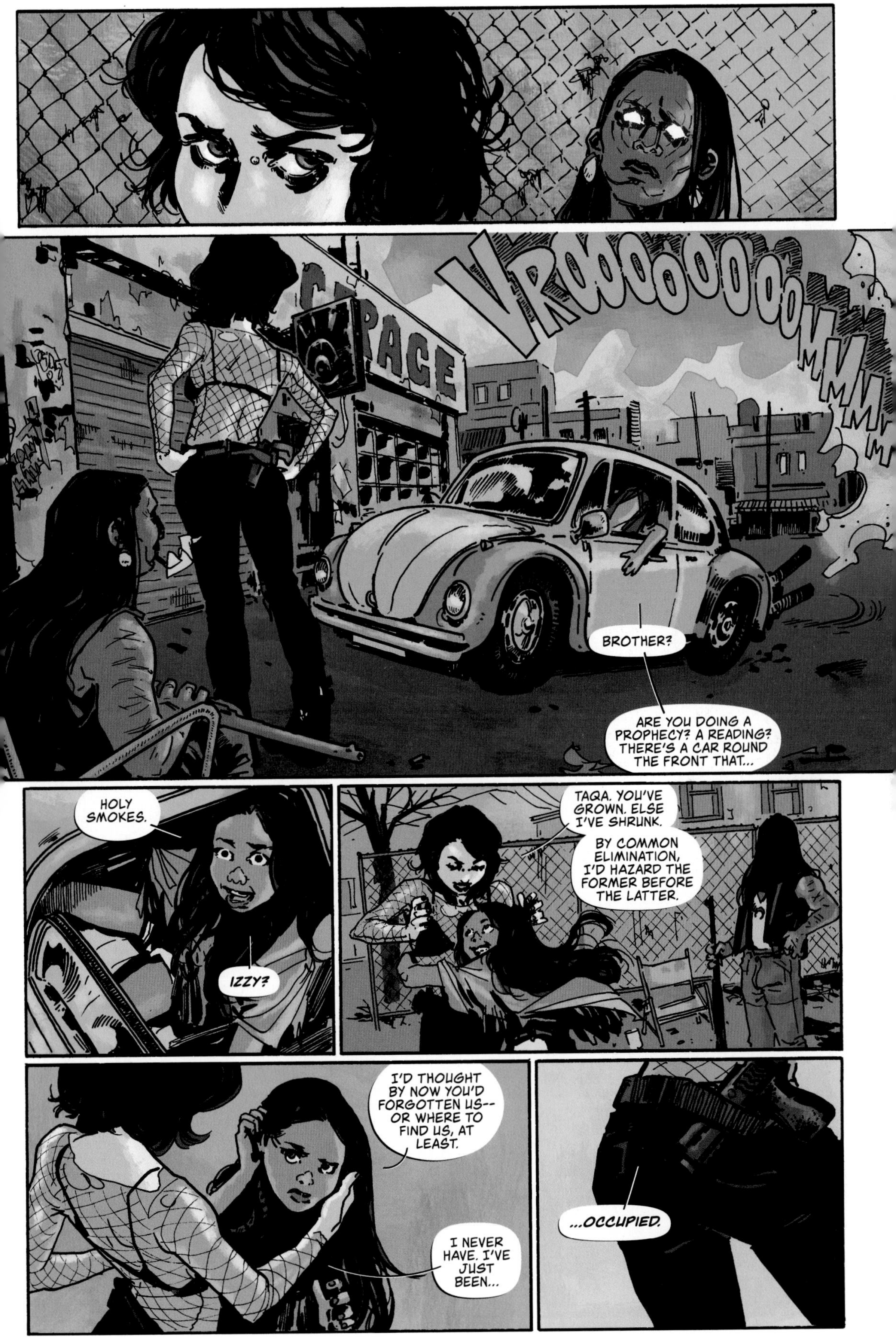
VROOOOOOOOMMMMM
BROTHER?
ARE YOU DOING A PROPHECY? A READING? THERE'S A CAR ROUND THE FRONT THAT...
HOLY SMOKES.
IZZY?
TAQA. YOU'VE GROWN. ELSE I'VE SHRUNK.
BY COMMON ELIMINATION, I'D HAZARD THE FORMER BEFORE THE LATTER.
I'D THOUGHT BY NOW YOU'D FORGOTTEN US-- OR WHERE TO FIND US, AT LEAST.
I NEVER HAVE. I'VE JUST BEEN...
...OCCUPIED.

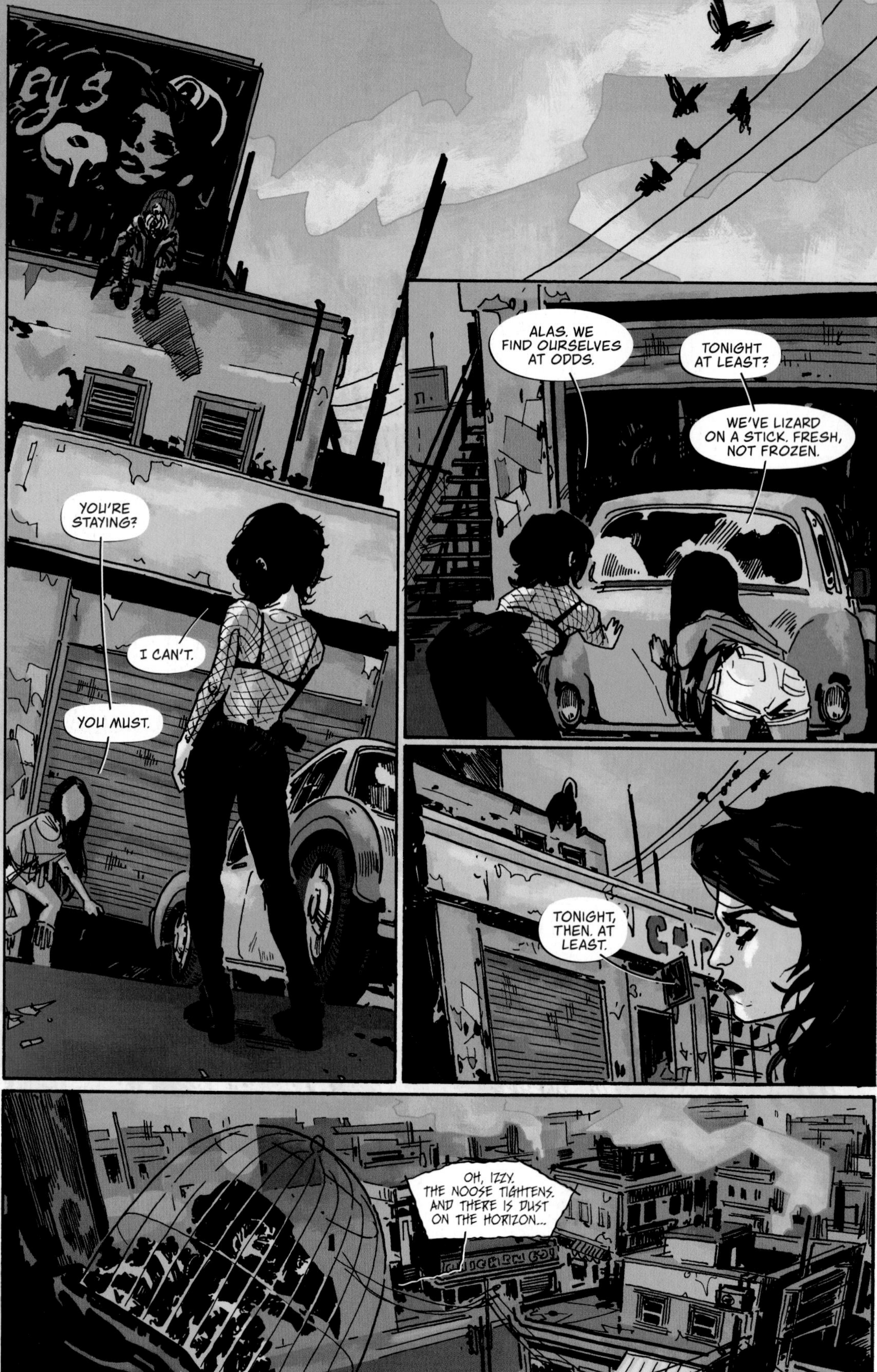
YOU'RE STAYING?
I CAN'T.
YOU MUST.
ALAS. WE FIND OURSELVES AT ODDS.
TONIGHT AT LEAST?
WE'VE LIZARD ON A STICK. FRESH, NOT FROZEN.
TONIGHT, THEN. AT LEAST.
OH, IZZY. THE NOOSE TIGHTENS. AND THERE IS DUST ON THE HORIZON...

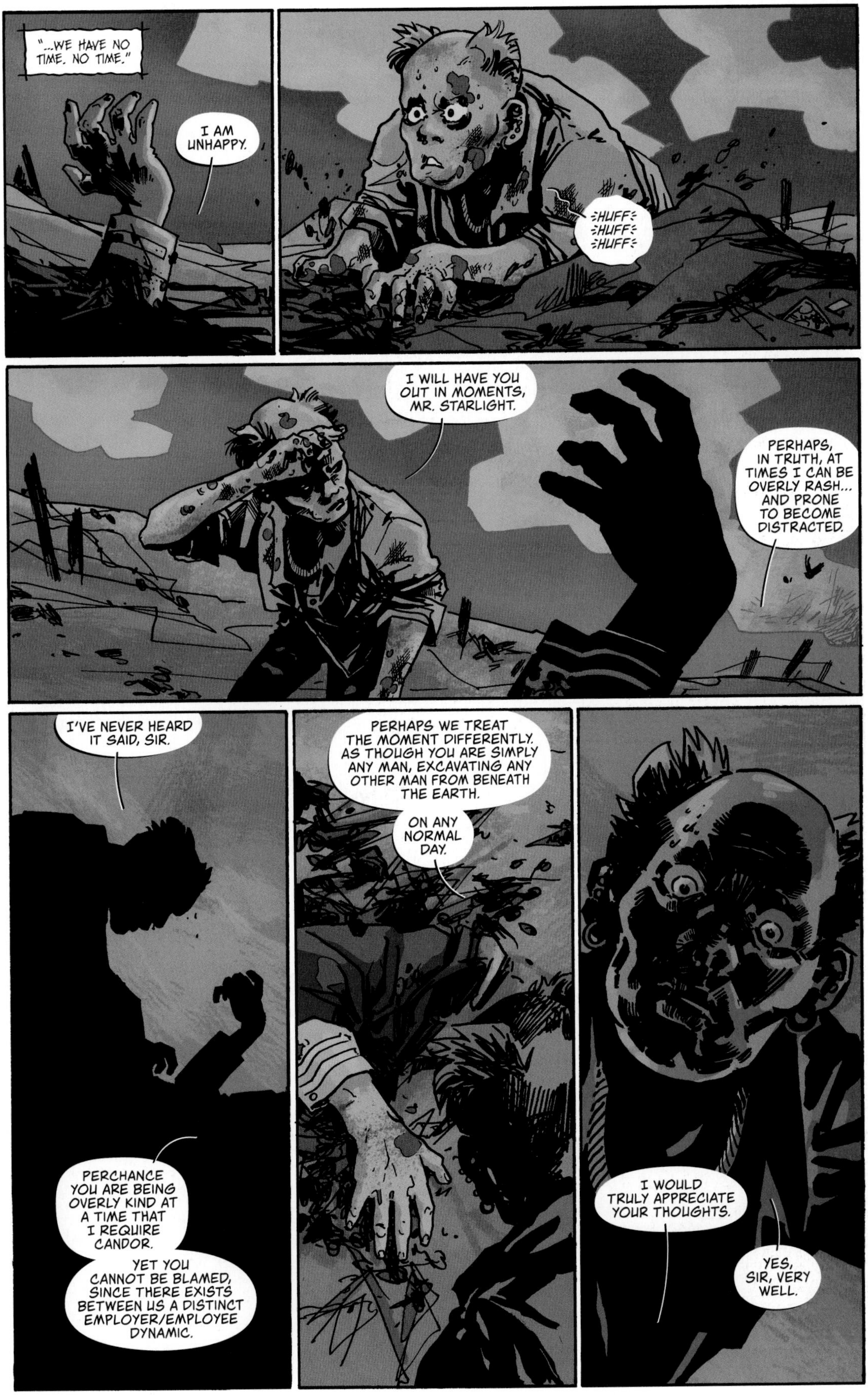
"...WE HAVE NO TIME. NO TIME."
I AM UNHAPPY.
HUFF HUFF HUFF
I WILL HAVE YOU OUT IN MOMENTS, MR. STARLIGHT.
PERHAPS, IN TRUTH, AT TIMES I CAN BE OVERLY RASH... AND PRONE TO BECOME DISTRACTED.
I'VE NEVER HEARD IT SAID, SIR.
PERCHANCE YOU ARE BEING OVERLY KIND AT A TIME THAT I REQUIRE CANDOR.
YET YOU CANNOT BE BLAMED, SINCE THERE EXISTS BETWEEN US A DISTINCT EMPLOYER/EMPLOYEE DYNAMIC.
PERHAPS WE TREAT THE MOMENT DIFFERENTLY. AS THOUGH YOU ARE SIMPLY ANY MAN, EXCAVATING ANY OTHER MAN FROM BENEATH THE EARTH.
ON ANY NORMAL DAY.
I WOULD TRULY APPRECIATE YOUR THOUGHTS.
YES, SIR, VERY WELL.

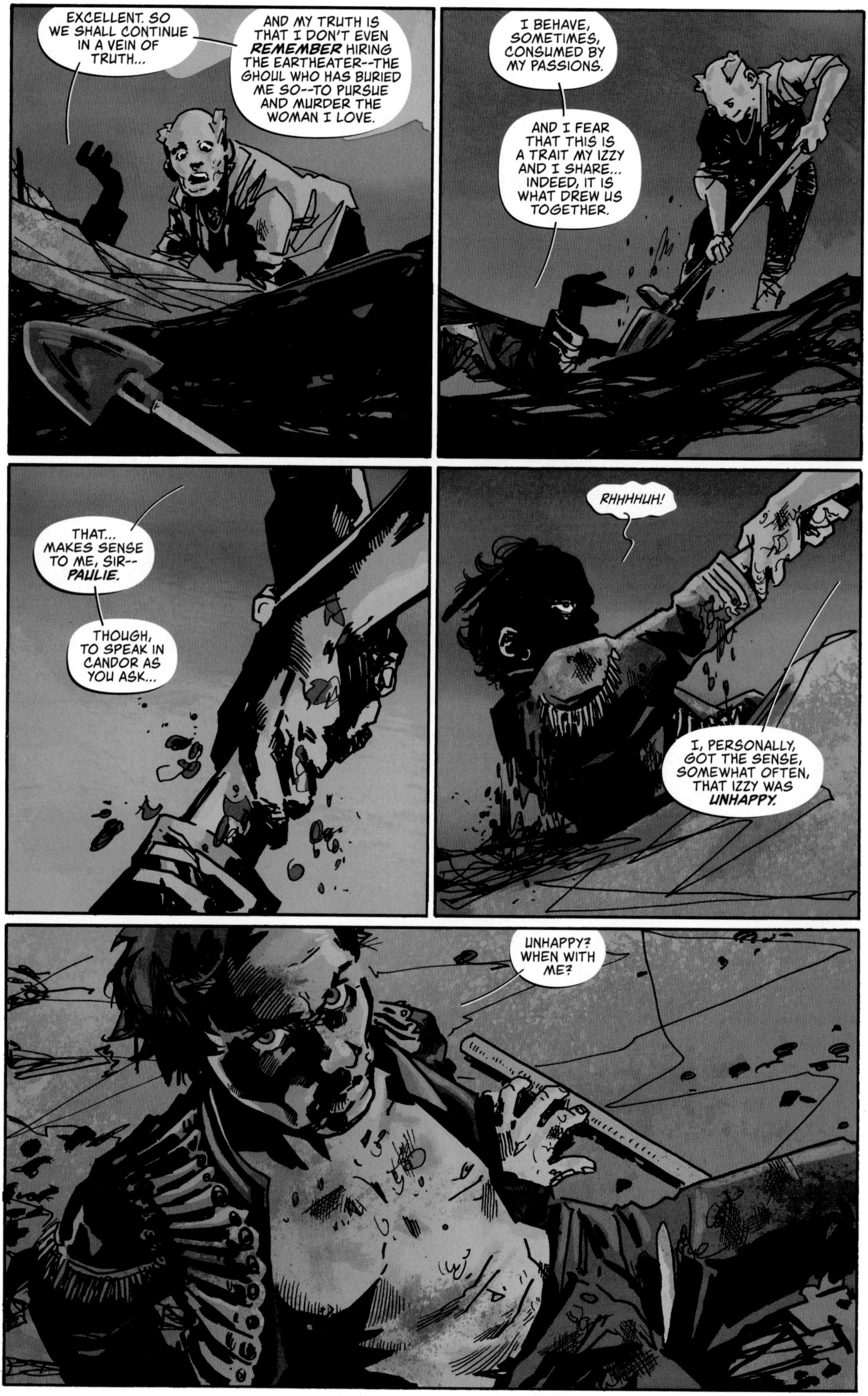

EXCELLENT. SO WE SHALL CONTINUE IN A VEIN OF TRUTH...
AND MY TRUTH IS THAT I DON'T EVEN REMEMBER HIRING THE EARTHEATER--THE GHOUL WHO HAS BURIED ME SO--TO PURSUE AND MURDER THE WOMAN I LOVE.
I BEHAVE, SOMETIMES, CONSUMED BY MY PASSIONS.
AND I FEAR THAT THIS IS A TRAIT MY IZZY AND I SHARE... INDEED, IT IS WHAT DREW US TOGETHER.
THAT... MAKES SENSE TO ME, SIR-- PAULIE.
THOUGH, TO SPEAK IN CANDOR AS YOU ASK...
RHHHHUH!
I, PERSONALLY, GOT THE SENSE, SOMEWHAT OFTEN, THAT IZZY WAS UNHAPPY.
UNHAPPY? WHEN WITH ME?

YOU SEE NOW WHAT I SAY?

I ACT WITH MY PASSIONS.

AND NOW, LOOK, I'VE FOSTERED THE START OF A VENDETTA BETWEEN YOU AND I NOW, TOO.

A RESOLUTION, THEN--TO FINISH WHAT I BEGIN.

IZZY **SHALL** END.

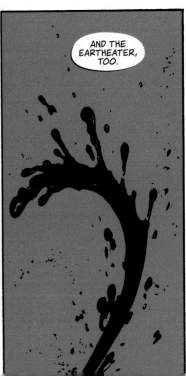

AND THE EARTHEATER, TOO.

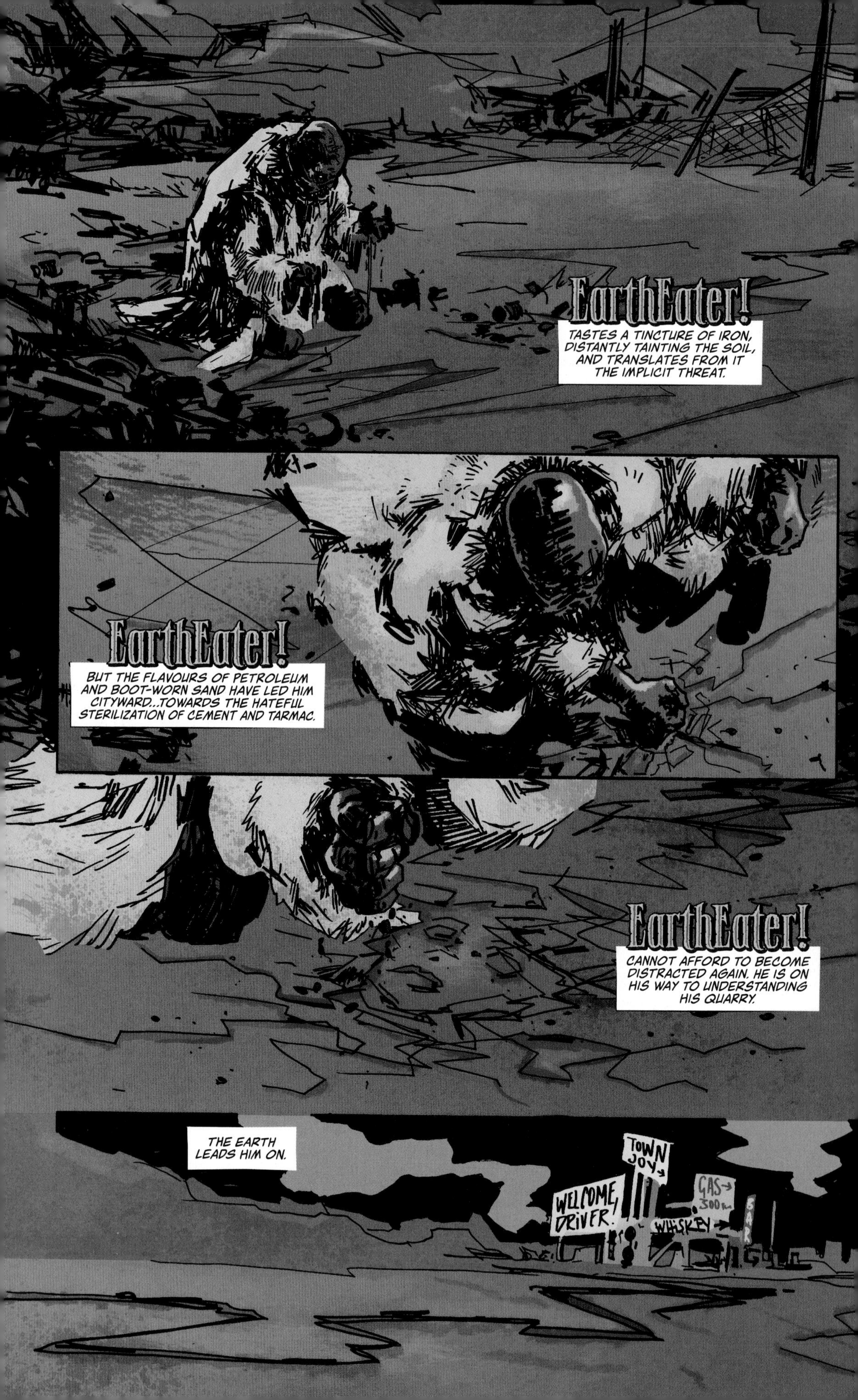
EarthEater!
TASTES A TINCTURE OF IRON, DISTANTLY TAINTING THE SOIL, AND TRANSLATES FROM IT THE IMPLICIT THREAT.
EarthEater!
BUT THE FLAVOURS OF PETROLEUM AND BOOT-WORN SAND HAVE LED HIM CITYWARD...TOWARDS THE HATEFUL STERILIZATION OF CEMENT AND TARMAC.
EarthEater!
CANNOT AFFORD TO BECOME DISTRACTED AGAIN. HE IS ON HIS WAY TO UNDERSTANDING HIS QUARRY.
THE EARTH LEADS HIM ON.
TOWN JOY
WELCOME, DRIVER!
GAS 300
WHISKEY

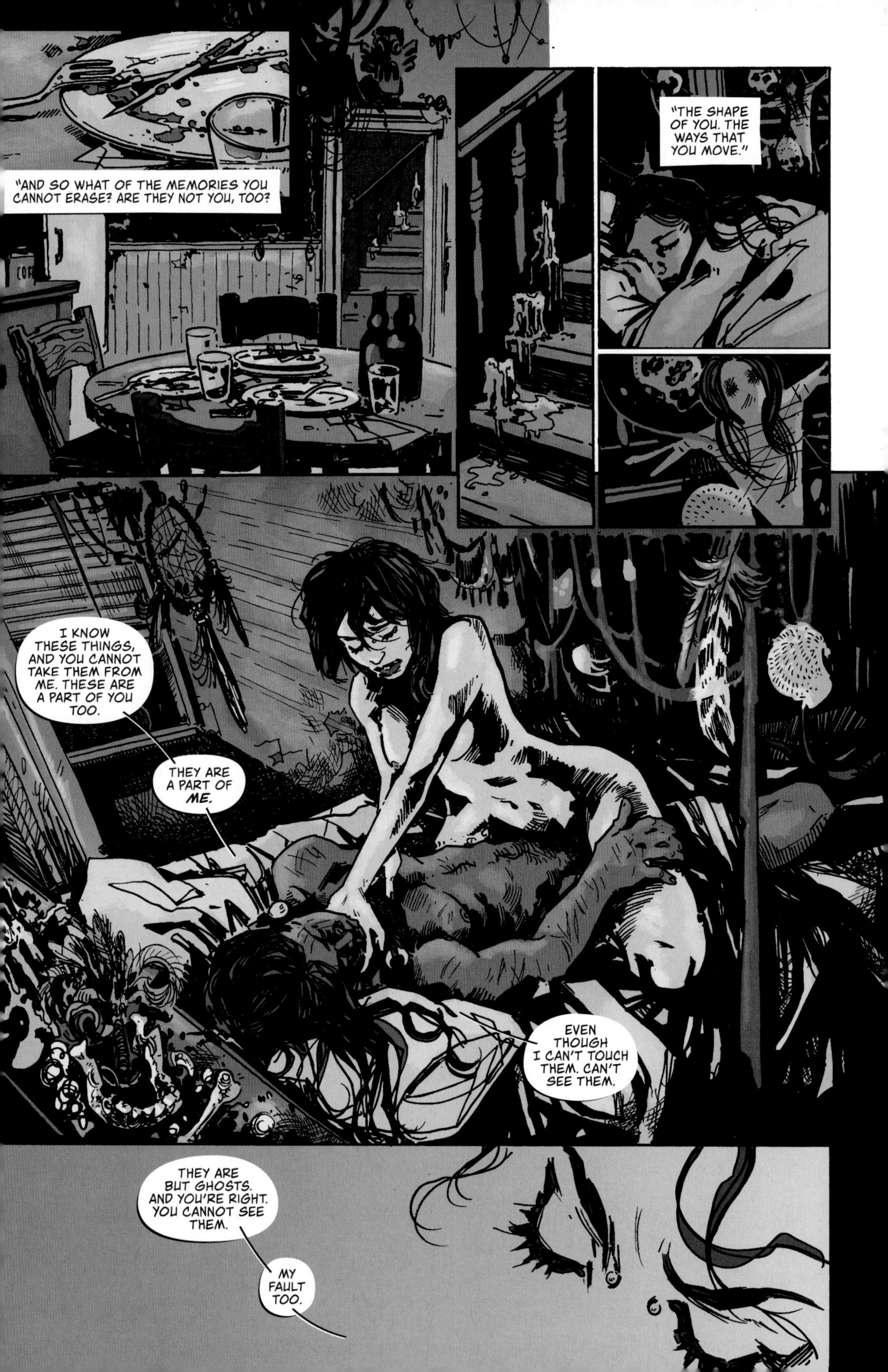
"AND SO WHAT OF THE MEMORIES YOU CANNOT ERASE? ARE THEY NOT YOU, TOO?
"THE SHAPE OF YOU. THE WAYS THAT YOU MOVE."
I KNOW THESE THINGS, AND YOU CANNOT TAKE THEM FROM ME. THESE ARE A PART OF YOU TOO.
THEY ARE A PART OF *ME.*
EVEN THOUGH I CAN'T TOUCH THEM. CAN'T SEE THEM.
THEY ARE BUT GHOSTS. AND YOU'RE RIGHT. YOU CANNOT SEE THEM.
MY FAULT TOO.

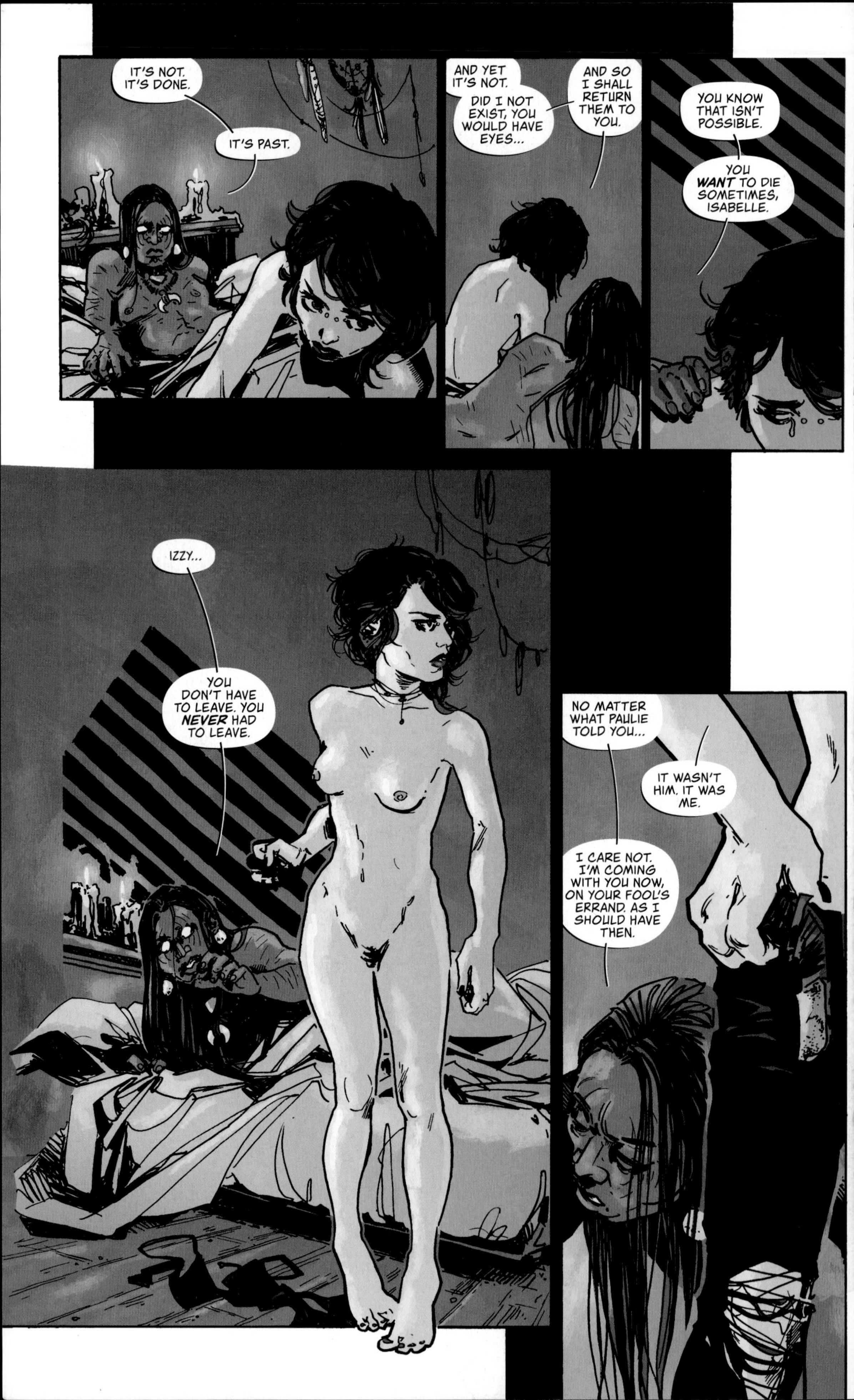
IT'S NOT. IT'S DONE.
IT'S PAST.
AND YET IT'S NOT.
DID I NOT EXIST, YOU WOULD HAVE EYES...
AND SO I SHALL RETURN THEM TO YOU.
YOU KNOW THAT ISN'T POSSIBLE.
YOU **WANT** TO DIE SOMETIMES, ISABELLE.
IZZY...
YOU DON'T HAVE TO LEAVE. YOU **NEVER** HAD TO LEAVE.
NO MATTER WHAT PAULIE TOLD YOU...
IT WASN'T HIM. IT WAS ME.
I CARE NOT. I'M COMING WITH YOU NOW, ON YOUR FOOL'S ERRAND. AS I SHOULD HAVE THEN.

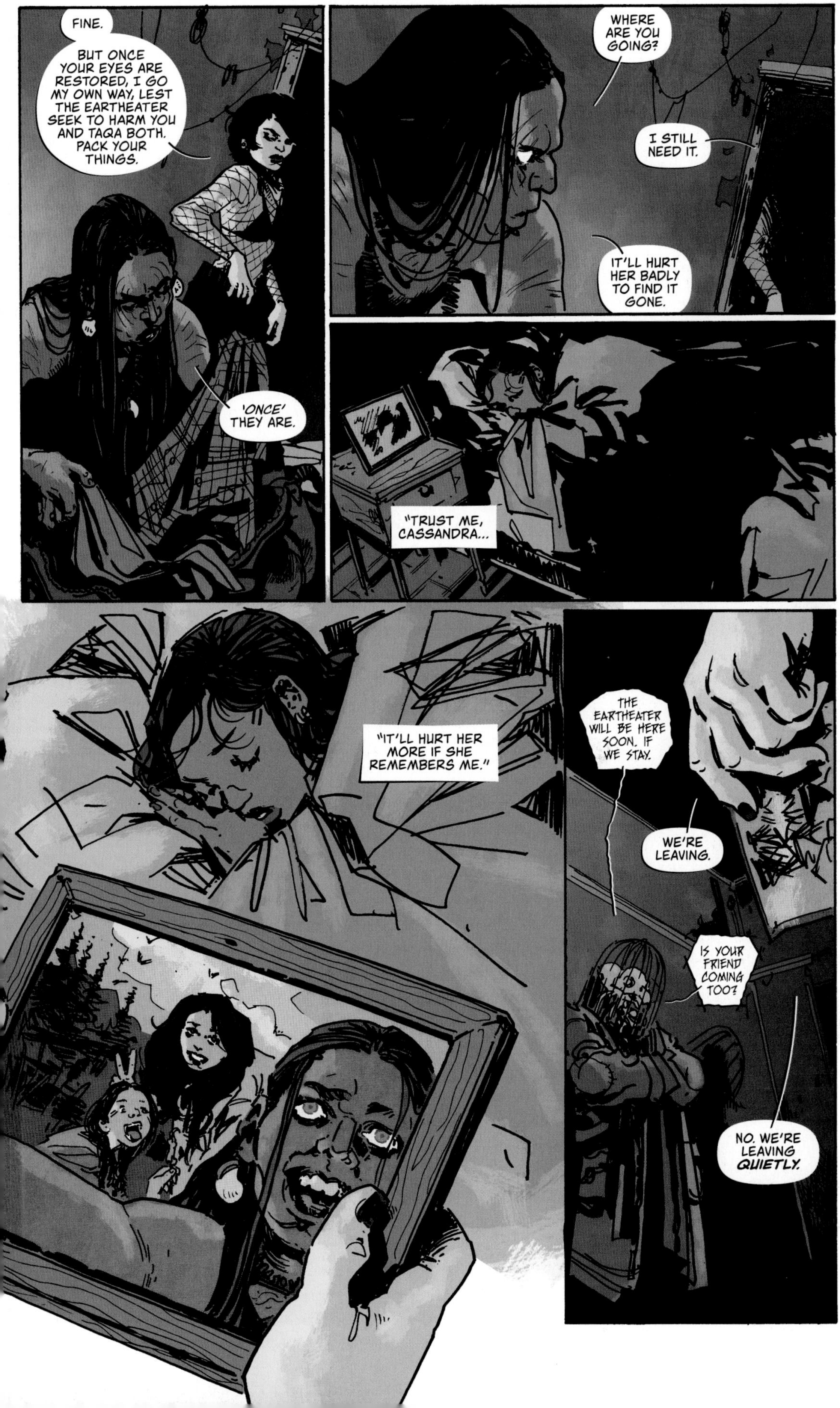
FINE.
BUT ONCE YOUR EYES ARE RESTORED, I GO MY OWN WAY, LEST THE EARTHEATER SEEK TO HARM YOU AND TAQA BOTH. PACK YOUR THINGS.
'ONCE' THEY ARE.
WHERE ARE YOU GOING?
I STILL NEED IT.
IT'LL HURT HER BADLY TO FIND IT GONE.
"TRUST ME, CASSANDRA...
"IT'LL HURT HER MORE IF SHE REMEMBERS ME."
THE EARTHEATER WILL BE HERE SOON. IF WE STAY.
WE'RE LEAVING.
IS YOUR FRIEND COMING TOO?
NO. WE'RE LEAVING *QUIETLY.*

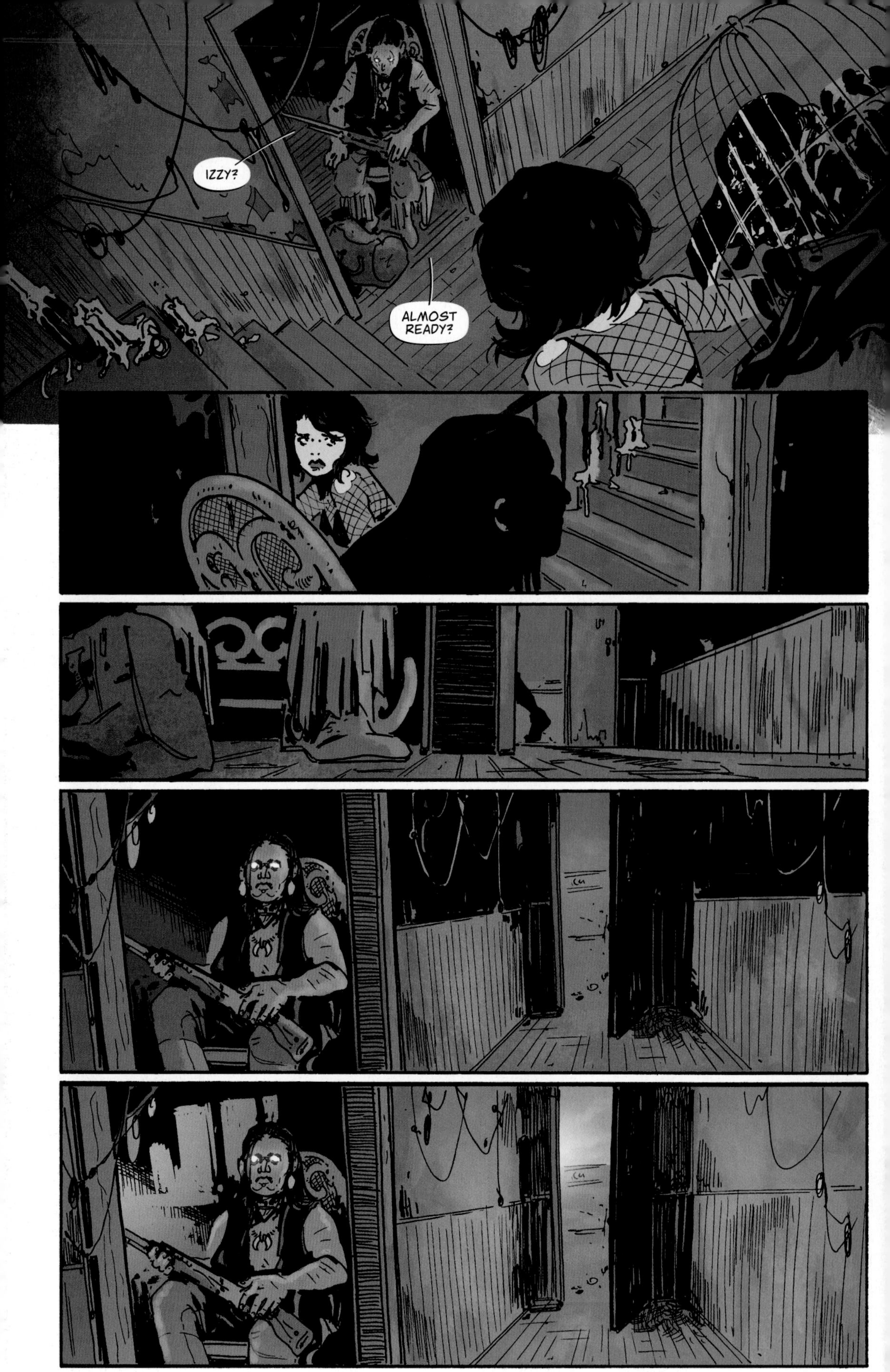
IZZY?
ALMOST READY?

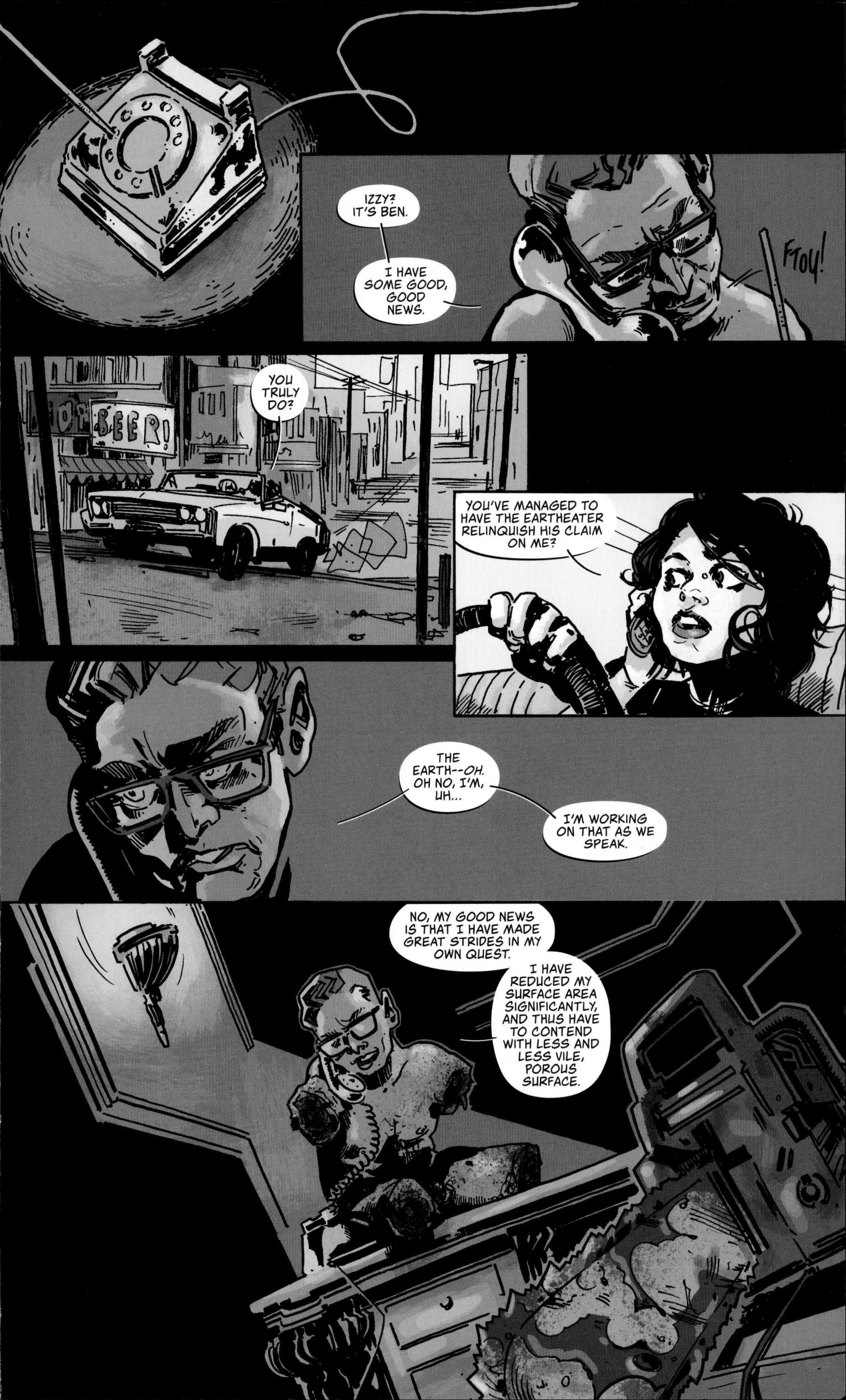
IZZY? IT'S BEN.
I HAVE SOME GOOD, GOOD NEWS.
FTOU!
YOU TRULY DO?
BEER!
YOU'VE MANAGED TO HAVE THE EARTHEATER RELINQUISH HIS CLAIM ON ME?
THE EARTH--OH. OH NO, I'M, UH...
I'M WORKING ON THAT AS WE SPEAK.
NO, MY GOOD NEWS IS THAT I HAVE MADE GREAT STRIDES IN MY OWN QUEST.
I HAVE REDUCED MY SURFACE AREA SIGNIFICANTLY, AND THUS HAVE TO CONTEND WITH LESS AND LESS VILE, POROUS SURFACE.

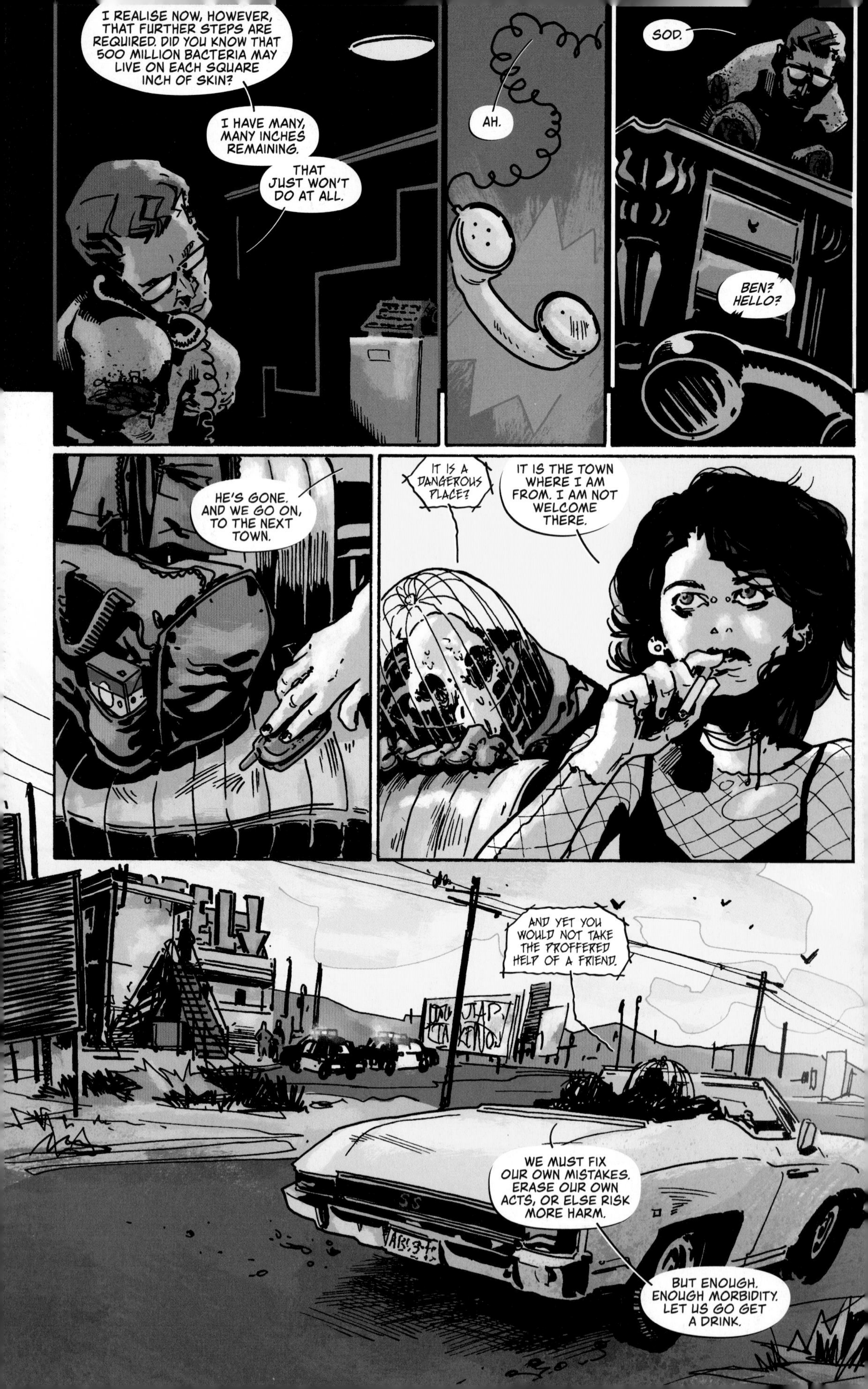
I REALISE NOW, HOWEVER, THAT FURTHER STEPS ARE REQUIRED. DID YOU KNOW THAT 500 MILLION BACTERIA MAY LIVE ON EACH SQUARE INCH OF SKIN?
I HAVE MANY, MANY INCHES REMAINING.
THAT JUST WON'T DO AT ALL.
AH.
SOD.
BEN? HELLO?
HE'S GONE. AND WE GO ON, TO THE NEXT TOWN.
IT IS A DANGEROUS PLACE?
IT IS THE TOWN WHERE I AM FROM. I AM NOT WELCOME THERE.
AND YET YOU WOULD NOT TAKE THE PROFFERED HELP OF A FRIEND.
WE MUST FIX OUR OWN MISTAKES. ERASE OUR OWN ACTS, OR ELSE RISK MORE HARM.
BUT ENOUGH. ENOUGH MORBIDITY. LET US GO GET A DRINK.

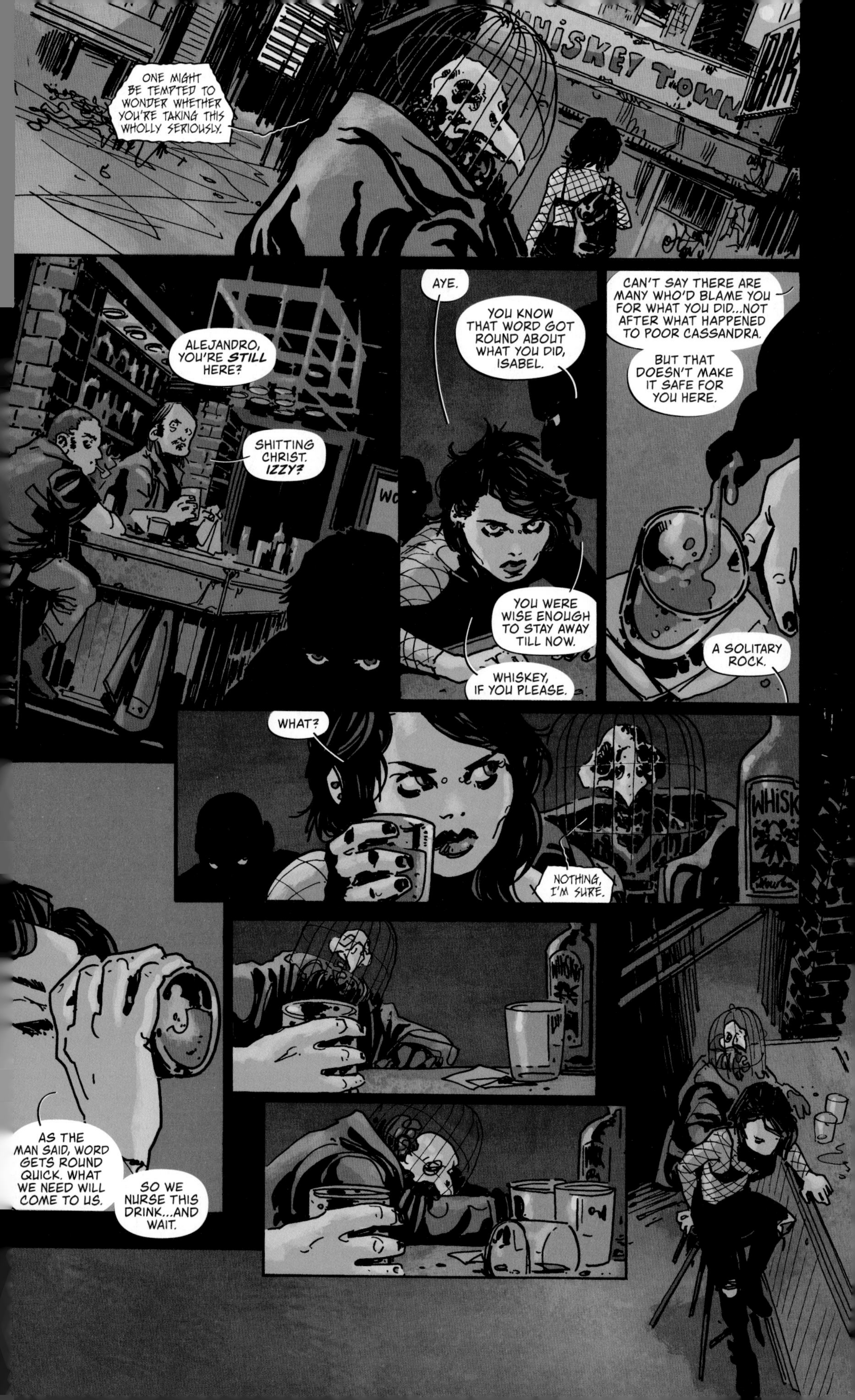
WHISKEY TOWN
ONE MIGHT BE TEMPTED TO WONDER WHETHER YOU'RE TAKING THIS WHOLLY SERIOUSLY.
ALEJANDRO, YOU'RE **STILL** HERE?
SHITTING CHRIST. ***IZZY?***
AYE.
YOU KNOW THAT WORD GOT ROUND ABOUT WHAT YOU DID, ISABEL.
YOU WERE WISE ENOUGH TO STAY AWAY TILL NOW.
WHISKEY, IF YOU PLEASE.
CAN'T SAY THERE ARE MANY WHO'D BLAME YOU FOR WHAT YOU DID...NOT AFTER WHAT HAPPENED TO POOR CASSANDRA.
BUT THAT DOESN'T MAKE IT SAFE FOR YOU HERE.
A SOLITARY ROCK.
WHAT?
NOTHING, I'M SURE.
AS THE MAN SAID, WORD GETS ROUND QUICK. WHAT WE NEED WILL COME TO US.
SO WE NURSE THIS DRINK...AND WAIT.

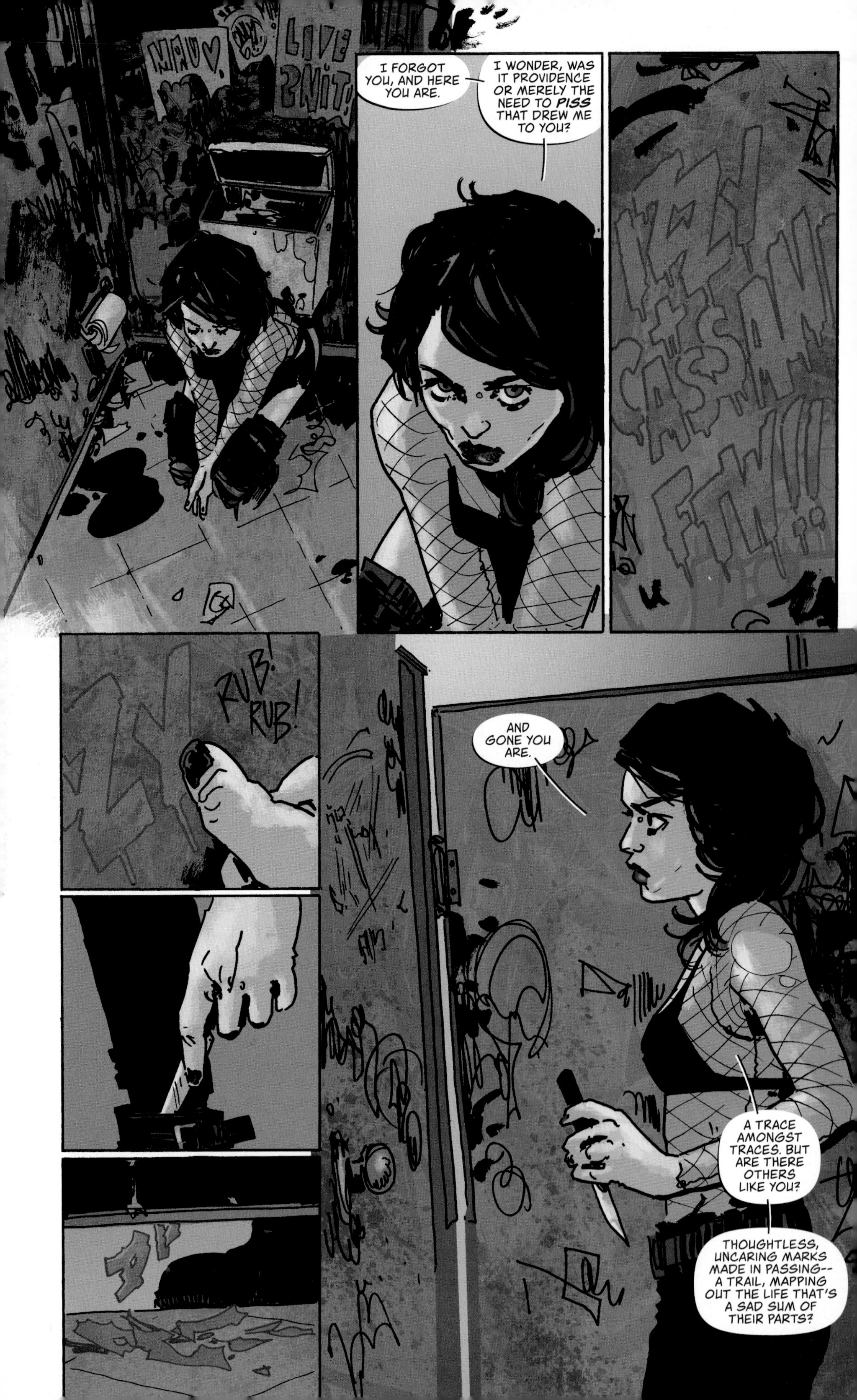
I FORGOT YOU, AND HERE YOU ARE.
I WONDER, WAS IT PROVIDENCE OR MERELY THE NEED TO *PISS* THAT DREW ME TO YOU?
RUB! RUB!
AND GONE YOU ARE.
A TRACE AMONGST TRACES. BUT ARE THERE OTHERS LIKE YOU?
THOUGHTLESS, UNCARING MARKS MADE IN PASSING-- A TRAIL, MAPPING OUT THE LIFE THAT'S A SAD SUM OF THEIR PARTS?

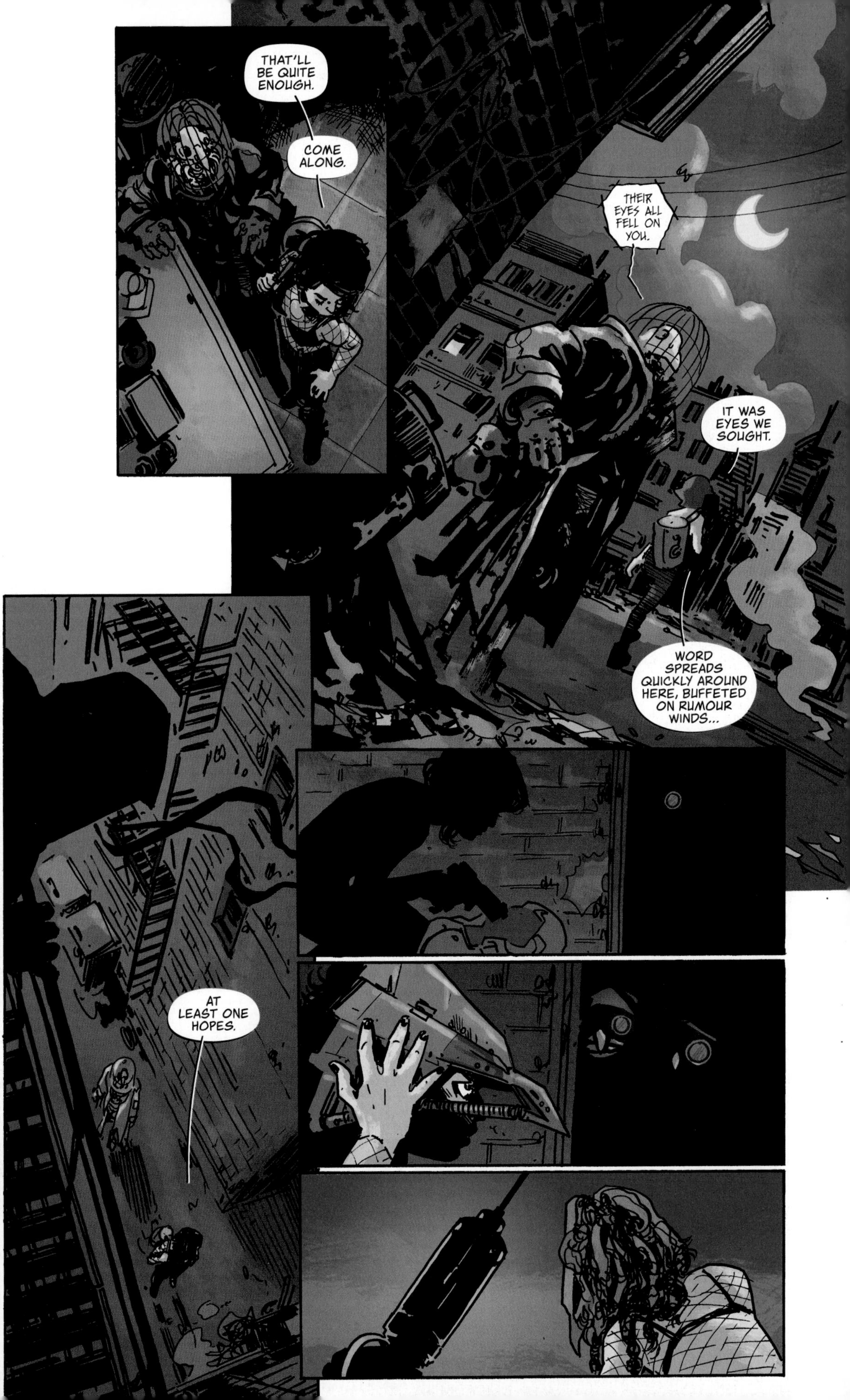
THAT'LL BE QUITE ENOUGH.
COME ALONG.
THEIR EYES ALL FELL ON YOU.
IT WAS EYES WE SOUGHT.
WORD SPREADS QUICKLY AROUND HERE, BUFFETED ON RUMOUR WINDS...
AT LEAST ONE HOPES.

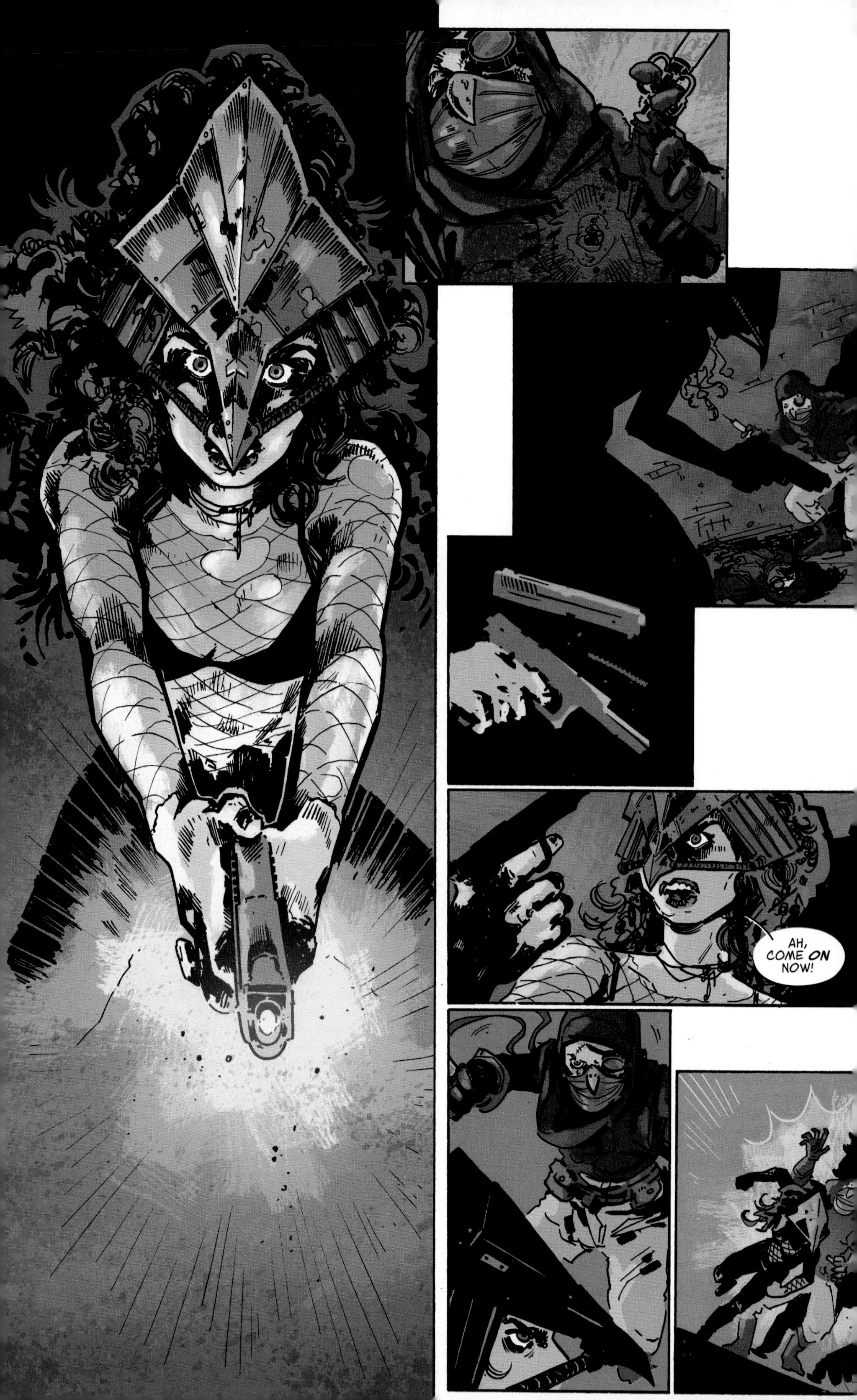
AH, COME ON NOW!

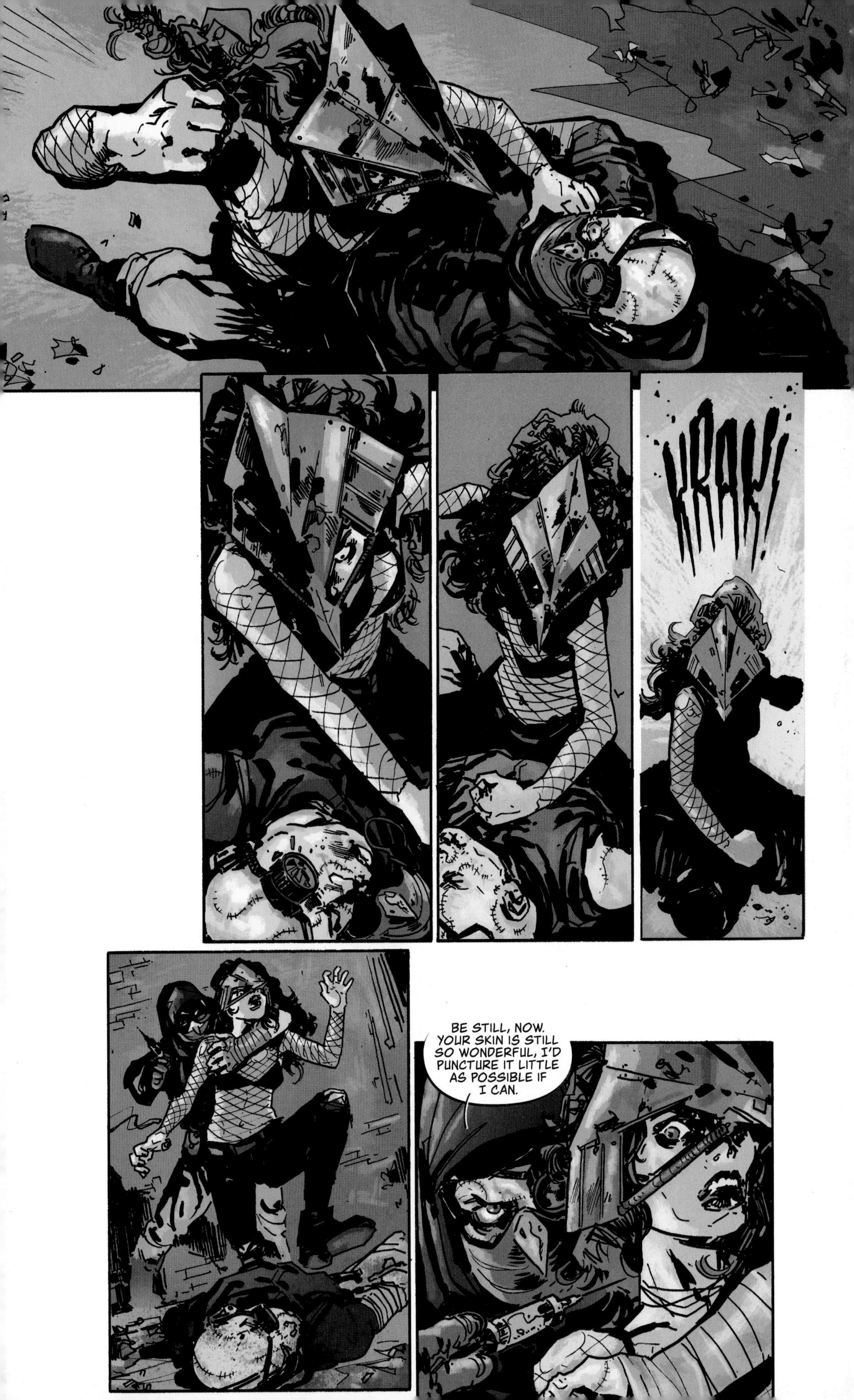
KRAK!
BE STILL, NOW. YOUR SKIN IS STILL SO WONDERFUL, I'D PUNCTURE IT LITTLE AS POSSIBLE IF I CAN.

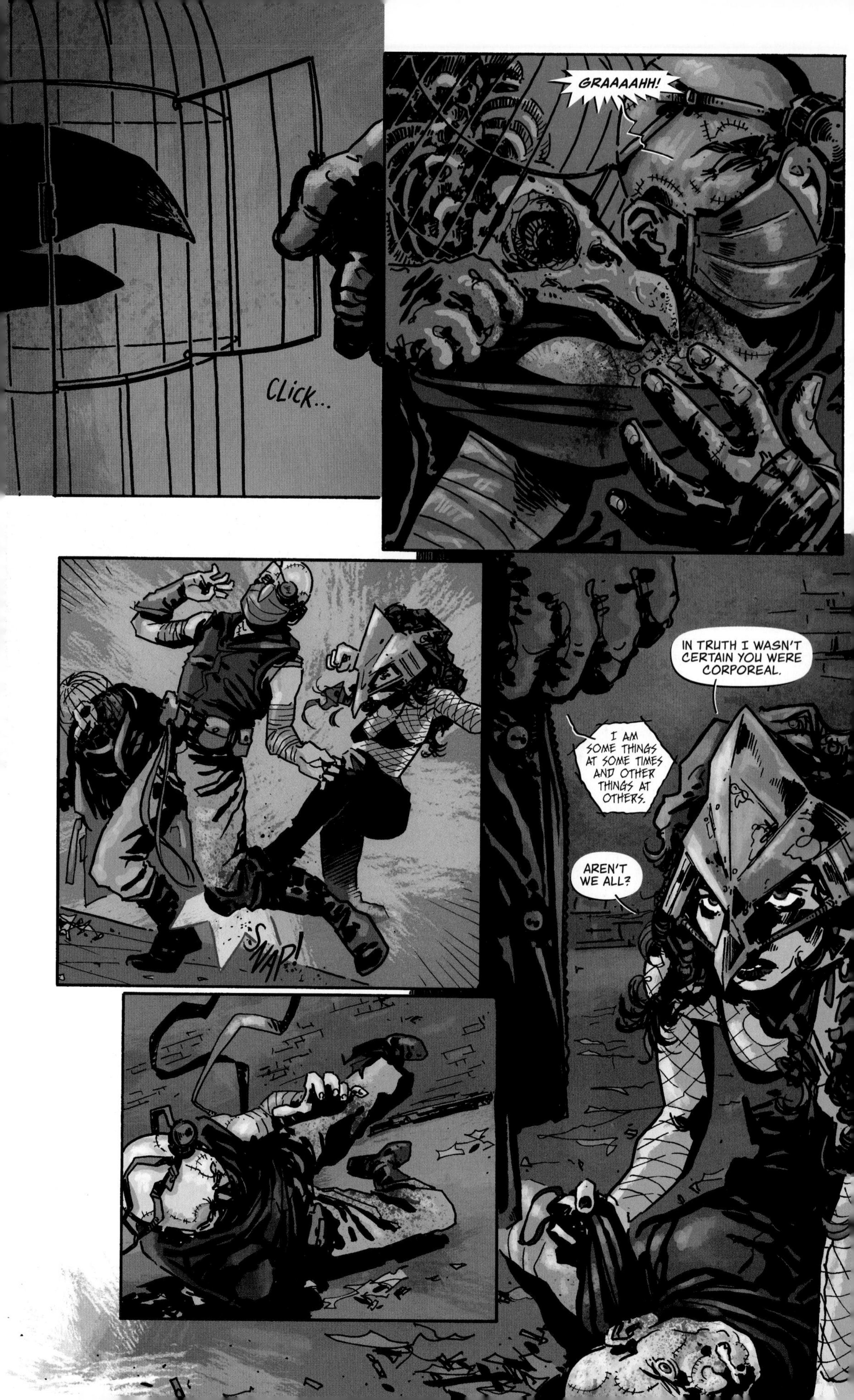
CLICK...
GRAAAAHH!
SNAP!
IN TRUTH I WASN'T CERTAIN YOU WERE CORPOREAL.
I AM SOME THINGS AT SOME TIMES AND OTHER THINGS AT OTHERS.
AREN'T WE ALL?

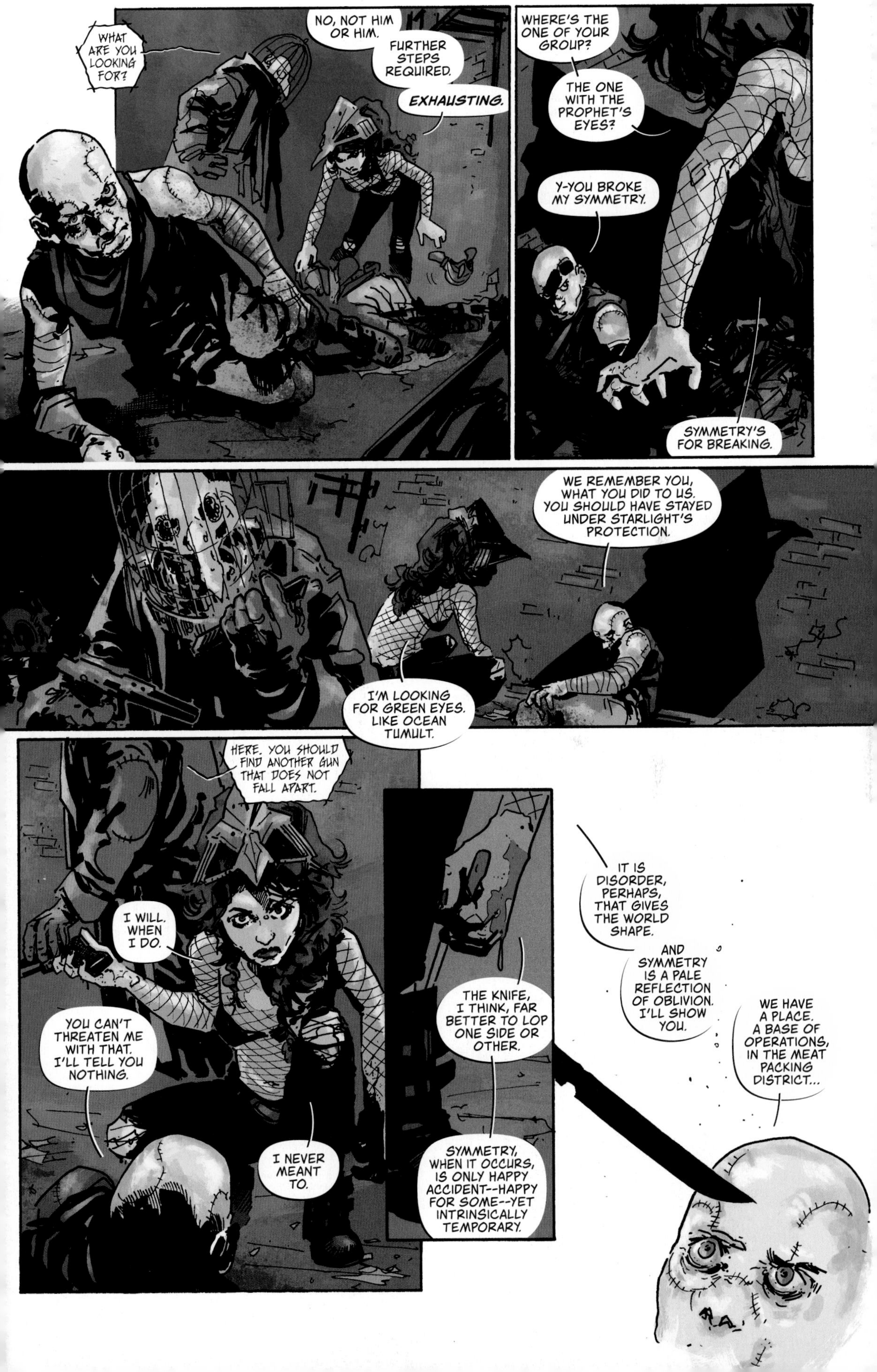
WHAT ARE YOU LOOKING FOR?
NO, NOT HIM OR HIM.
FURTHER STEPS REQUIRED.
EXHAUSTING.
WHERE'S THE ONE OF YOUR GROUP?
THE ONE WITH THE PROPHET'S EYES?
Y-YOU BROKE MY SYMMETRY.
SYMMETRY'S FOR BREAKING.
WE REMEMBER YOU, WHAT YOU DID TO US. YOU SHOULD HAVE STAYED UNDER STARLIGHT'S PROTECTION.
I'M LOOKING FOR GREEN EYES. LIKE OCEAN TUMULT.
HERE. YOU SHOULD FIND ANOTHER GUN THAT DOES NOT FALL APART.
I WILL. WHEN I DO.
YOU CAN'T THREATEN ME WITH THAT. I'LL TELL YOU NOTHING.
I NEVER MEANT TO.
THE KNIFE, I THINK, FAR BETTER TO LOP ONE SIDE OR OTHER.
SYMMETRY, WHEN IT OCCURS, IS ONLY HAPPY ACCIDENT--HAPPY FOR SOME--YET INTRINSICALLY TEMPORARY.
IT IS DISORDER, PERHAPS, THAT GIVES THE WORLD SHAPE.
AND SYMMETRY IS A PALE REFLECTION OF OBLIVION. I'LL SHOW YOU.
WE HAVE A PLACE. A BASE OF OPERATIONS, IN THE MEAT PACKING DISTRICT...

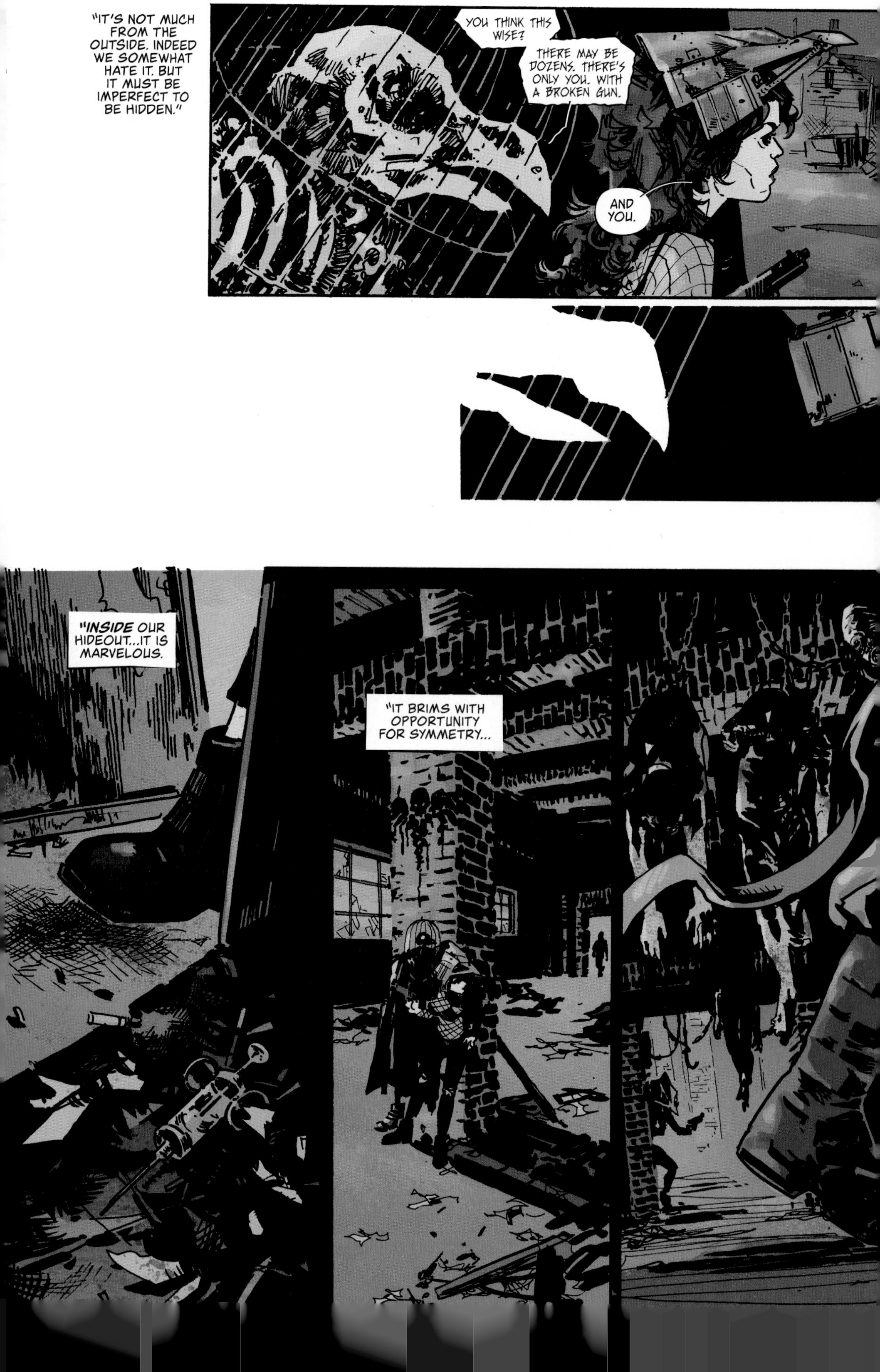
"IT'S NOT MUCH FROM THE OUTSIDE. INDEED WE SOMEWHAT HATE IT. BUT IT MUST BE IMPERFECT TO BE HIDDEN."
YOU THINK THIS WISE?
THERE MAY BE DOZENS. THERE'S ONLY YOU. WITH A BROKEN GUN.
AND YOU.
"INSIDE OUR HIDEOUT...IT IS MARVELOUS.
"IT BRIMS WITH OPPORTUNITY FOR SYMMETRY...

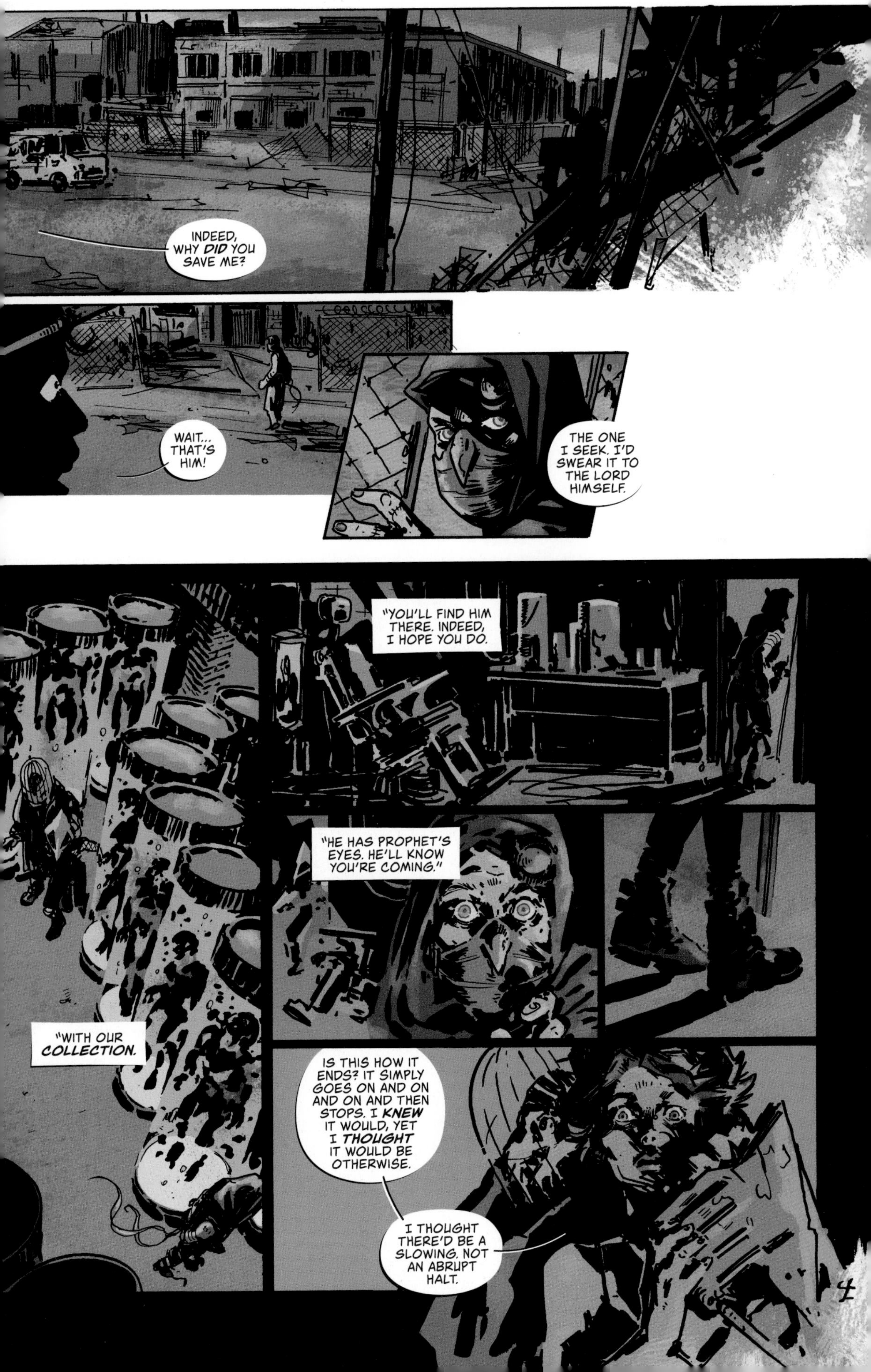
INDEED, WHY DID YOU SAVE ME?
WAIT... THAT'S HIM!
THE ONE I SEEK. I'D SWEAR IT TO THE LORD HIMSELF.
"YOU'LL FIND HIM THERE. INDEED, I HOPE YOU DO.
"HE HAS PROPHET'S EYES. HE'LL KNOW YOU'RE COMING."
"WITH OUR COLLECTION.
IS THIS HOW IT ENDS? IT SIMPLY GOES ON AND ON AND ON AND THEN STOPS. I KNEW IT WOULD, YET I THOUGHT IT WOULD BE OTHERWISE.
I THOUGHT THERE'D BE A SLOWING. NOT AN ABRUPT HALT.
4

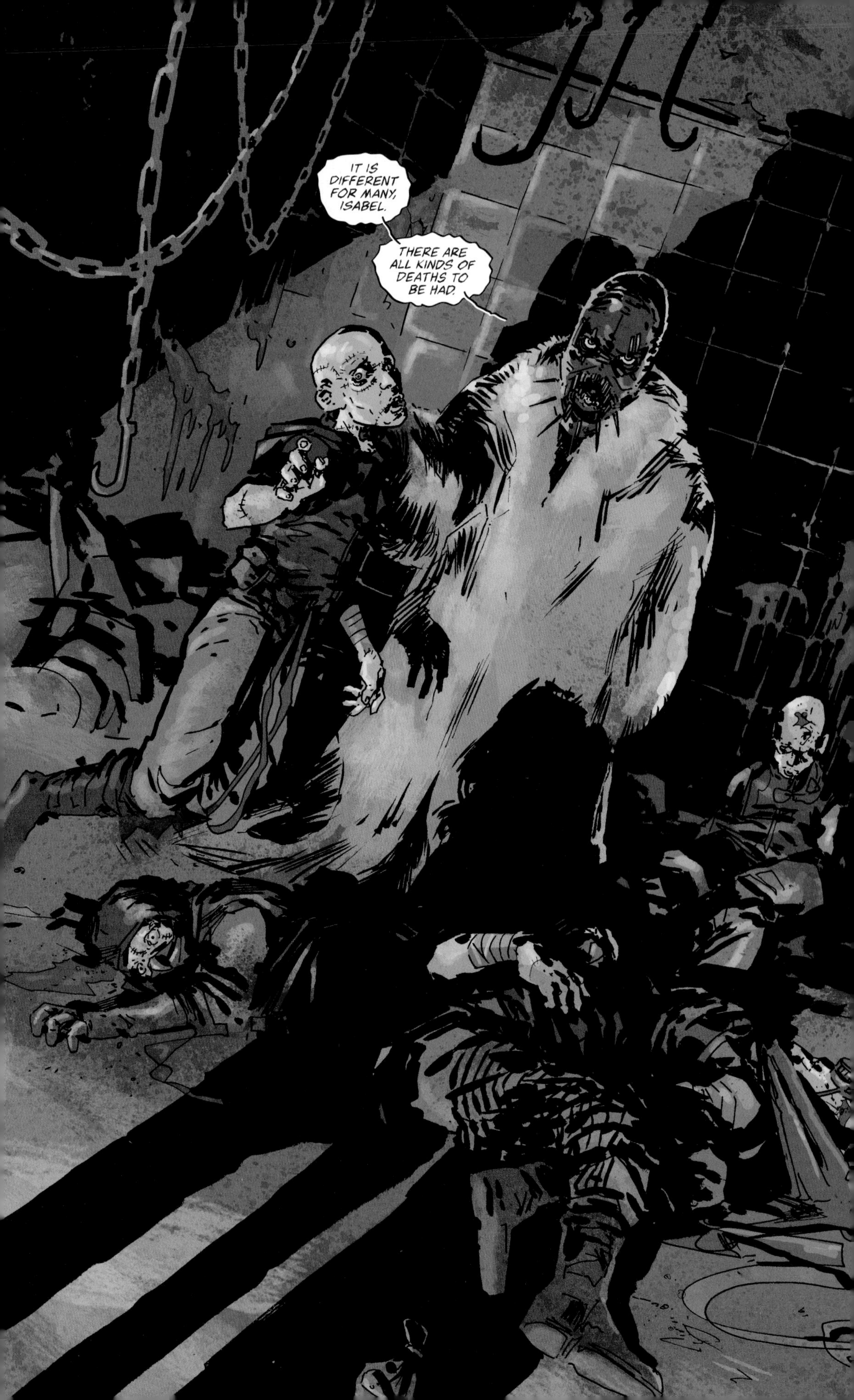
IT IS DIFFERENT FOR MANY, ISABEL.
THERE ARE ALL KINDS OF DEATHS TO BE HAD.

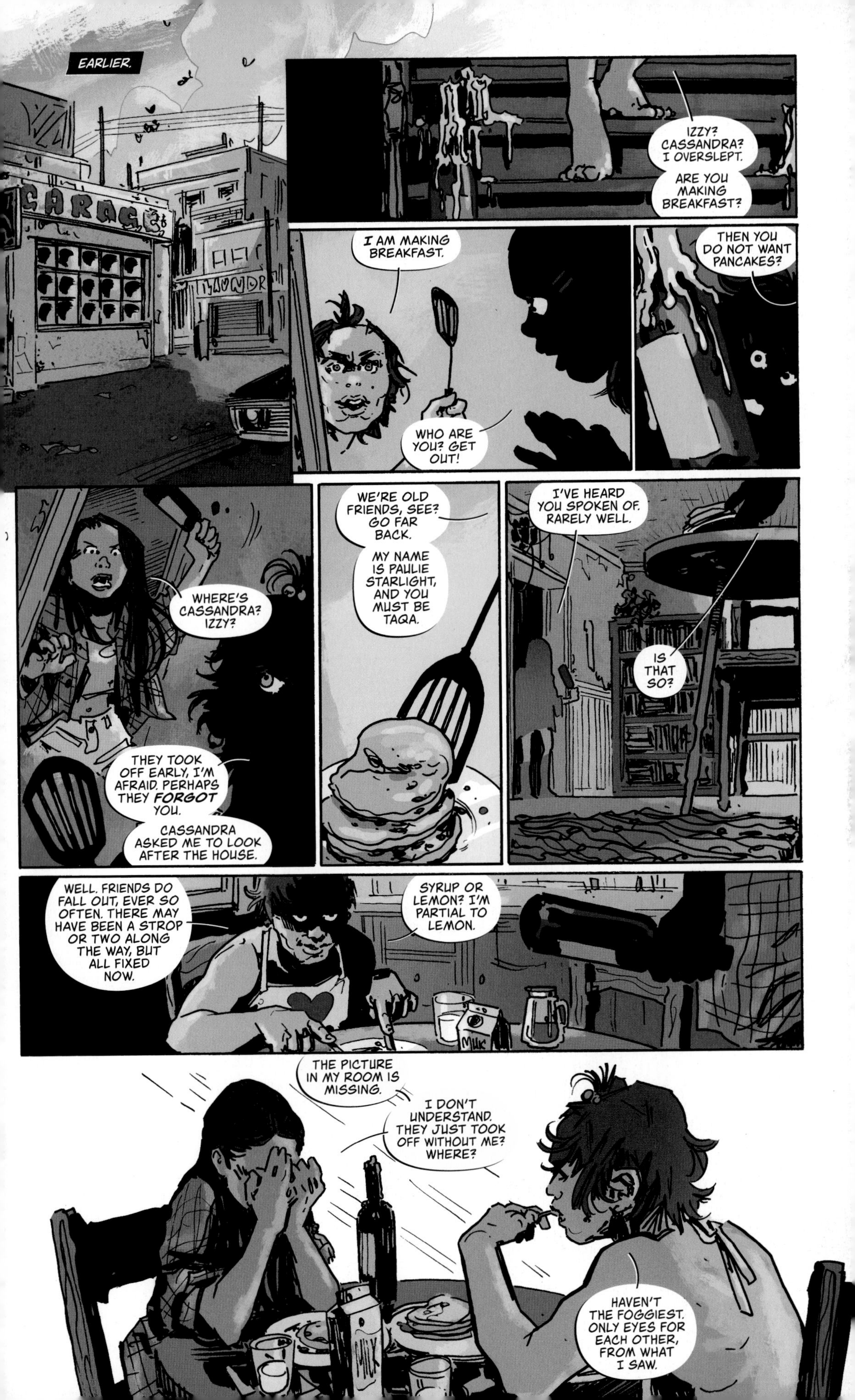
EARLIER.
GARAGE
LAUNDR
IZZY? CASSANDRA? I OVERSLEPT.
ARE YOU MAKING BREAKFAST?
I AM MAKING BREAKFAST.
WHO ARE YOU? GET OUT!
THEN YOU DO NOT WANT PANCAKES?
WHERE'S CASSANDRA? IZZY?
THEY TOOK OFF EARLY, I'M AFRAID. PERHAPS THEY FORGOT YOU.
CASSANDRA ASKED ME TO LOOK AFTER THE HOUSE.
WE'RE OLD FRIENDS, SEE? GO FAR BACK.
MY NAME IS PAULIE STARLIGHT, AND YOU MUST BE TAQA.
I'VE HEARD YOU SPOKEN OF. RARELY WELL.
IS THAT SO?
WELL. FRIENDS DO FALL OUT, EVER SO OFTEN. THERE MAY HAVE BEEN A STROP OR TWO ALONG THE WAY, BUT ALL FIXED NOW.
SYRUP OR LEMON? I'M PARTIAL TO LEMON.
MILK
THE PICTURE IN MY ROOM IS MISSING.
I DON'T UNDERSTAND. THEY JUST TOOK OFF WITHOUT ME? WHERE?
HAVEN'T THE FOGGIEST. ONLY EYES FOR EACH OTHER, FROM WHAT I SAW.
MILK

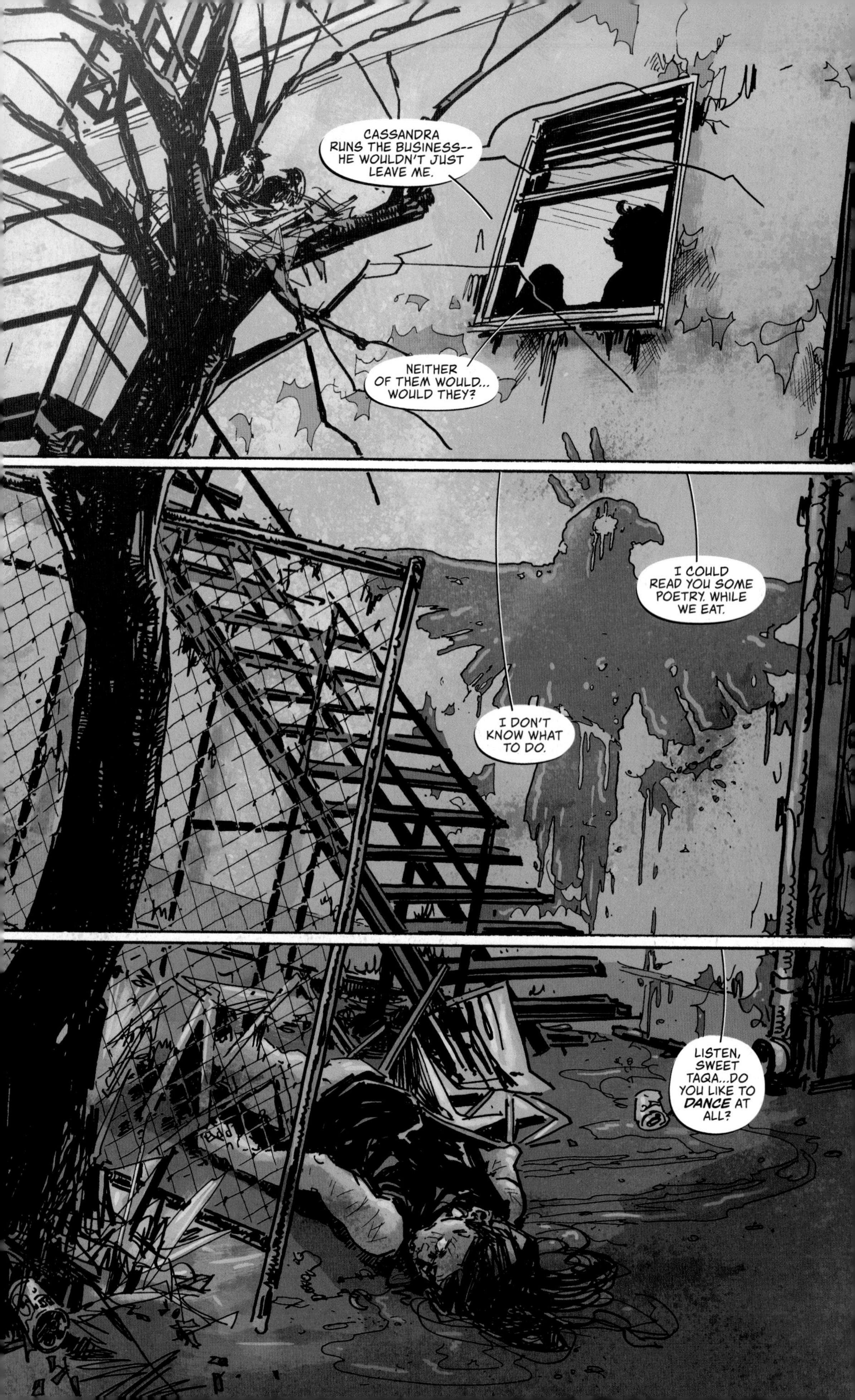
CASSANDRA RUNS THE BUSINESS-- HE WOULDN'T JUST LEAVE ME.
NEITHER OF THEM WOULD... WOULD THEY?
I COULD READ YOU SOME POETRY. WHILE WE EAT.
I DON'T KNOW WHAT TO DO.
LISTEN, SWEET TAQA...DO YOU LIKE TO DANCE AT ALL?

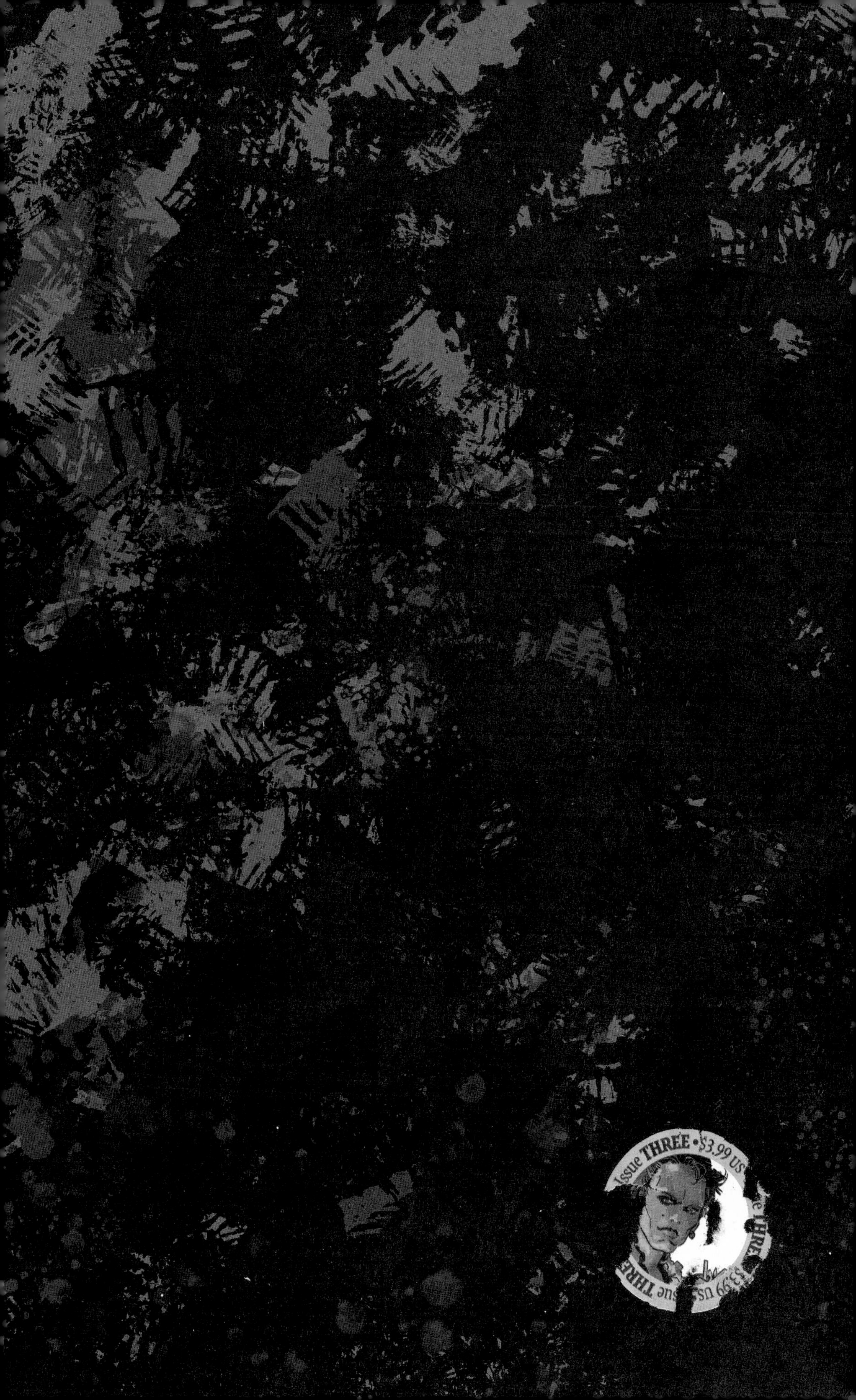

Issue THREE •$3.99 US

"glad to see you
GO GO GO GO GOODBYE"
— THE RAMONES

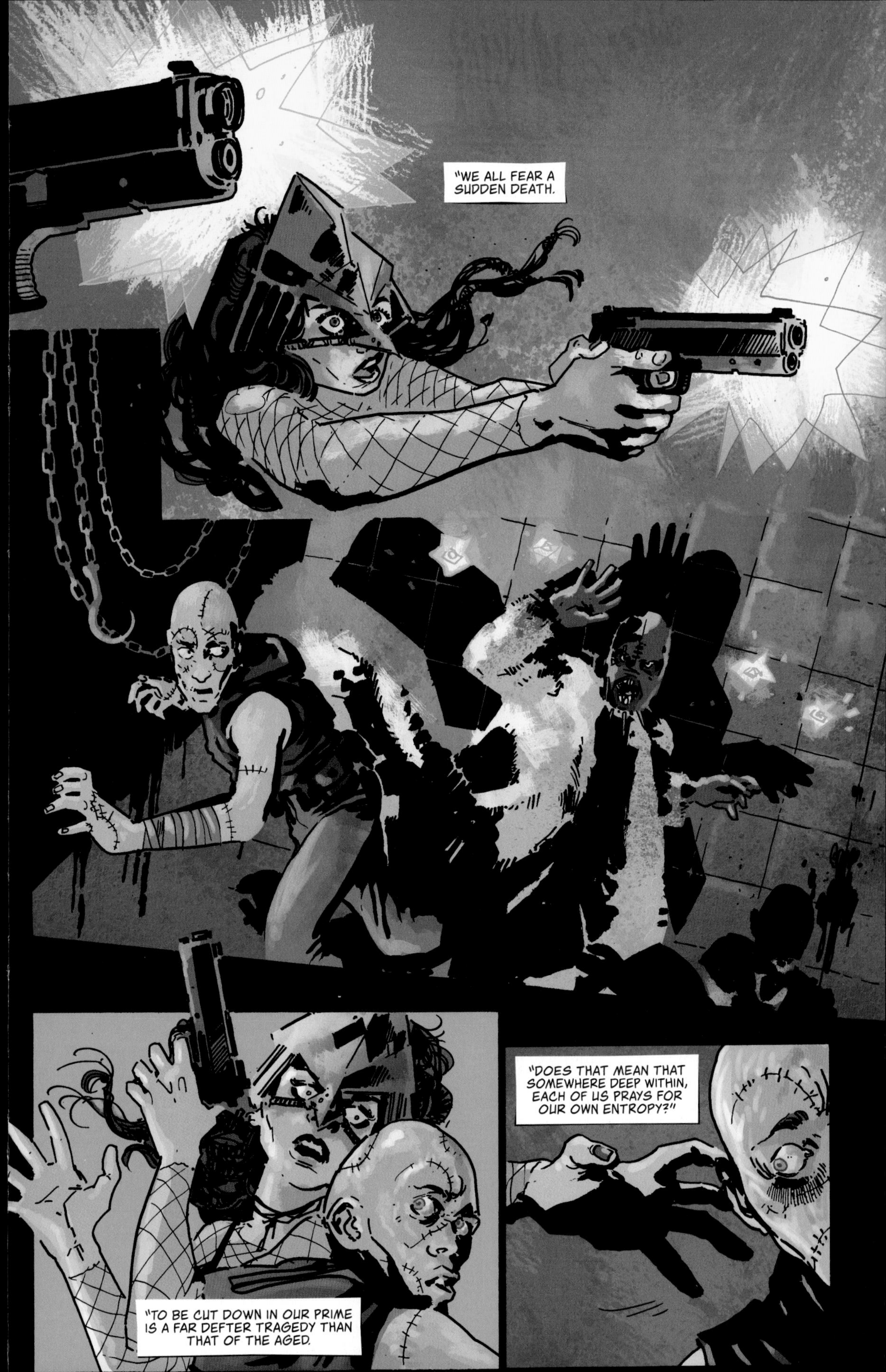
"WE ALL FEAR A SUDDEN DEATH.
"TO BE CUT DOWN IN OUR PRIME IS A FAR DEFTER TRAGEDY THAN THAT OF THE AGED.
"DOES THAT MEAN THAT SOMEWHERE DEEP WITHIN, EACH OF US PRAYS FOR OUR OWN ENTROPY?"

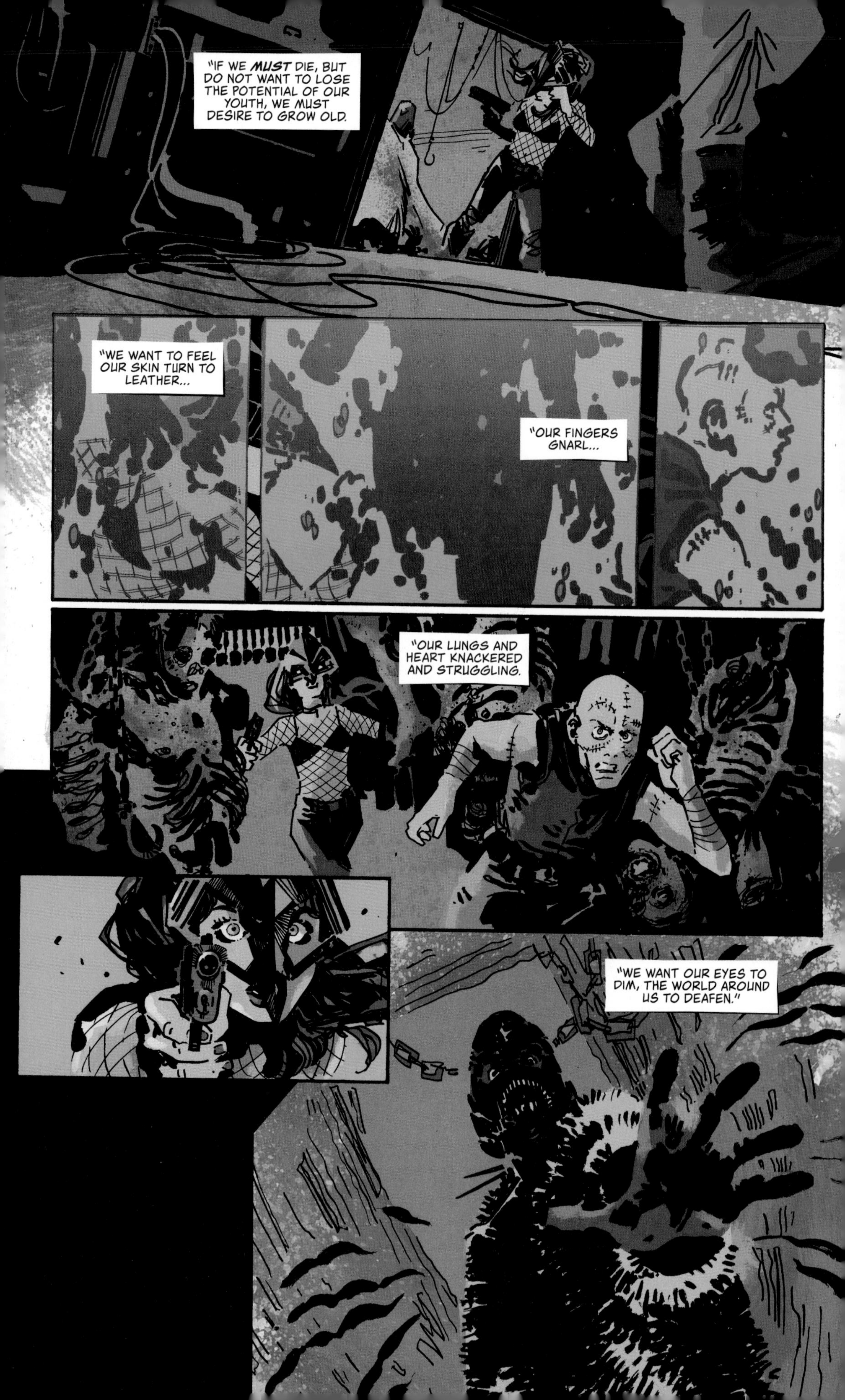
"IF WE MUST DIE, BUT DO NOT WANT TO LOSE THE POTENTIAL OF OUR YOUTH, WE MUST DESIRE TO GROW OLD.
"WE WANT TO FEEL OUR SKIN TURN TO LEATHER...
"OUR FINGERS GNARL...
"OUR LUNGS AND HEART KNACKERED AND STRUGGLING.
"WE WANT OUR EYES TO DIM, THE WORLD AROUND US TO DEAFEN."

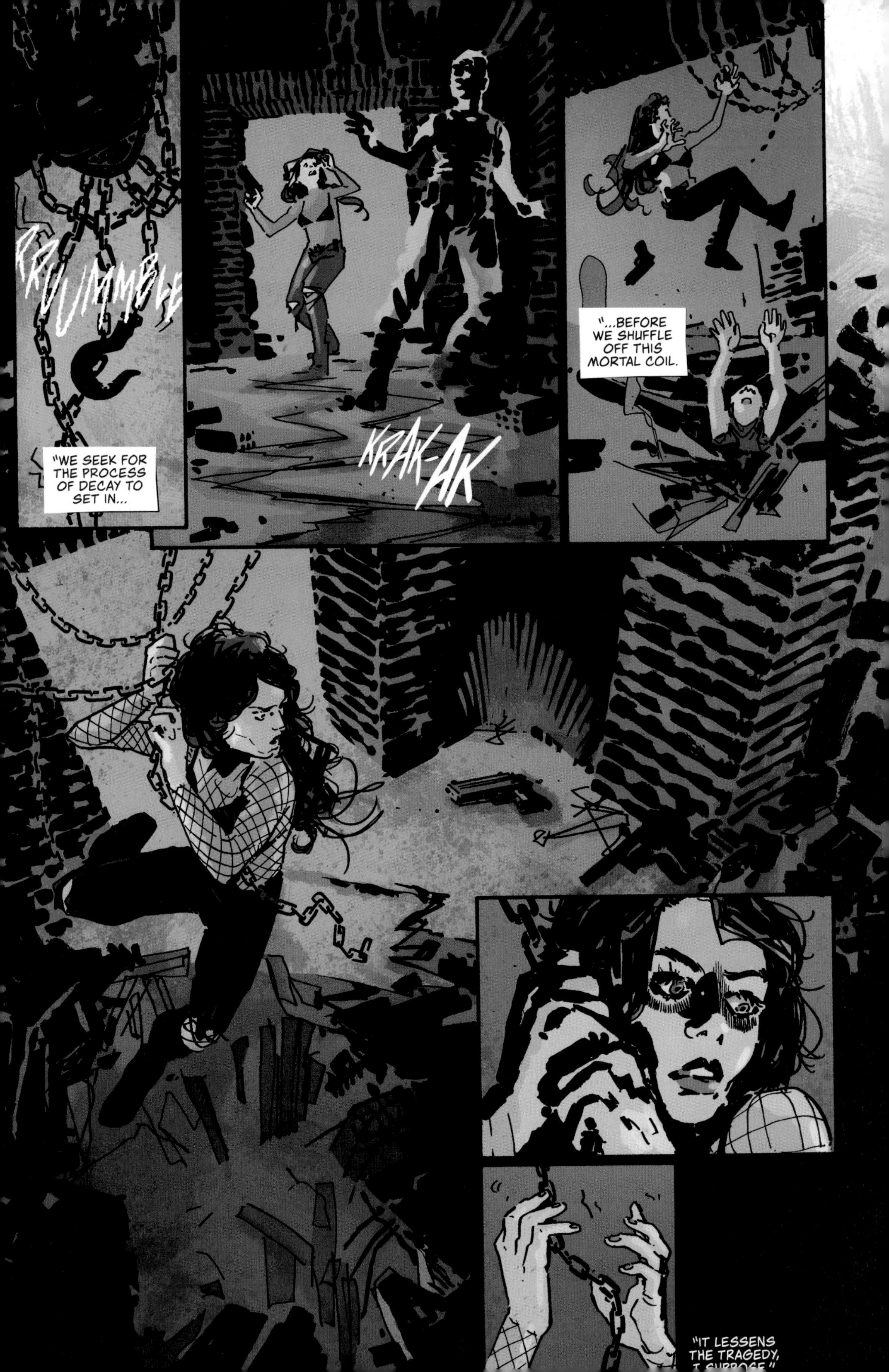
RRUUMMBLE
"WE SEEK FOR THE PROCESS OF DECAY TO SET IN...
KRAK-AK
"...BEFORE WE SHUFFLE OFF THIS MORTAL COIL.
"IT LESSENS THE TRAGEDY,

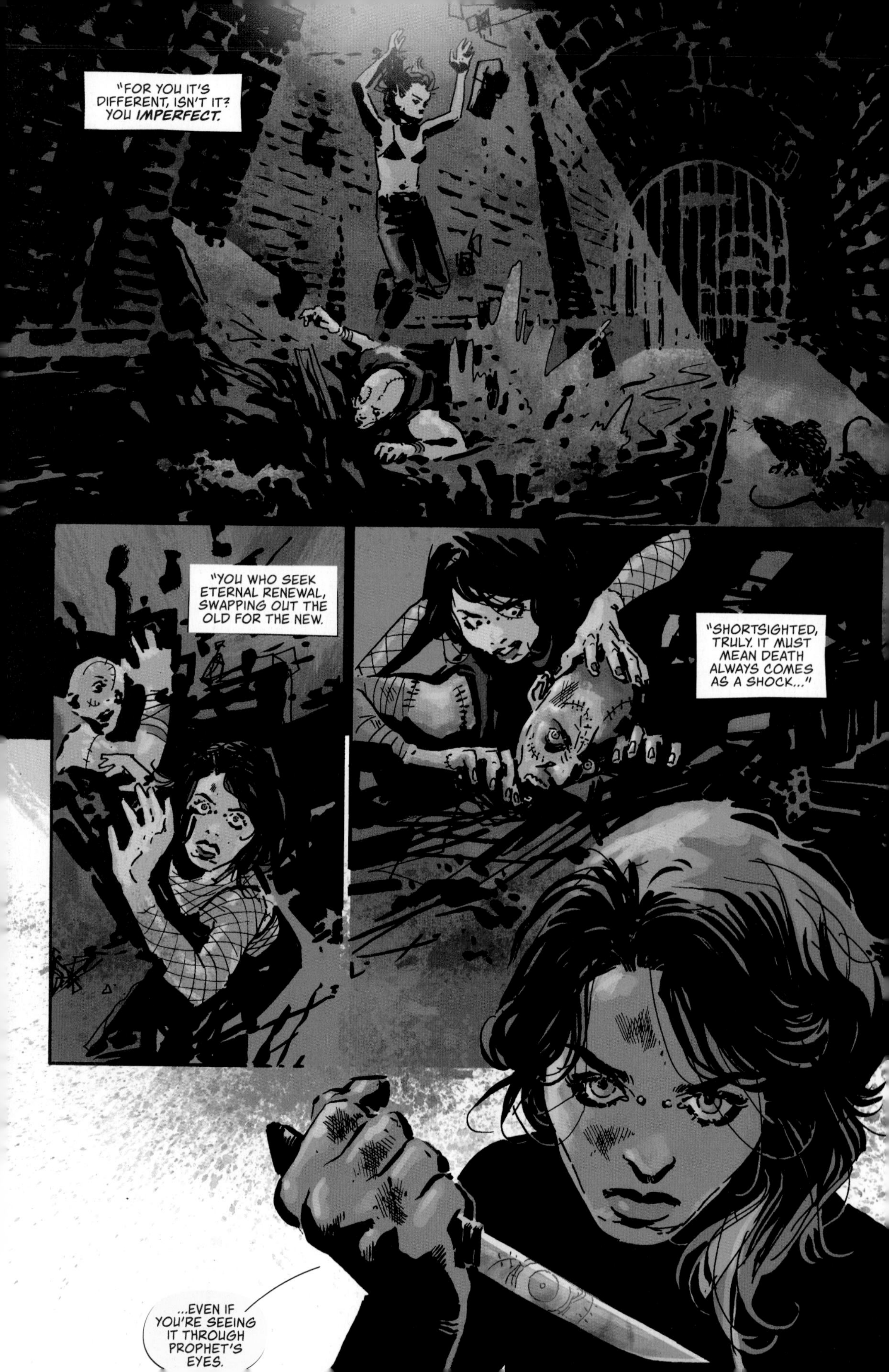
"FOR YOU IT'S DIFFERENT, ISN'T IT? YOU IMPERFECT.
"YOU WHO SEEK ETERNAL RENEWAL, SWAPPING OUT THE OLD FOR THE NEW.
"SHORTSIGHTED, TRULY. IT MUST MEAN DEATH ALWAYS COMES AS A SHOCK..."
...EVEN IF YOU'RE SEEING IT THROUGH PROPHET'S EYES.

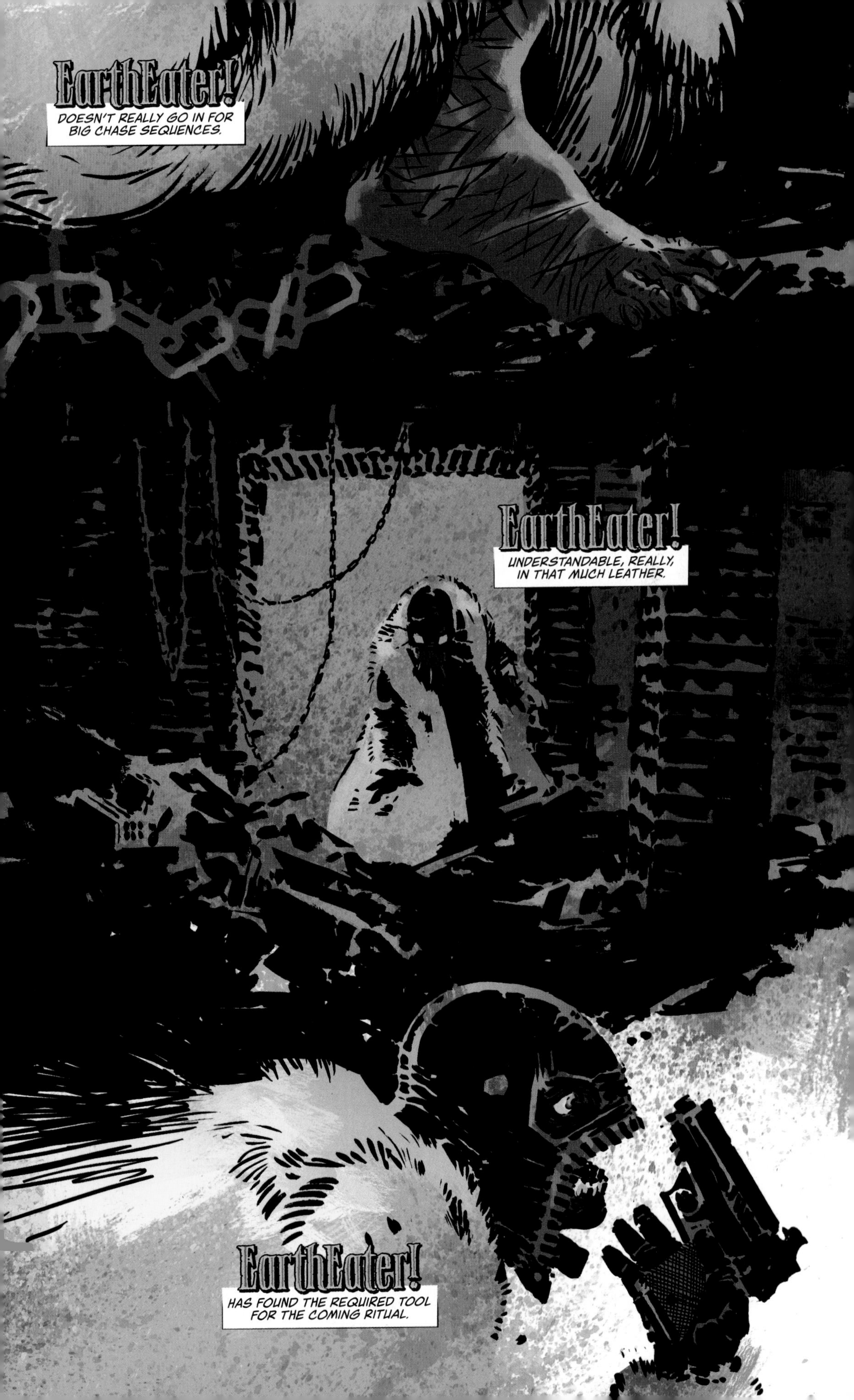
EarthEater!
DOESN'T REALLY GO IN FOR BIG CHASE SEQUENCES.
EarthEater!
UNDERSTANDABLE, REALLY, IN THAT MUCH LEATHER.
EarthEater!
HAS FOUND THE REQUIRED TOOL FOR THE COMING RITUAL.

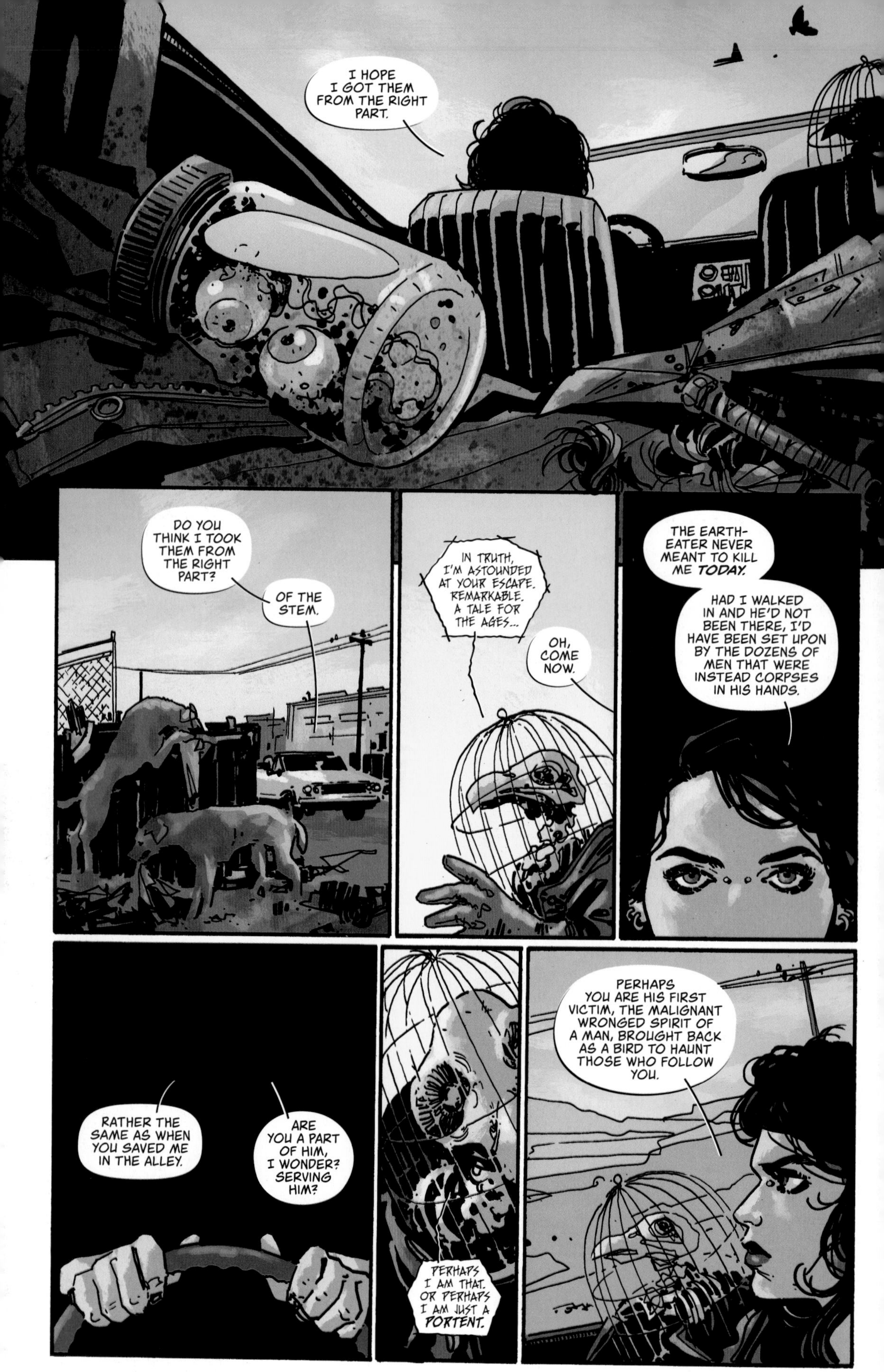
I HOPE I GOT THEM FROM THE RIGHT PART.
DO YOU THINK I TOOK THEM FROM THE RIGHT PART?
OF THE STEM.
IN TRUTH, I'M ASTOUNDED AT YOUR ESCAPE. REMARKABLE. A TALE FOR THE AGES...
OH, COME NOW.
THE EARTH-EATER NEVER MEANT TO KILL ME TODAY.
HAD I WALKED IN AND HE'D NOT BEEN THERE, I'D HAVE BEEN SET UPON BY THE DOZENS OF MEN THAT WERE INSTEAD CORPSES IN HIS HANDS.
RATHER THE SAME AS WHEN YOU SAVED ME IN THE ALLEY.
ARE YOU A PART OF HIM, I WONDER? SERVING HIM?
PERHAPS I AM THAT. OR PERHAPS I AM JUST A PORTENT.
PERHAPS YOU ARE HIS FIRST VICTIM, THE MALIGNANT WRONGED SPIRIT OF A MAN, BROUGHT BACK AS A BIRD TO HAUNT THOSE WHO FOLLOW YOU.

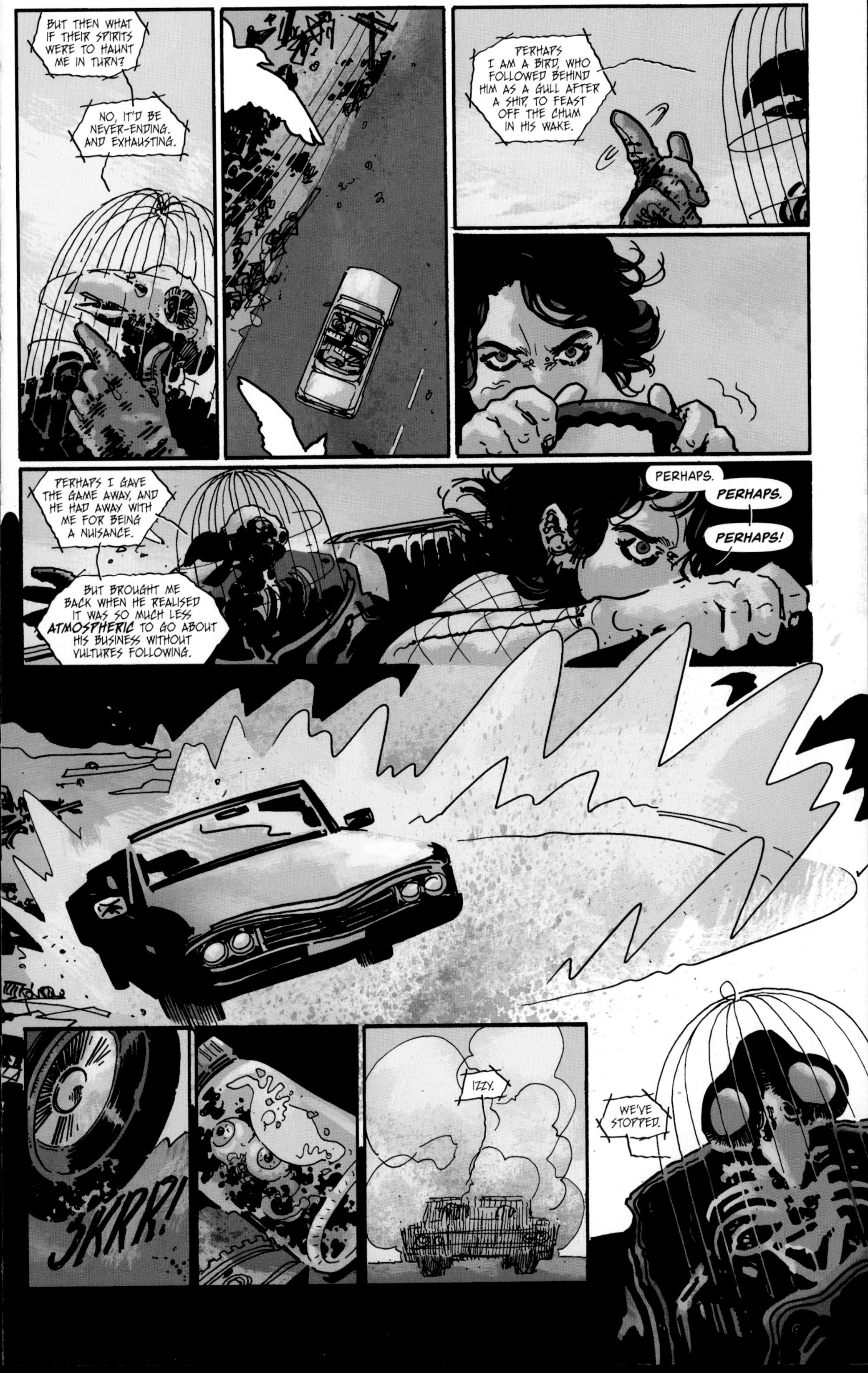
BUT THEN WHAT IF THEIR SPIRITS WERE TO HAUNT ME IN TURN?
NO, IT'D BE NEVER-ENDING. AND EXHAUSTING.
PERHAPS I AM A BIRD, WHO FOLLOWED BEHIND HIM AS A GULL AFTER A SHIP, TO FEAST OFF THE CHUM IN HIS WAKE.
PERHAPS I GAVE THE GAME AWAY, AND HE HAD AWAY WITH ME FOR BEING A NUISANCE.
BUT BROUGHT ME BACK WHEN HE REALISED IT WAS SO MUCH LESS ATMOSPHERIC TO GO ABOUT HIS BUSINESS WITHOUT VULTURES FOLLOWING.
PERHAPS.
PERHAPS.
PERHAPS!
SKRR!
IZZY.
WE'VE STOPPED.

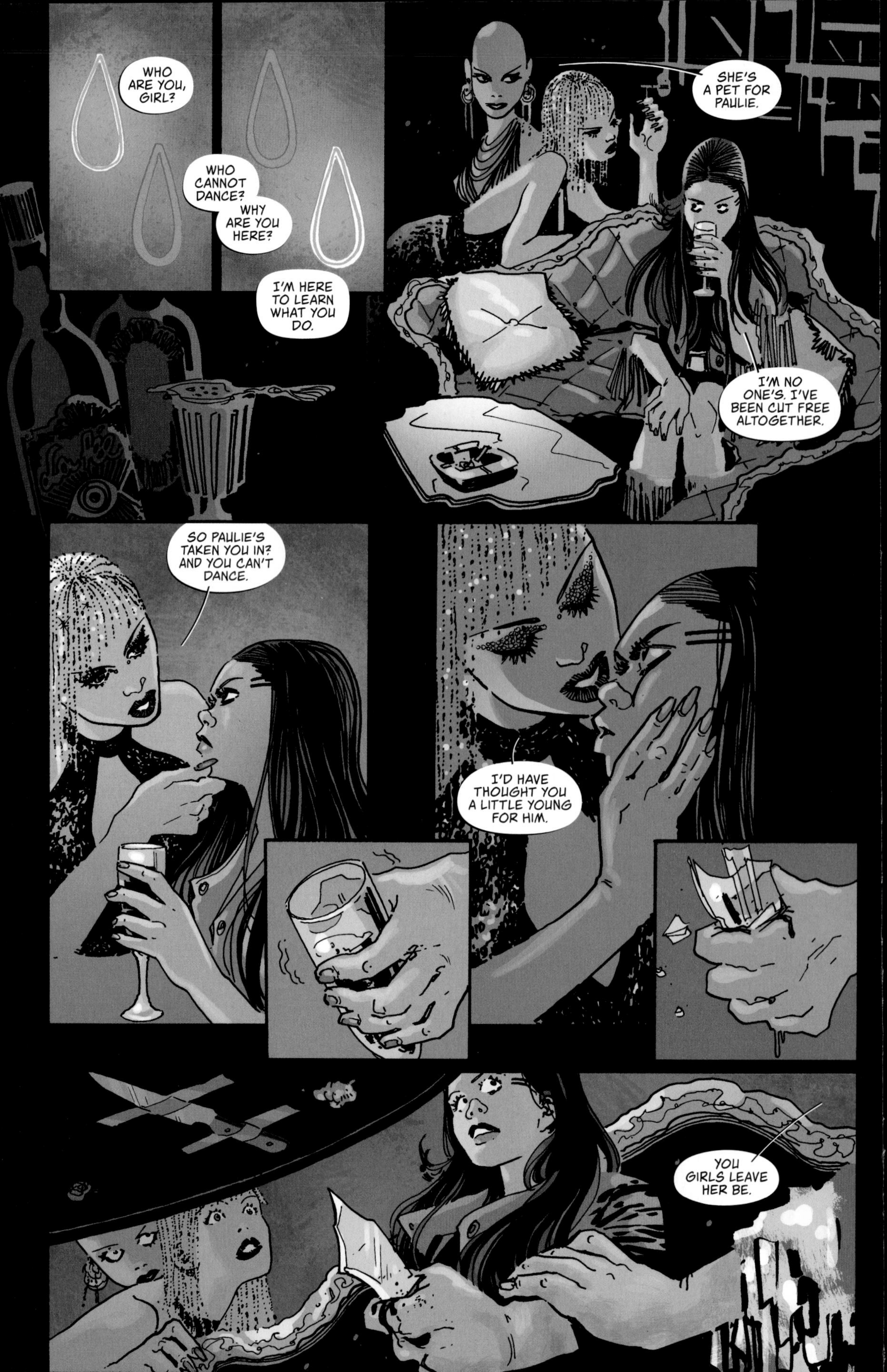
WHO ARE YOU, GIRL?
WHO CANNOT DANCE?
WHY ARE YOU HERE?
I'M HERE TO LEARN WHAT YOU DO.
SHE'S A PET FOR PAULIE.
I'M NO ONE'S. I'VE BEEN CUT FREE ALTOGETHER.
SO PAULIE'S TAKEN YOU IN? AND YOU CAN'T DANCE.
I'D HAVE THOUGHT YOU A LITTLE YOUNG FOR HIM.
YOU GIRLS LEAVE HER BE.

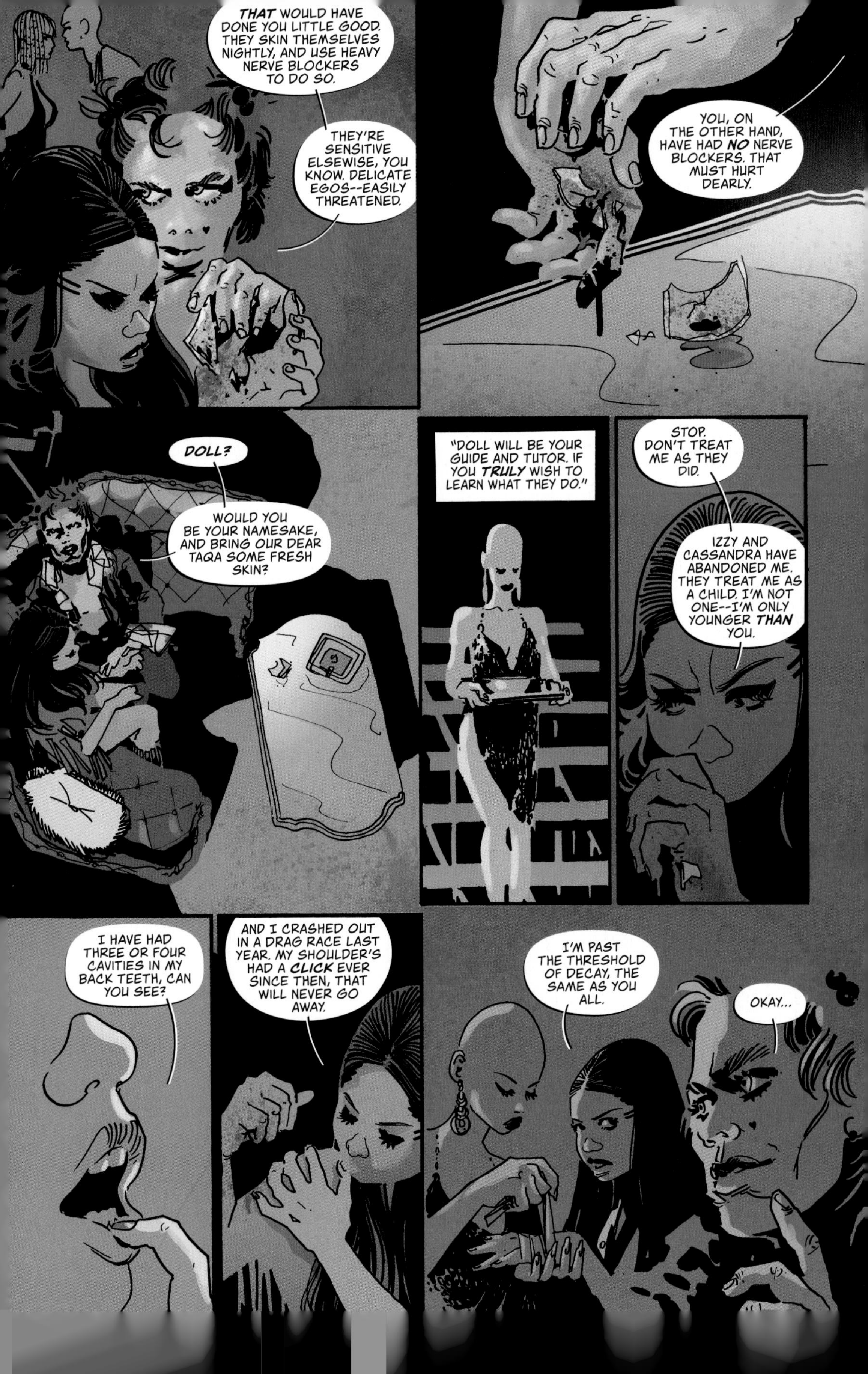
THAT WOULD HAVE DONE YOU LITTLE GOOD. THEY SKIN THEMSELVES NIGHTLY, AND USE HEAVY NERVE BLOCKERS TO DO SO.
THEY'RE SENSITIVE ELSEWISE, YOU KNOW. DELICATE EGOS--EASILY THREATENED.
YOU, ON THE OTHER HAND, HAVE HAD NO NERVE BLOCKERS. THAT MUST HURT DEARLY.
DOLL?
WOULD YOU BE YOUR NAMESAKE, AND BRING OUR DEAR TAQA SOME FRESH SKIN?
"DOLL WILL BE YOUR GUIDE AND TUTOR. IF YOU TRULY WISH TO LEARN WHAT THEY DO."
STOP. DON'T TREAT ME AS THEY DID.
IZZY AND CASSANDRA HAVE ABANDONED ME. THEY TREAT ME AS A CHILD. I'M NOT ONE--I'M ONLY YOUNGER THAN YOU.
I HAVE HAD THREE OR FOUR CAVITIES IN MY BACK TEETH, CAN YOU SEE?
AND I CRASHED OUT IN A DRAG RACE LAST YEAR. MY SHOULDER'S HAD A CLICK EVER SINCE THEN, THAT WILL NEVER GO AWAY.
I'M PAST THE THRESHOLD OF DECAY, THE SAME AS YOU ALL.
OKAY...

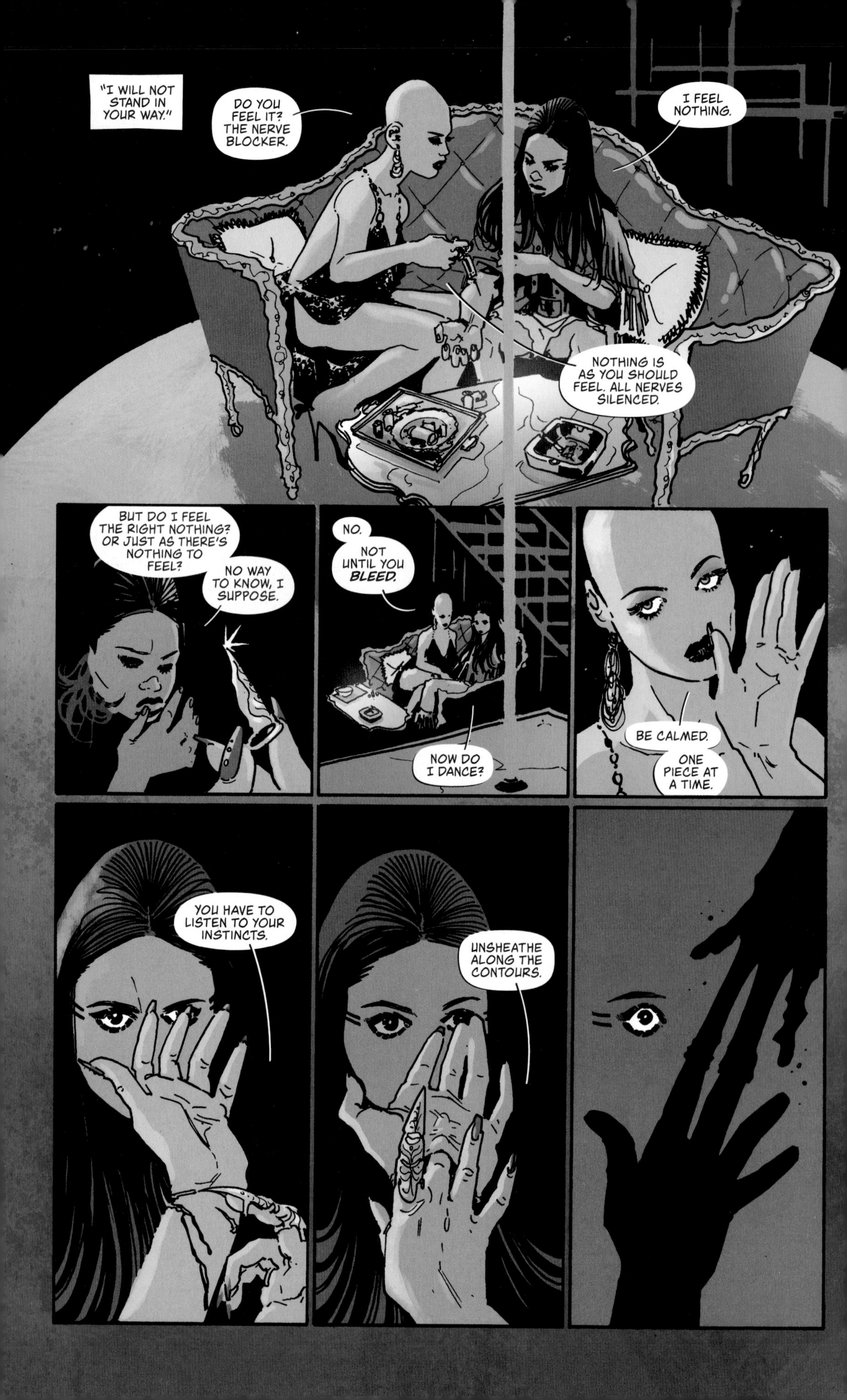
"I WILL NOT STAND IN YOUR WAY."
DO YOU FEEL IT? THE NERVE BLOCKER.
I FEEL NOTHING.
NOTHING IS AS YOU SHOULD FEEL. ALL NERVES SILENCED.
BUT DO I FEEL THE RIGHT NOTHING? OR JUST AS THERE'S NOTHING TO FEEL?
NO WAY TO KNOW, I SUPPOSE.
NO.
NOT UNTIL YOU BLEED.
NOW DO I DANCE?
BE CALMED.
ONE PIECE AT A TIME.
YOU HAVE TO LISTEN TO YOUR INSTINCTS.
UNSHEATHE ALONG THE CONTOURS.

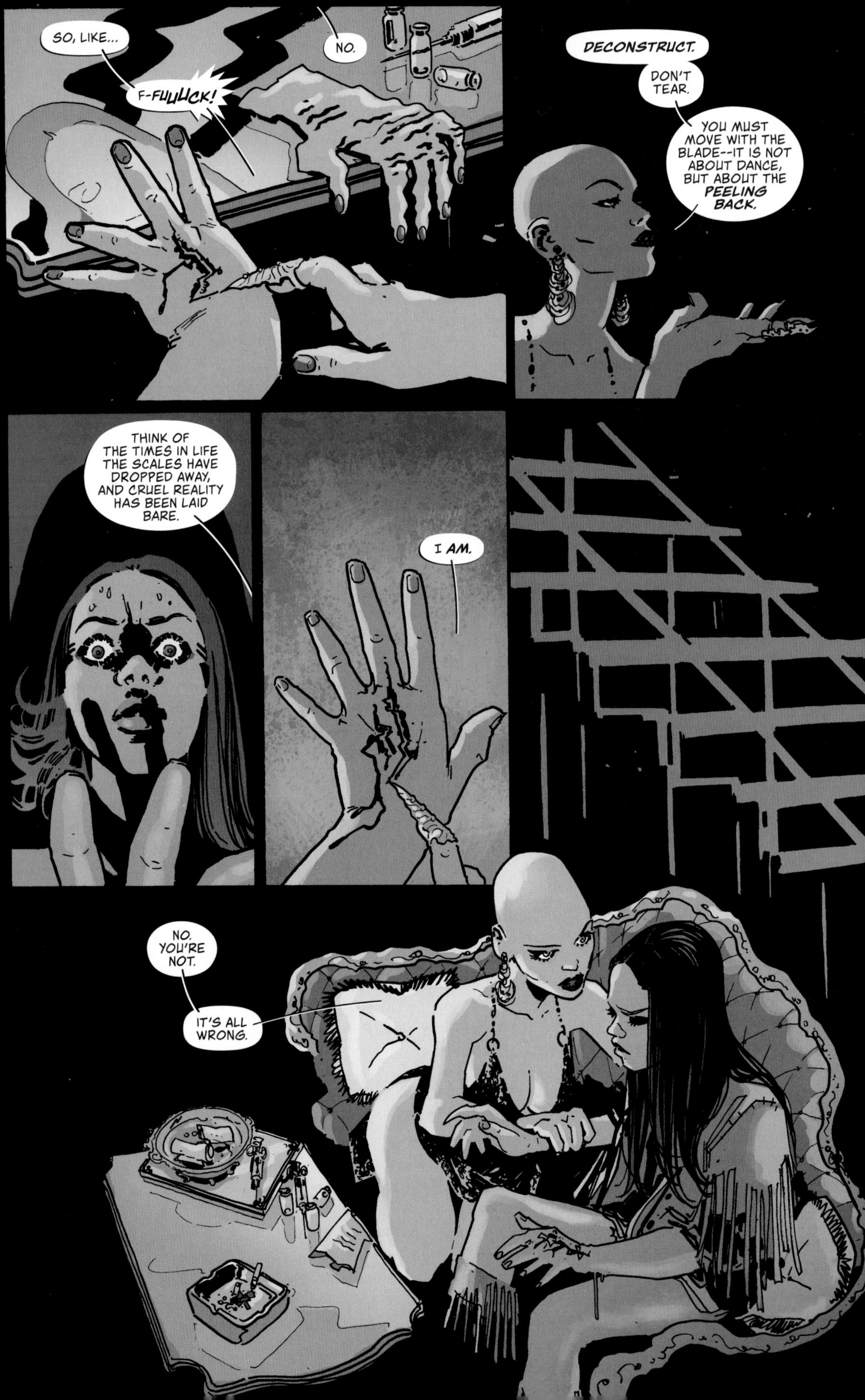
SO, LIKE...
F-FUUUCK!
NO.
DECONSTRUCT.
DON'T TEAR.
YOU MUST MOVE WITH THE BLADE--IT IS NOT ABOUT DANCE, BUT ABOUT THE PEELING BACK.
THINK OF THE TIMES IN LIFE THE SCALES HAVE DROPPED AWAY, AND CRUEL REALITY HAS BEEN LAID BARE.
I AM.
NO. YOU'RE NOT.
IT'S ALL WRONG.

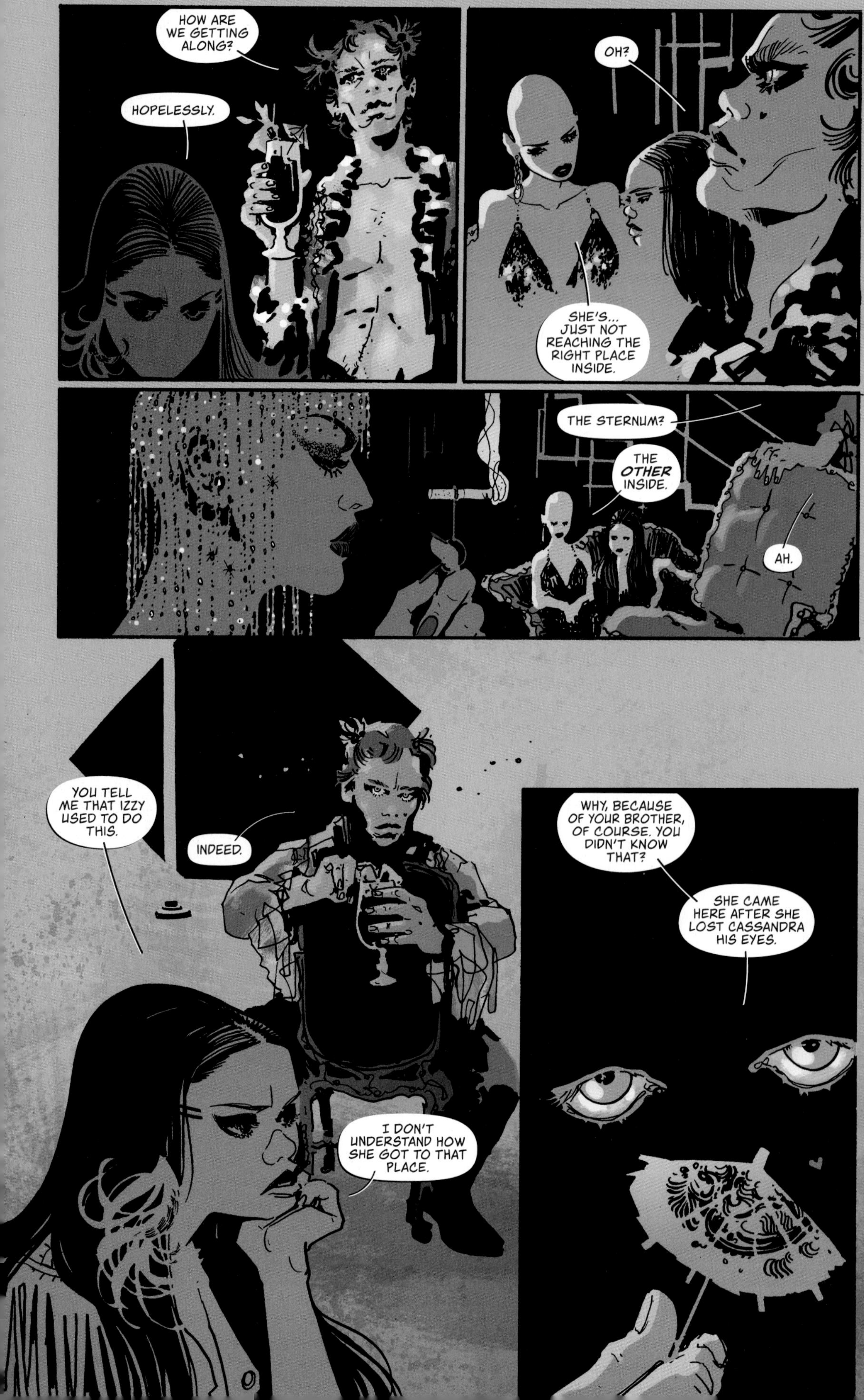
HOW ARE WE GETTING ALONG?
HOPELESSLY.
OH?
SHE'S... JUST NOT REACHING THE RIGHT PLACE INSIDE.
THE STERNUM?
THE *OTHER* INSIDE.
AH.
YOU TELL ME THAT IZZY USED TO DO THIS.
INDEED.
I DON'T UNDERSTAND HOW SHE GOT TO THAT PLACE.
WHY, BECAUSE OF YOUR BROTHER, OF COURSE. YOU DIDN'T KNOW THAT?
SHE CAME HERE AFTER SHE LOST CASSANDRA HIS EYES.

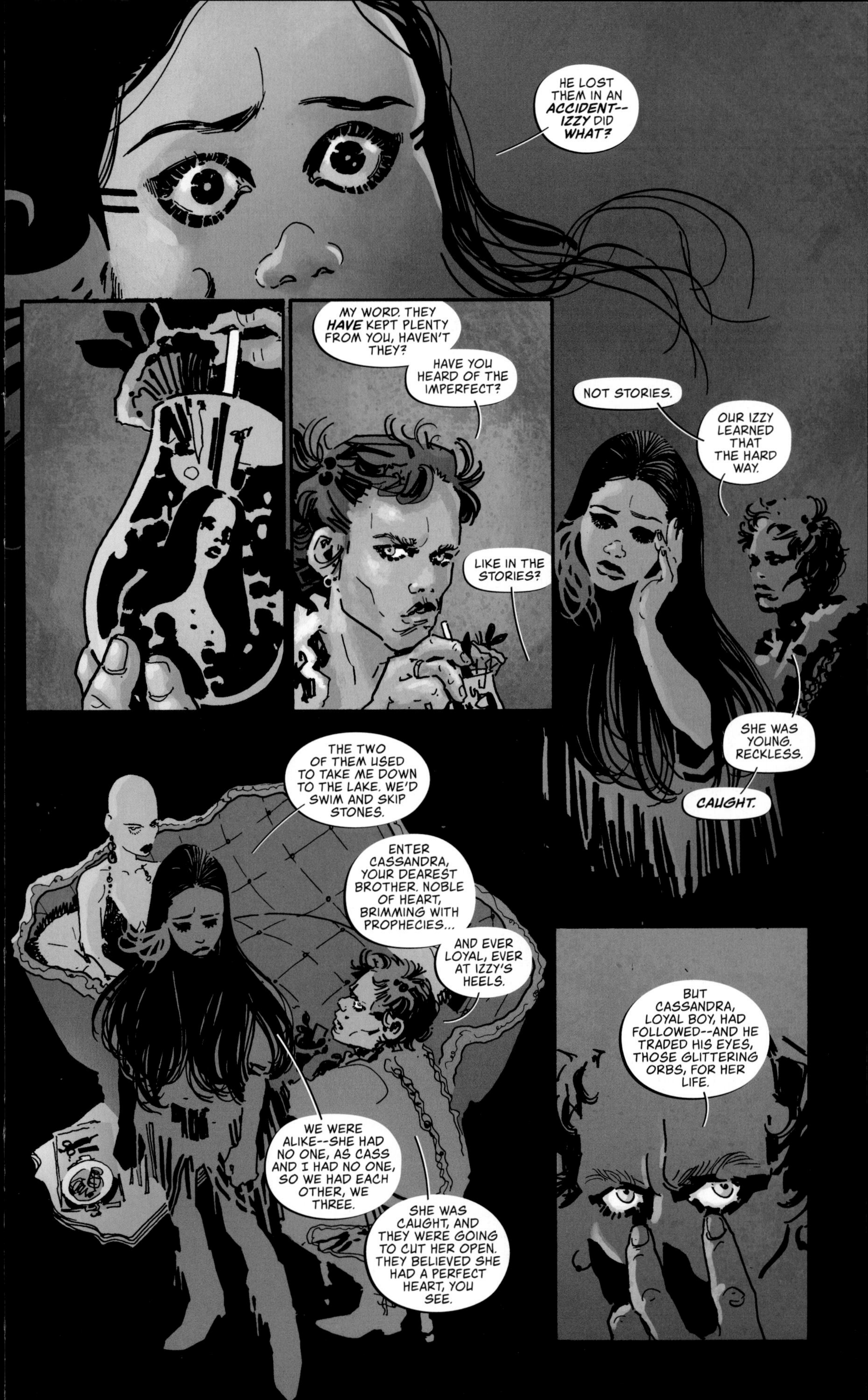
HE LOST THEM IN AN ACCIDENT-- IZZY DID WHAT?
MY WORD. THEY HAVE KEPT PLENTY FROM YOU, HAVEN'T THEY?
HAVE YOU HEARD OF THE IMPERFECT?
LIKE IN THE STORIES?
NOT STORIES.
OUR IZZY LEARNED THAT THE HARD WAY.
SHE WAS YOUNG. RECKLESS.
CAUGHT.
THE TWO OF THEM USED TO TAKE ME DOWN TO THE LAKE. WE'D SWIM AND SKIP STONES.
ENTER CASSANDRA, YOUR DEAREST BROTHER. NOBLE OF HEART, BRIMMING WITH PROPHECIES...
AND EVER LOYAL, EVER AT IZZY'S HEELS.
WE WERE ALIKE--SHE HAD NO ONE, AS CASS AND I HAD NO ONE, SO WE HAD EACH OTHER, WE THREE.
SHE WAS CAUGHT, AND THEY WERE GOING TO CUT HER OPEN. THEY BELIEVED SHE HAD A PERFECT HEART, YOU SEE.
BUT CASSANDRA, LOYAL BOY, HAD FOLLOWED--AND HE TRADED HIS EYES, THOSE GLITTERING ORBS, FOR HER LIFE.

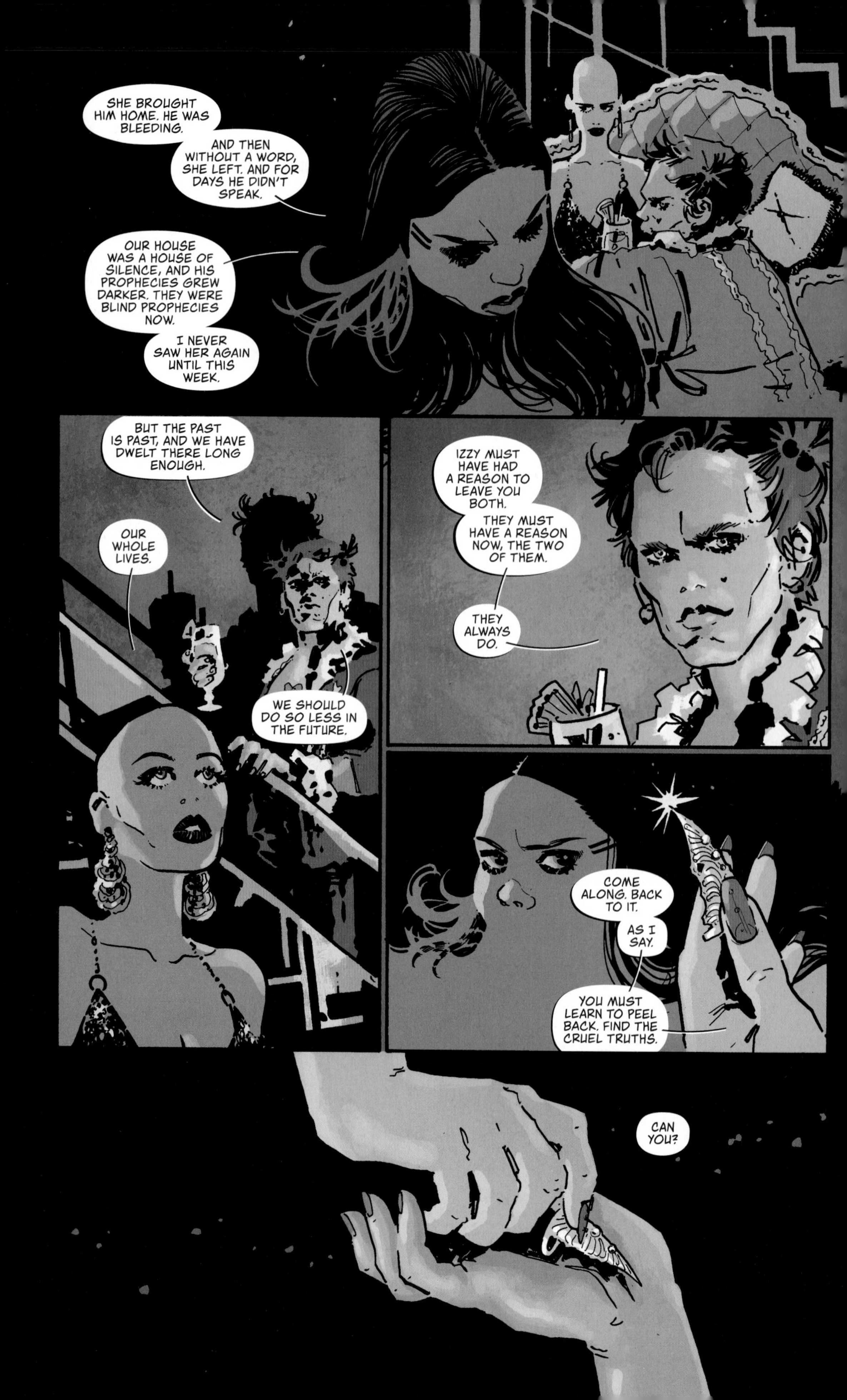
SHE BROUGHT HIM HOME. HE WAS BLEEDING.
AND THEN WITHOUT A WORD, SHE LEFT. AND FOR DAYS HE DIDN'T SPEAK.
OUR HOUSE WAS A HOUSE OF SILENCE, AND HIS PROPHECIES GREW DARKER. THEY WERE BLIND PROPHECIES NOW.
I NEVER SAW HER AGAIN UNTIL THIS WEEK.
BUT THE PAST IS PAST, AND WE HAVE DWELT THERE LONG ENOUGH.
OUR WHOLE LIVES.
WE SHOULD DO SO LESS IN THE FUTURE.
IZZY MUST HAVE HAD A REASON TO LEAVE YOU BOTH.
THEY MUST HAVE A REASON NOW, THE TWO OF THEM.
THEY ALWAYS DO.
COME ALONG. BACK TO IT.
AS I SAY.
YOU MUST LEARN TO PEEL BACK. FIND THE CRUEL TRUTHS.
CAN YOU?

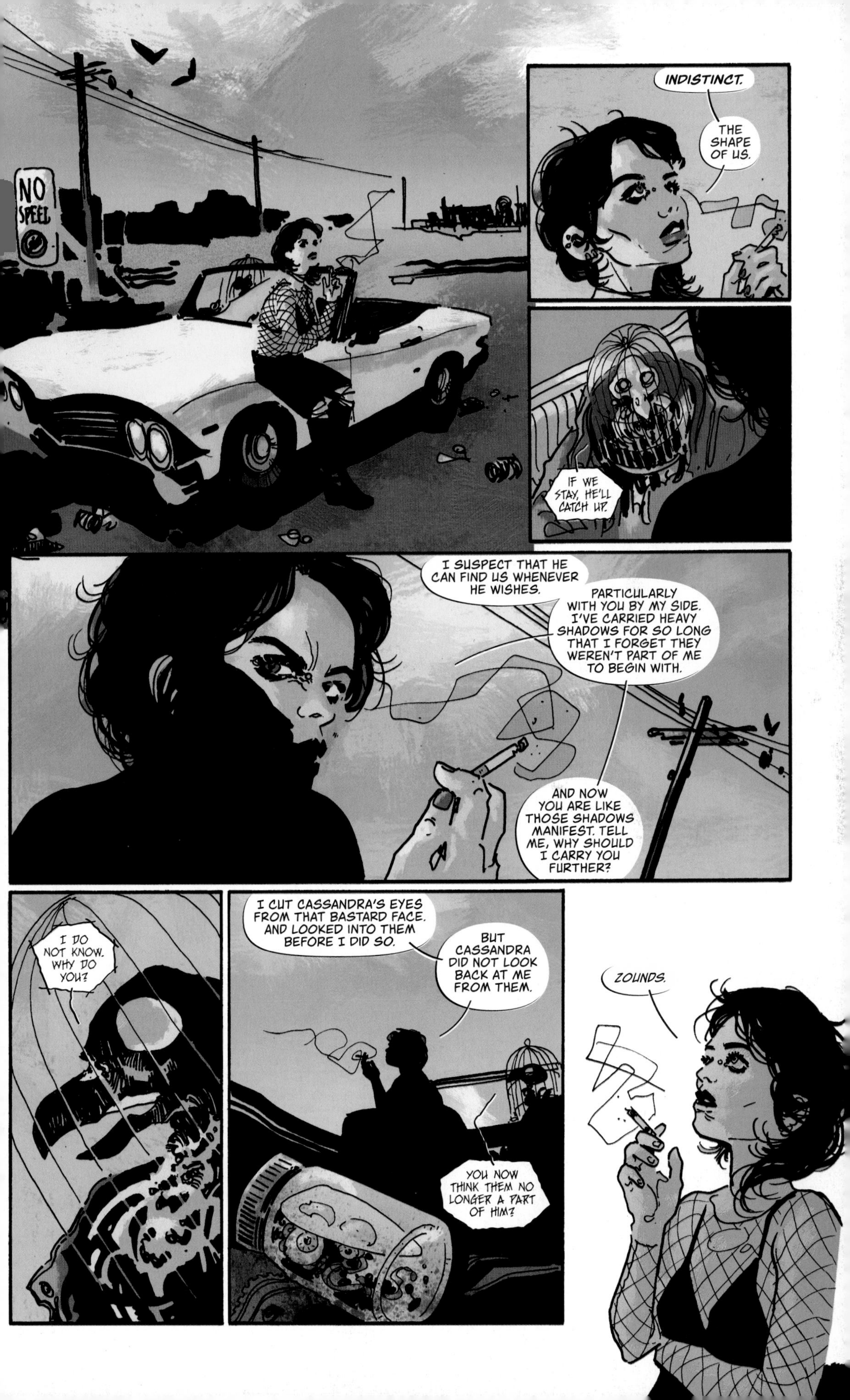
NO SPEEL
INDISTINCT.
THE SHAPE OF US.
IF WE STAY, HE'LL CATCH UP.
I SUSPECT THAT HE CAN FIND US WHENEVER HE WISHES.
PARTICULARLY WITH YOU BY MY SIDE. I'VE CARRIED HEAVY SHADOWS FOR SO LONG THAT I FORGET THEY WEREN'T PART OF ME TO BEGIN WITH.
AND NOW YOU ARE LIKE THOSE SHADOWS MANIFEST. TELL ME, WHY SHOULD I CARRY YOU FURTHER?
I DO NOT KNOW. WHY DO YOU?
I CUT CASSANDRA'S EYES FROM THAT BASTARD FACE. AND LOOKED INTO THEM BEFORE I DID SO.
BUT CASSANDRA DID NOT LOOK BACK AT ME FROM THEM.
YOU NOW THINK THEM NO LONGER A PART OF HIM?
ZOUNDS.

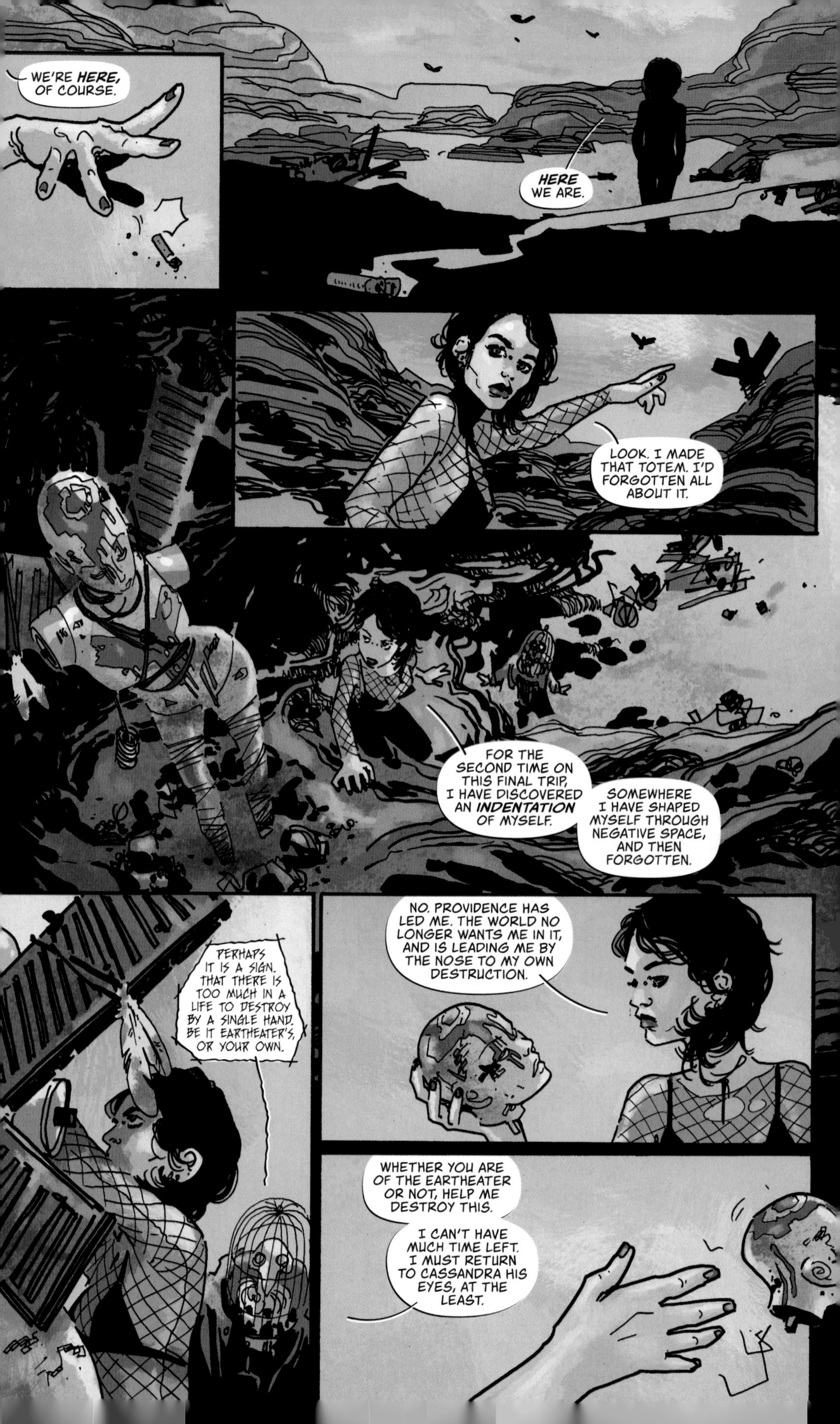
WE'RE ***HERE,*** OF COURSE.
HERE WE ARE.
LOOK. I MADE THAT TOTEM. I'D FORGOTTEN ALL ABOUT IT.
FOR THE SECOND TIME ON THIS FINAL TRIP, I HAVE DISCOVERED AN ***INDENTATION*** OF MYSELF.
SOMEWHERE I HAVE SHAPED MYSELF THROUGH NEGATIVE SPACE, AND THEN FORGOTTEN.
PERHAPS IT IS A SIGN. THAT THERE IS TOO MUCH IN A LIFE TO DESTROY BY A SINGLE HAND. BE IT EARTHEATER'S, OR YOUR OWN.
NO. PROVIDENCE HAS LED ME. THE WORLD NO LONGER WANTS ME IN IT, AND IS LEADING ME BY THE NOSE TO MY OWN DESTRUCTION.
WHETHER YOU ARE OF THE EARTHEATER OR NOT, HELP ME DESTROY THIS.
I CAN'T HAVE MUCH TIME LEFT. I MUST RETURN TO CASSANDRA HIS EYES, AT THE LEAST.

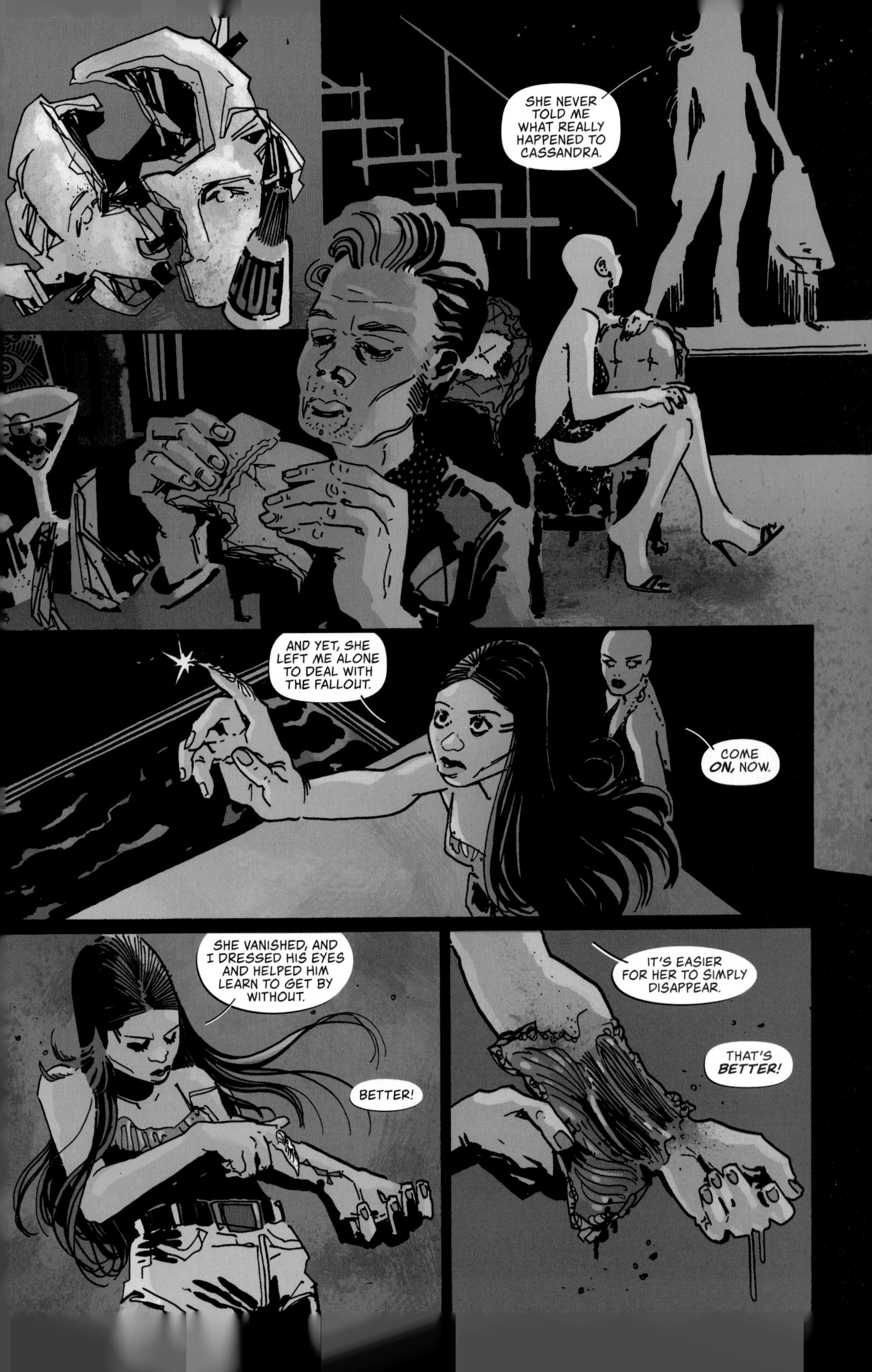
SHE NEVER TOLD ME WHAT REALLY HAPPENED TO CASSANDRA.
AND YET, SHE LEFT ME ALONE TO DEAL WITH THE FALLOUT.
COME ON, NOW.
SHE VANISHED, AND I DRESSED HIS EYES AND HELPED HIM LEARN TO GET BY WITHOUT.
BETTER!
IT'S EASIER FOR HER TO SIMPLY DISAPPEAR.
THAT'S BETTER!

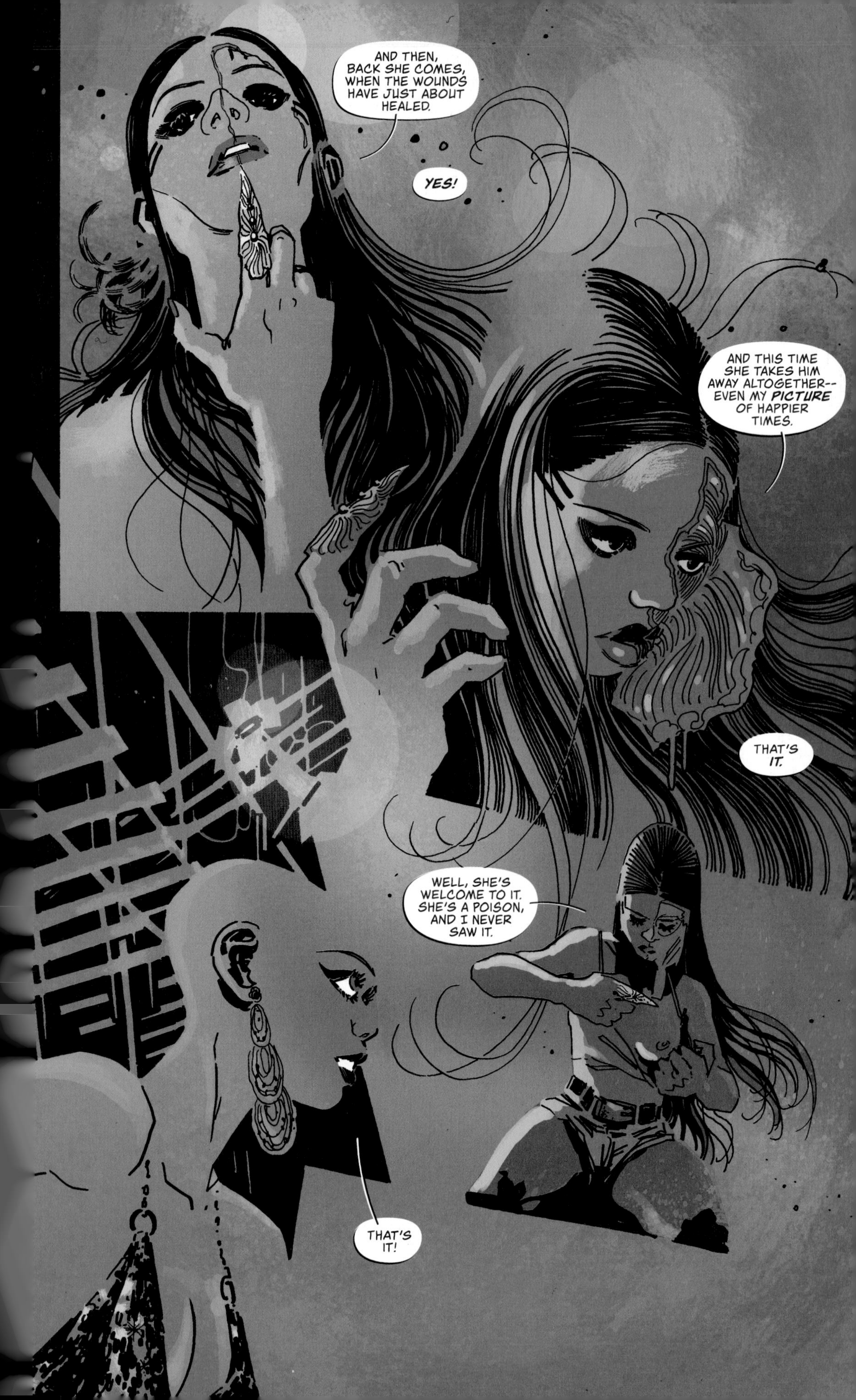
AND THEN, BACK SHE COMES, WHEN THE WOUNDS HAVE JUST ABOUT HEALED.
YES!
AND THIS TIME SHE TAKES HIM AWAY ALTOGETHER-- EVEN MY PICTURE OF HAPPIER TIMES.
THAT'S IT.
WELL, SHE'S WELCOME TO IT. SHE'S A POISON, AND I NEVER SAW IT.
THAT'S IT!

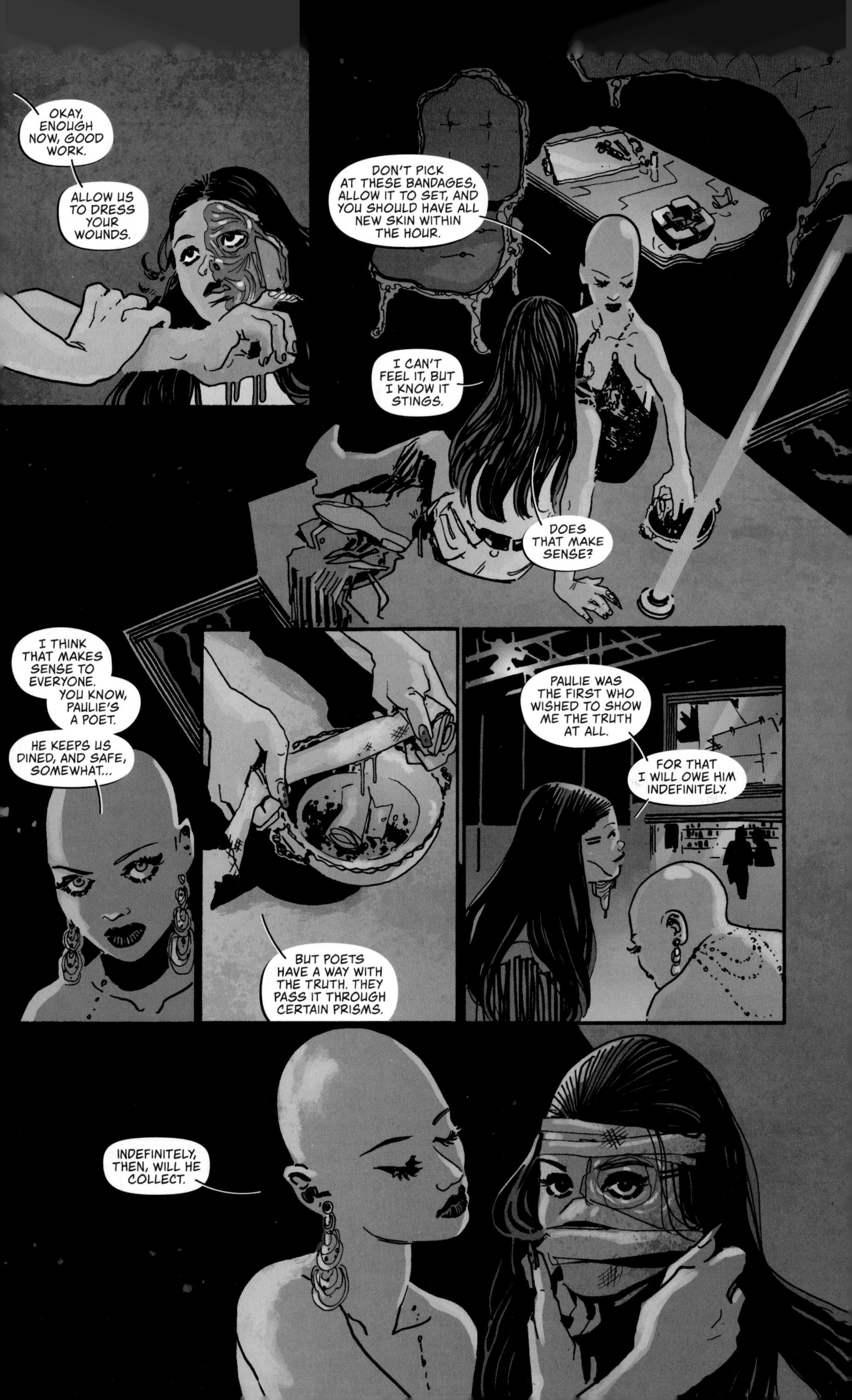
OKAY, ENOUGH NOW, GOOD WORK.
ALLOW US TO DRESS YOUR WOUNDS.
DON'T PICK AT THESE BANDAGES, ALLOW IT TO SET, AND YOU SHOULD HAVE ALL NEW SKIN WITHIN THE HOUR.
I CAN'T FEEL IT, BUT I KNOW IT STINGS.
DOES THAT MAKE SENSE?
I THINK THAT MAKES SENSE TO EVERYONE.
YOU KNOW, PAULIE'S A POET.
HE KEEPS US DINED, AND SAFE, SOMEWHAT...
BUT POETS HAVE A WAY WITH THE TRUTH. THEY PASS IT THROUGH CERTAIN PRISMS.
PAULIE WAS THE FIRST WHO WISHED TO SHOW ME THE TRUTH AT ALL.
FOR THAT I WILL OWE HIM INDEFINITELY.
INDEFINITELY, THEN, WILL HE COLLECT.

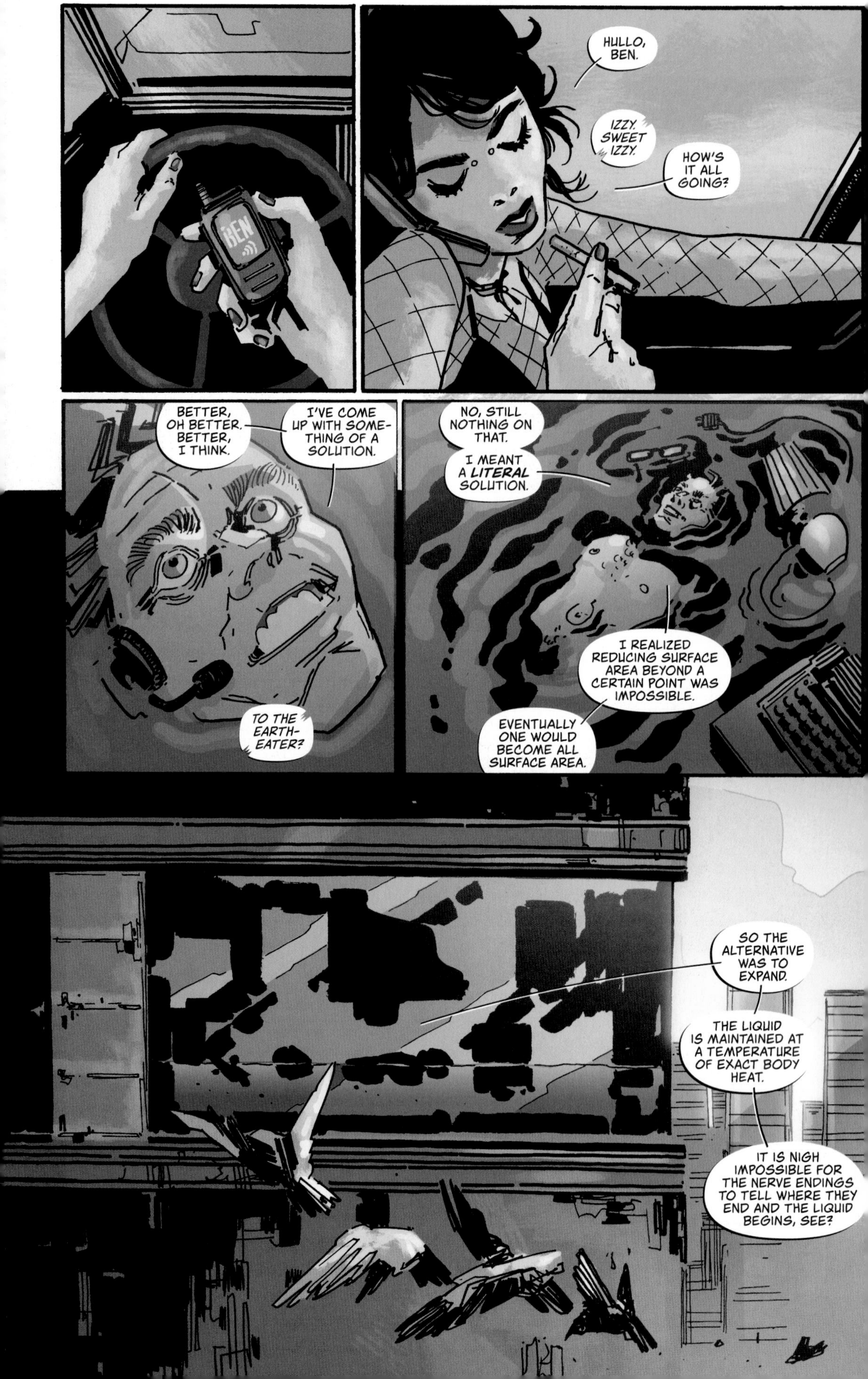

BEN
HULLO, BEN.
IZZY. SWEET IZZY.
HOW'S IT ALL GOING?
BETTER, OH BETTER. BETTER, I THINK.
I'VE COME UP WITH SOME-THING OF A SOLUTION.
TO THE EARTH-EATER?
NO, STILL NOTHING ON THAT.
I MEANT A *LITERAL* SOLUTION.
I REALIZED REDUCING SURFACE AREA BEYOND A CERTAIN POINT WAS IMPOSSIBLE.
EVENTUALLY ONE WOULD BECOME ALL SURFACE AREA.
SO THE ALTERNATIVE WAS TO EXPAND.
THE LIQUID IS MAINTAINED AT A TEMPERATURE OF EXACT BODY HEAT.
IT IS NIGH IMPOSSIBLE FOR THE NERVE ENDINGS TO TELL WHERE THEY END AND THE LIQUID BEGINS, SEE?

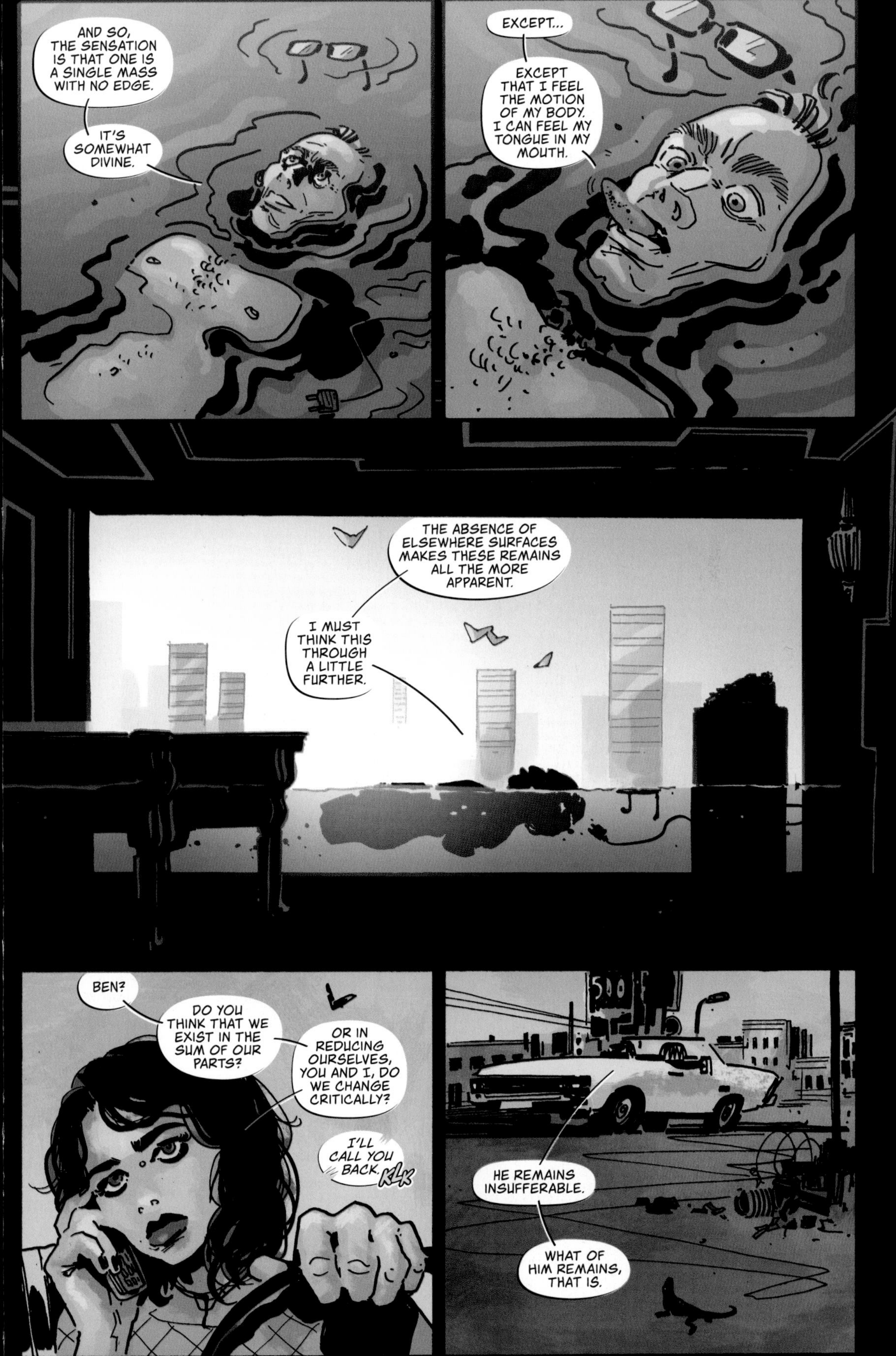
AND SO, THE SENSATION IS THAT ONE IS A SINGLE MASS WITH NO EDGE.
IT'S SOMEWHAT DIVINE.
EXCEPT...
EXCEPT THAT I FEEL THE MOTION OF MY BODY. I CAN FEEL MY TONGUE IN MY MOUTH.
THE ABSENCE OF ELSEWHERE SURFACES MAKES THESE REMAINS ALL THE MORE APPARENT.
I MUST THINK THIS THROUGH A LITTLE FURTHER.
BEN?
DO YOU THINK THAT WE EXIST IN THE SUM OF OUR PARTS?
OR IN REDUCING OURSELVES, YOU AND I, DO WE CHANGE CRITICALLY?
I'LL CALL YOU BACK.
KLK
HE REMAINS INSUFFERABLE.
WHAT OF HIM REMAINS, THAT IS.

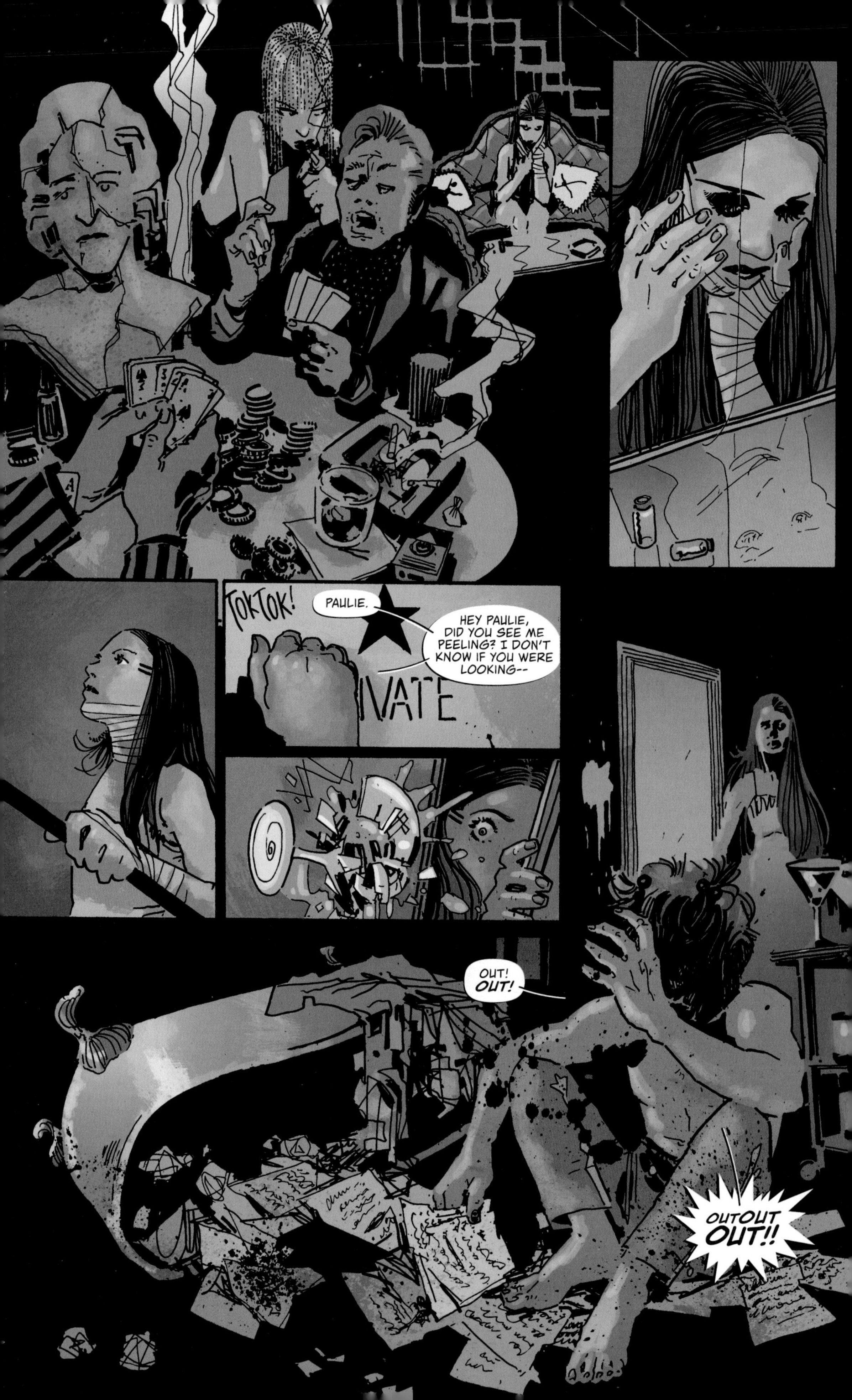
TOKTOK!
PAULIE.
HEY PAULIE, DID YOU SEE ME PEELING? I DON'T KNOW IF YOU WERE LOOKING--
IVATE
OUT! OUT!
OUTOUT OUT!!

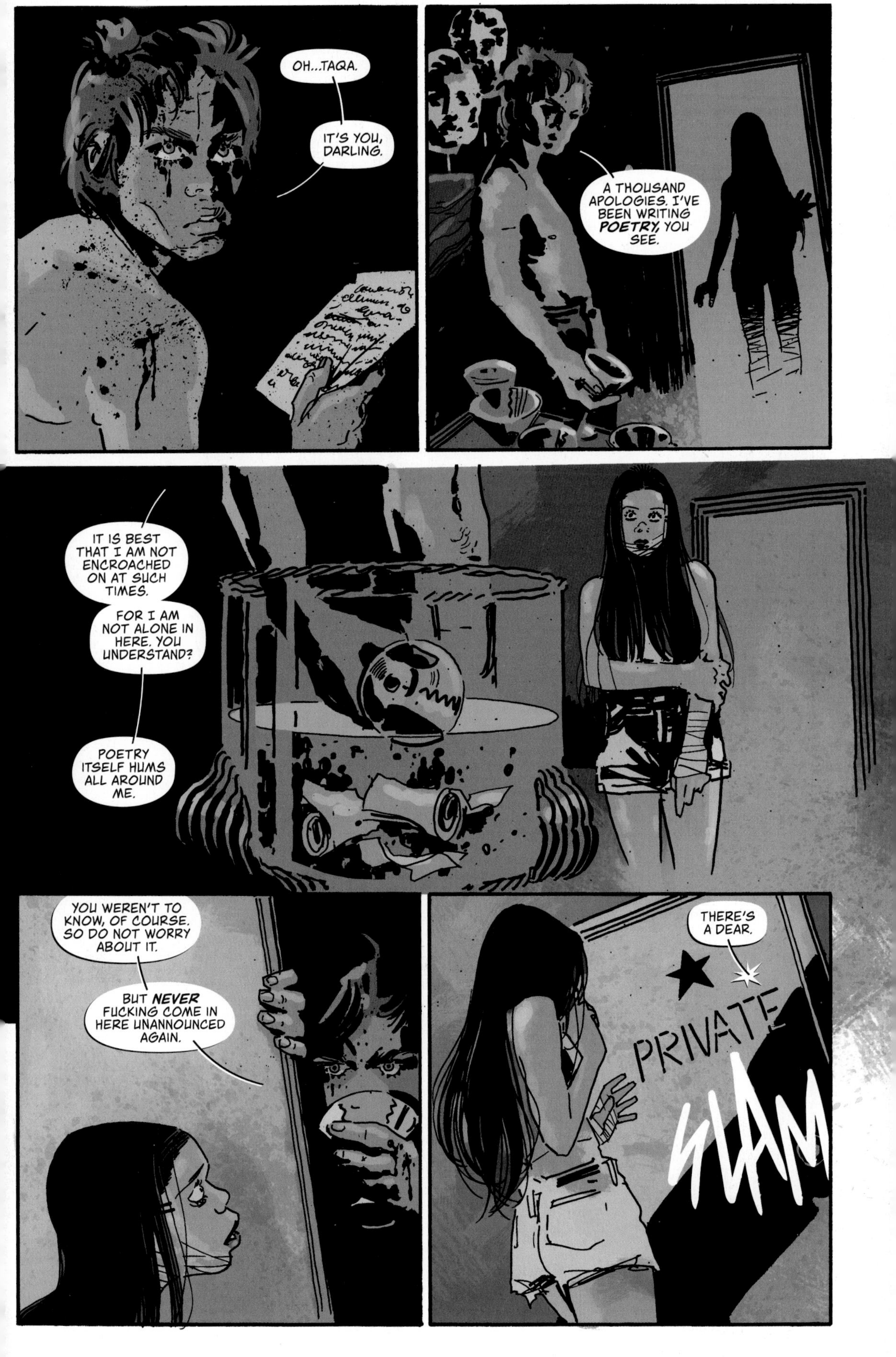
OH...TAQA.
IT'S YOU, DARLING.
A THOUSAND APOLOGIES. I'VE BEEN WRITING **POETRY,** YOU SEE.
IT IS BEST THAT I AM NOT ENCROACHED ON AT SUCH TIMES.
FOR I AM NOT ALONE IN HERE. YOU UNDERSTAND?
POETRY ITSELF HUMS ALL AROUND ME.
YOU WEREN'T TO KNOW, OF COURSE. SO DO NOT WORRY ABOUT IT.
BUT **NEVER** FUCKING COME IN HERE UNANNOUNCED AGAIN.
THERE'S A DEAR.
PRIVATE
SLAM

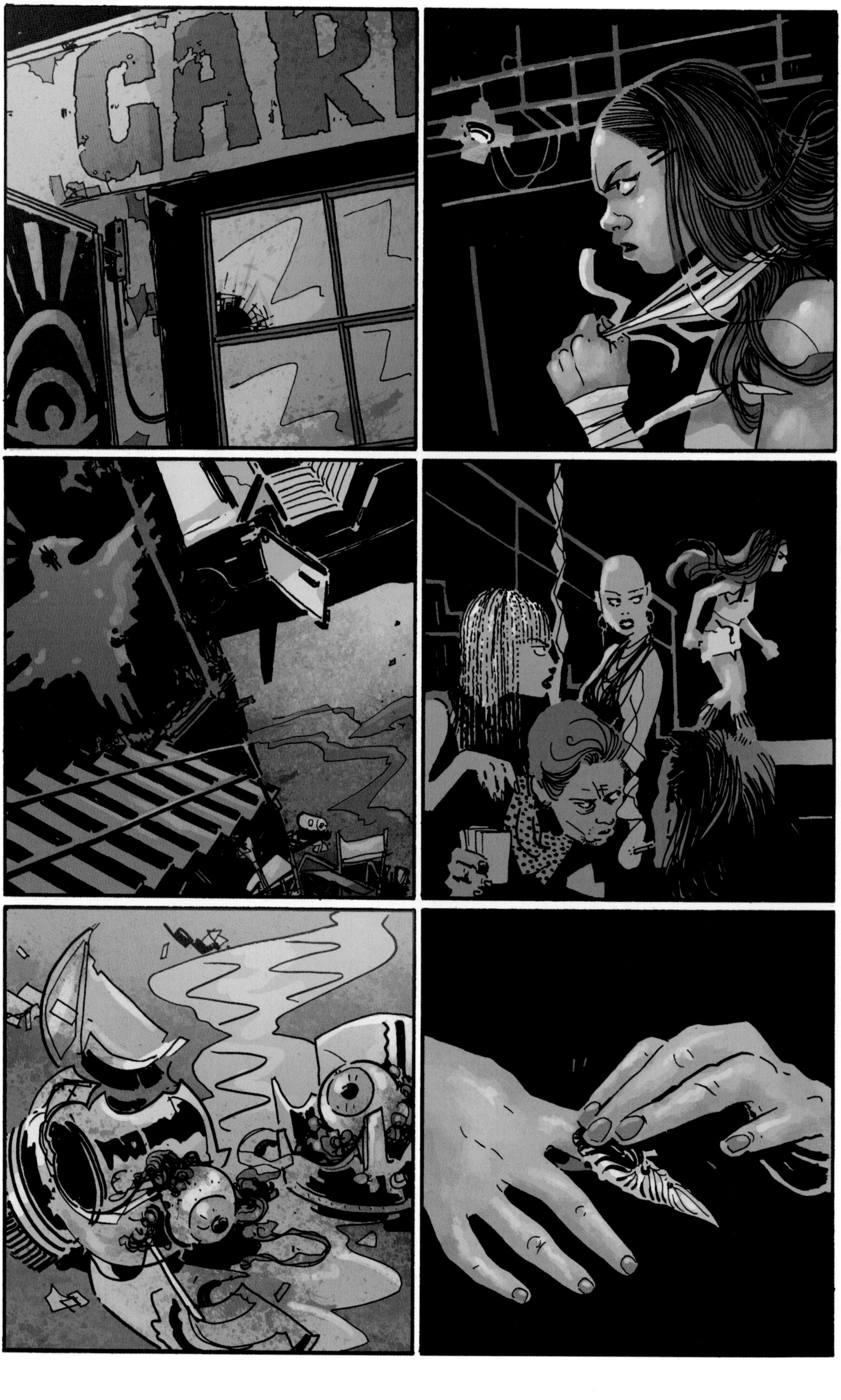

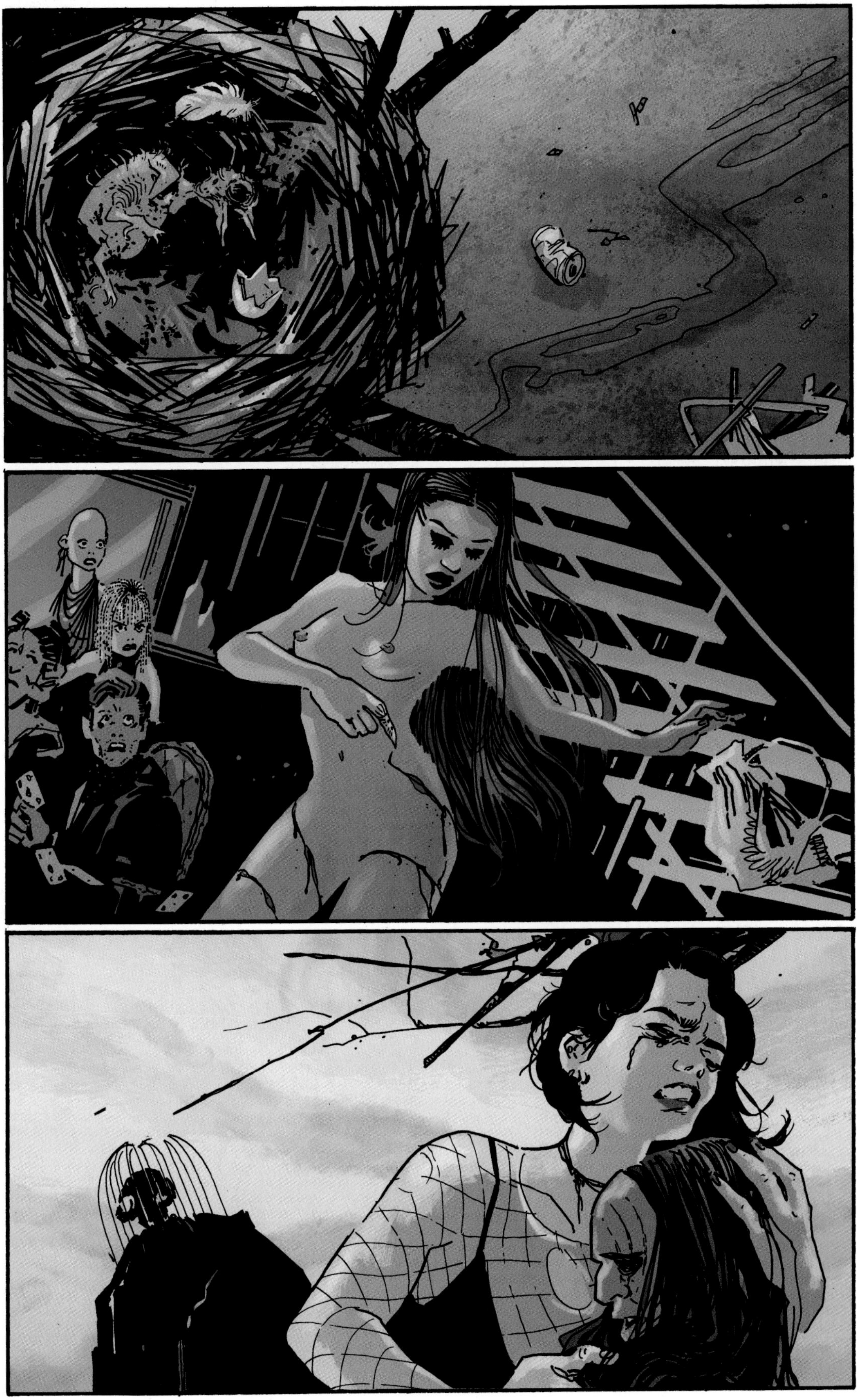

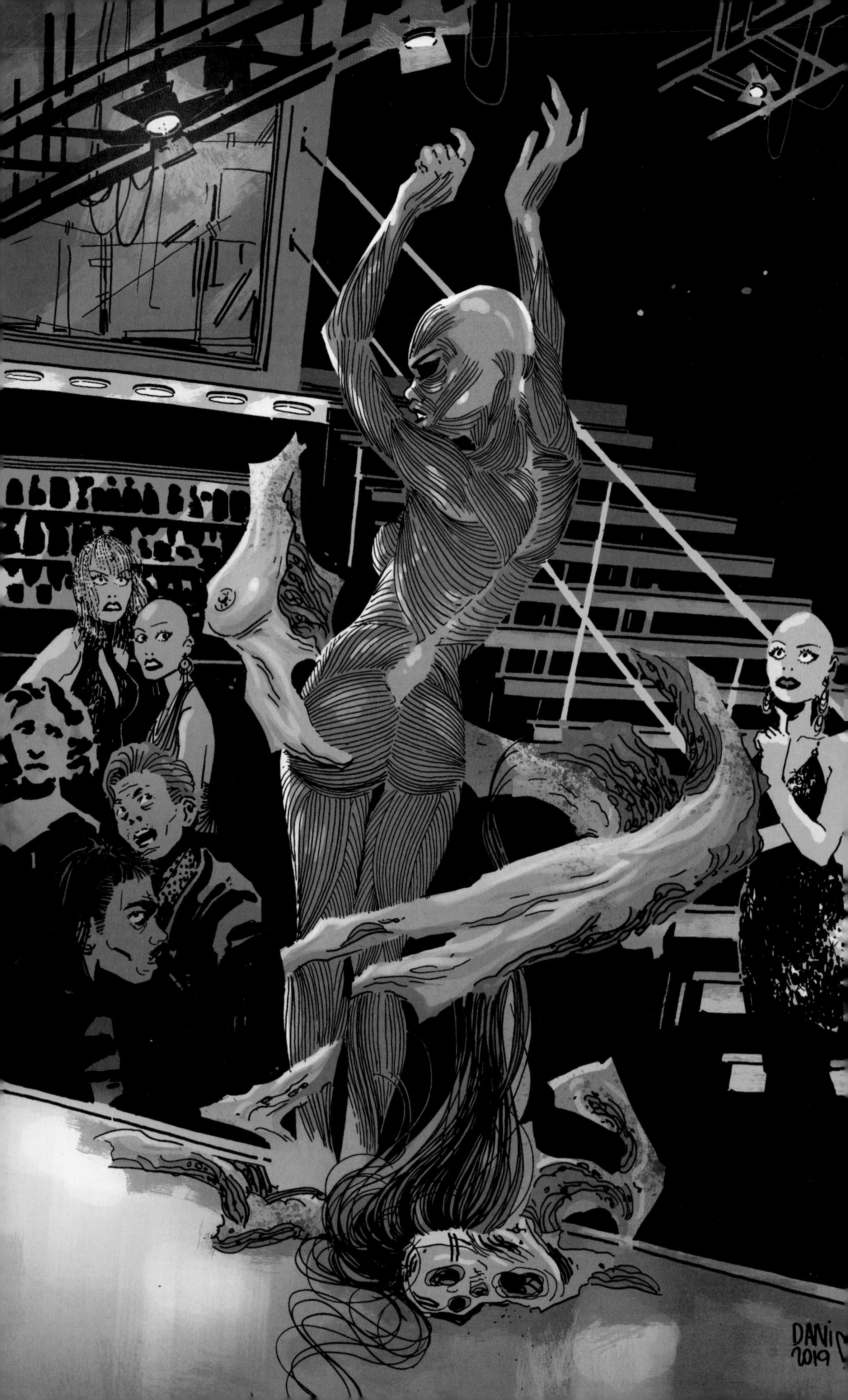
DANI
2019

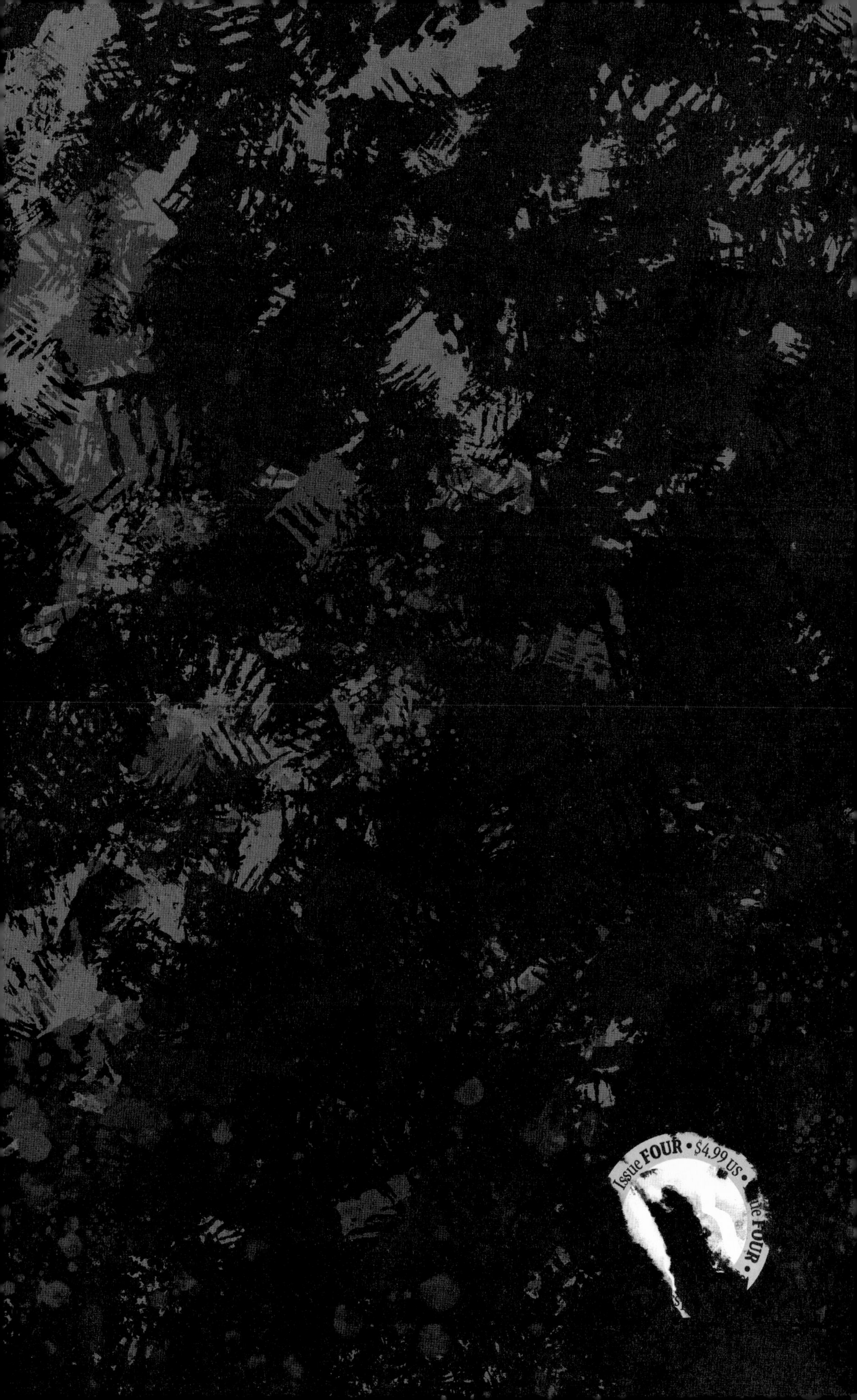

Issue FOUR • $4.99 US • ...e FOUR •

"This final scene I'll not see to the end –
MY DREAM IS FRAYING.**"**
—THE DEATH POEM OF CHOKO

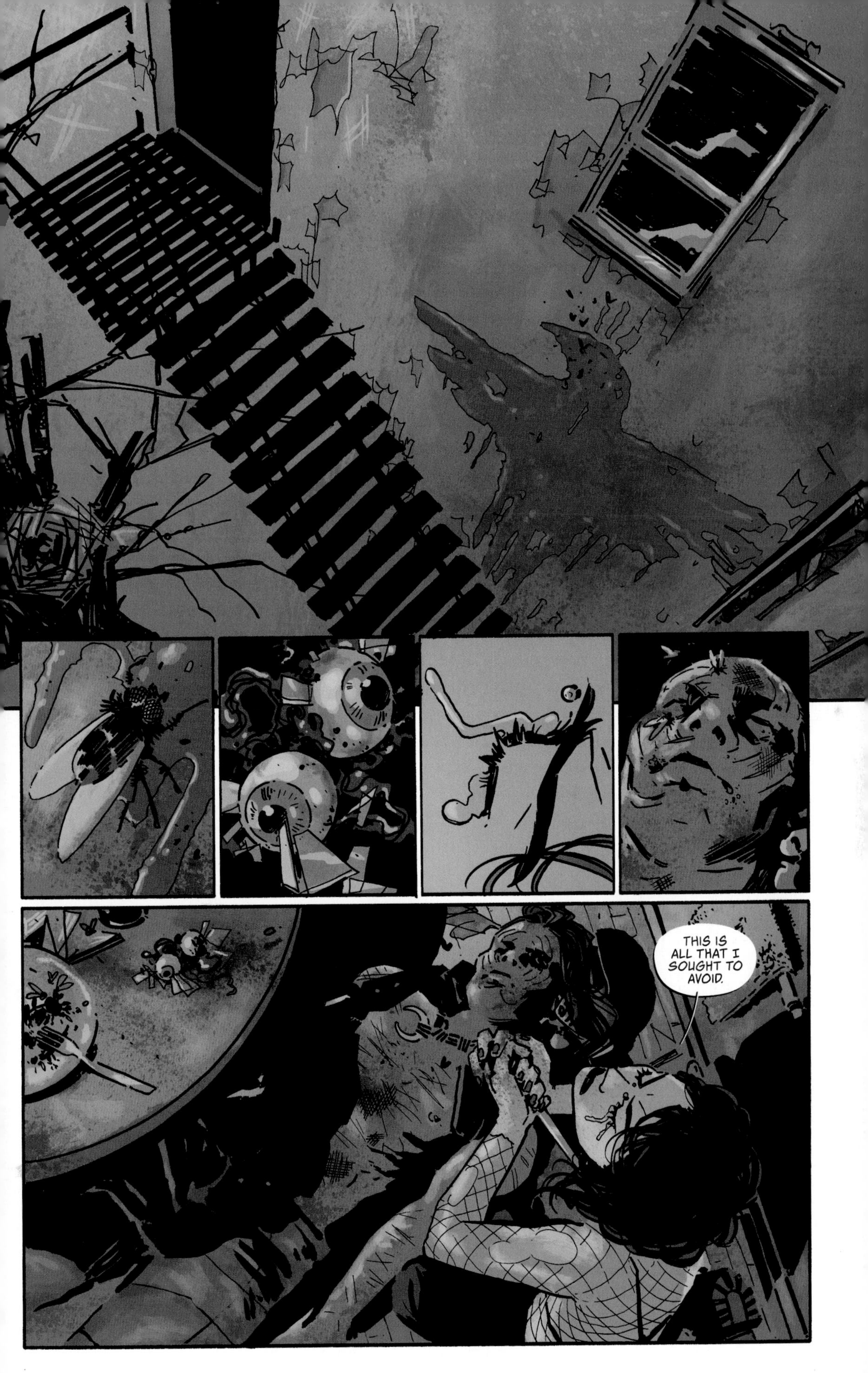
THIS IS ALL THAT I SOUGHT TO AVOID.

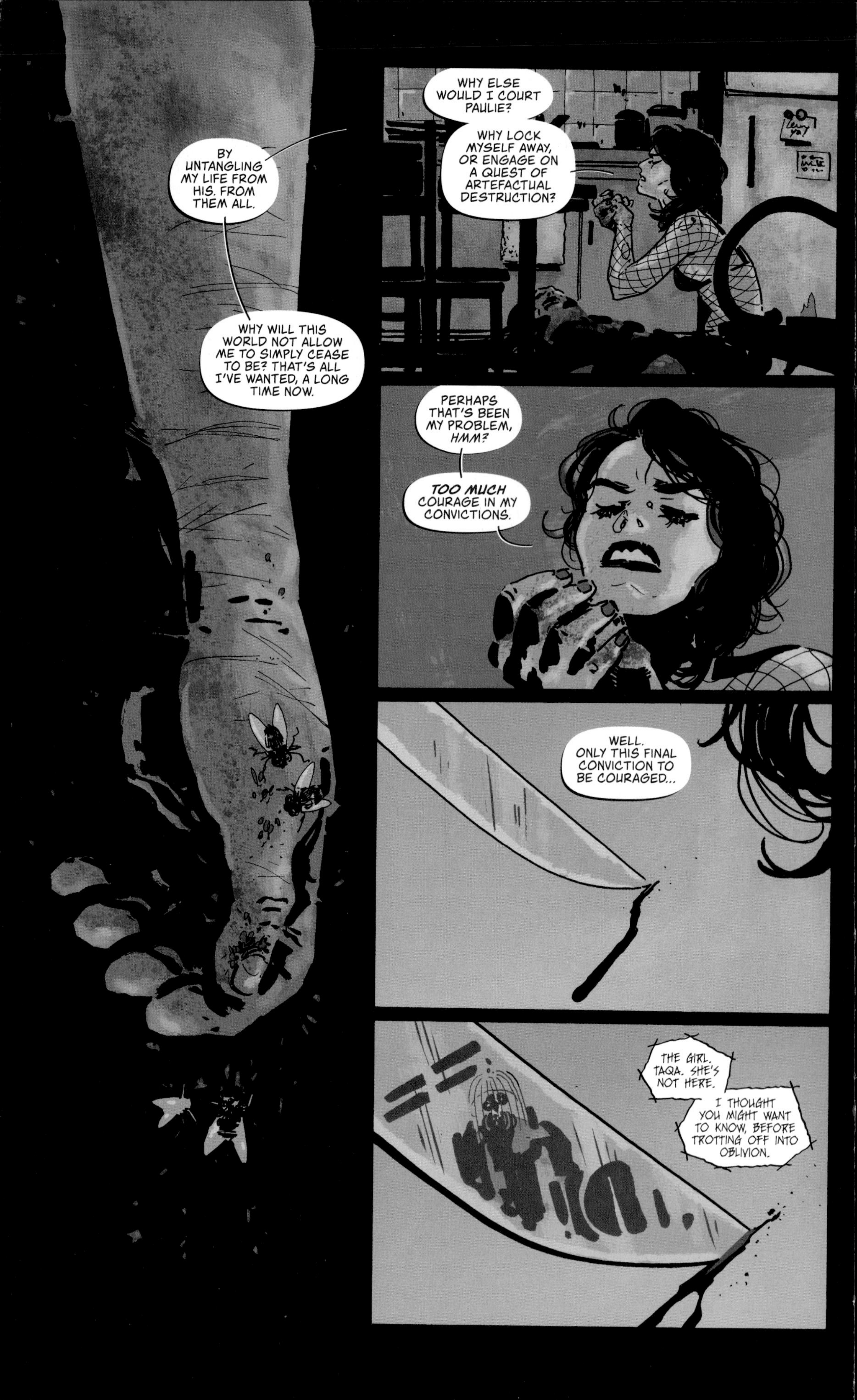
BY UNTANGLING MY LIFE FROM HIS. FROM THEM ALL.
WHY WILL THIS WORLD NOT ALLOW ME TO SIMPLY CEASE TO BE? THAT'S ALL I'VE WANTED, A LONG TIME NOW.
WHY ELSE WOULD I COURT PAULIE?
WHY LOCK MYSELF AWAY, OR ENGAGE ON A QUEST OF ARTEFACTUAL DESTRUCTION?
PERHAPS THAT'S BEEN MY PROBLEM, HMM?
TOO MUCH COURAGE IN MY CONVICTIONS.
WELL. ONLY THIS FINAL CONVICTION TO BE COURAGED...
THE GIRL. TAQA. SHE'S NOT HERE.
I THOUGHT YOU MIGHT WANT TO KNOW, BEFORE TROTTING OFF INTO OBLIVION.

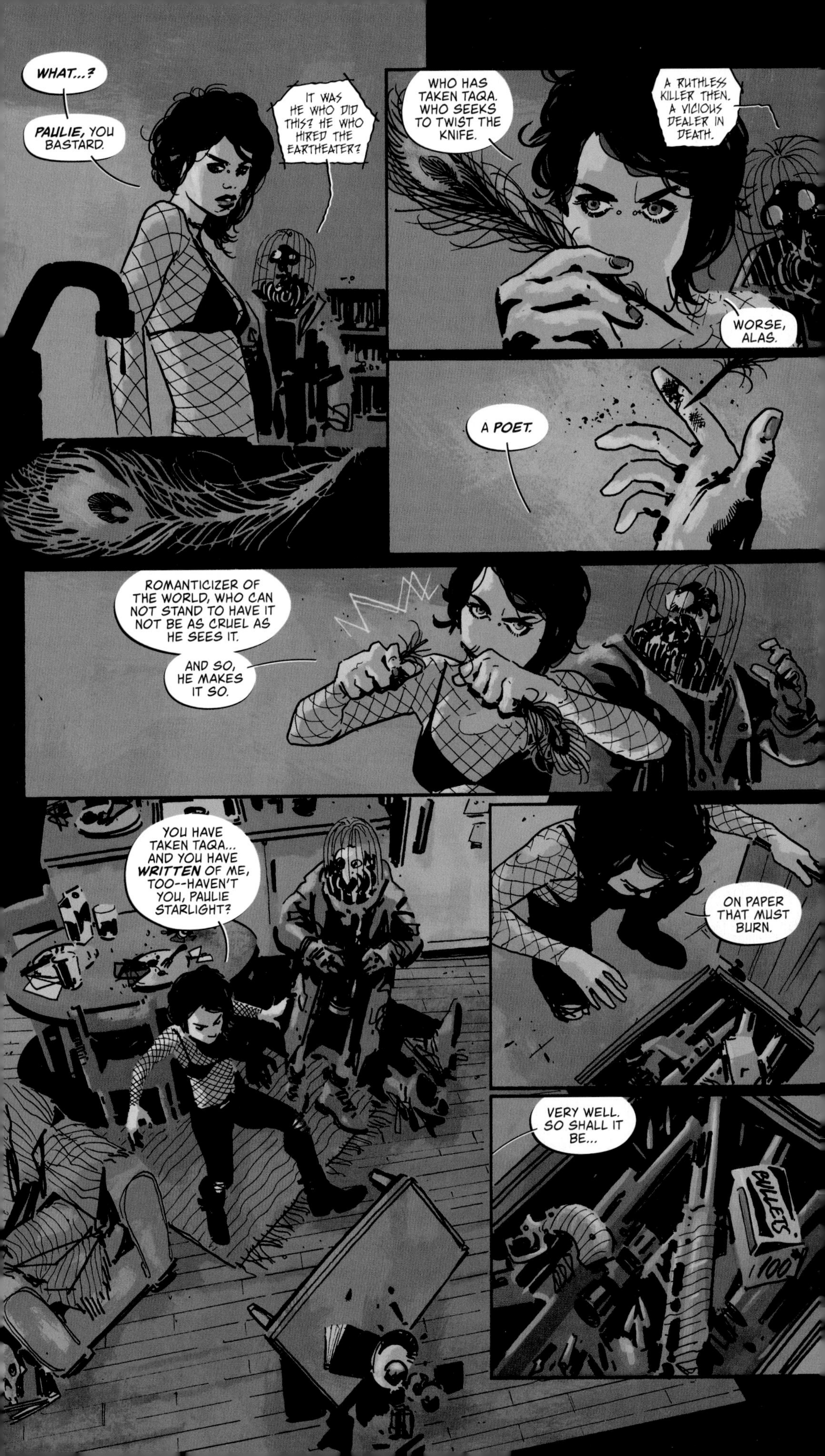

WHAT...?
PAULIE, YOU BASTARD.
IT WAS HE WHO DID THIS? HE WHO HIRED THE EARTHEATER?
WHO HAS TAKEN TAQA. WHO SEEKS TO TWIST THE KNIFE.
A RUTHLESS KILLER THEN. A VICIOUS DEALER IN DEATH.
WORSE, ALAS.
A POET.
ROMANTICIZER OF THE WORLD, WHO CAN NOT STAND TO HAVE IT NOT BE AS CRUEL AS HE SEES IT.
AND SO, HE MAKES IT SO.
YOU HAVE TAKEN TAQA... AND YOU HAVE WRITTEN OF ME, TOO--HAVEN'T YOU, PAULIE STARLIGHT?
ON PAPER THAT MUST BURN.
VERY WELL. SO SHALL IT BE...
BULLETS
100

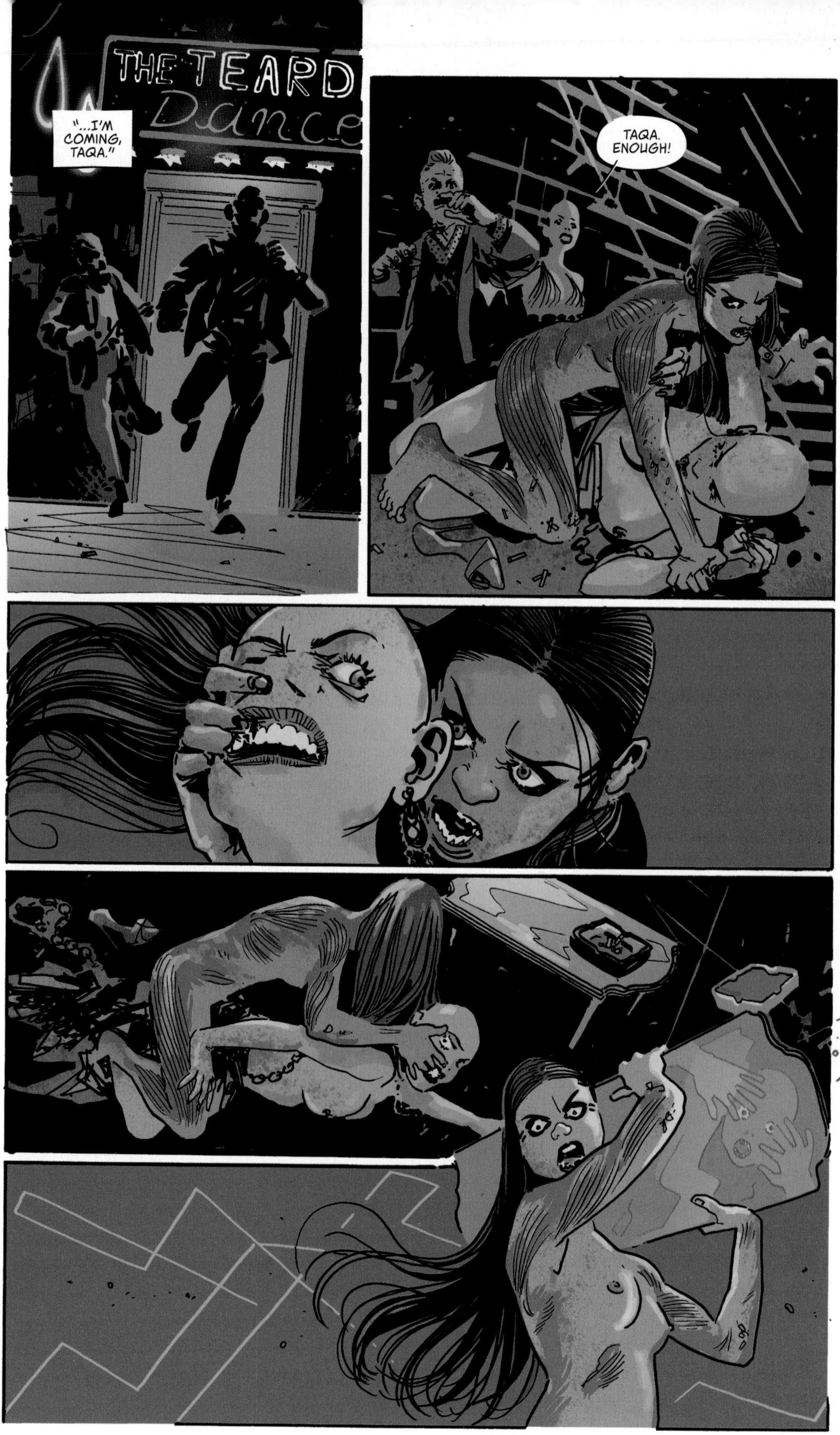
THE TEARD
Dance
"...I'M COMING, TAQA."
TAQA. ENOUGH!

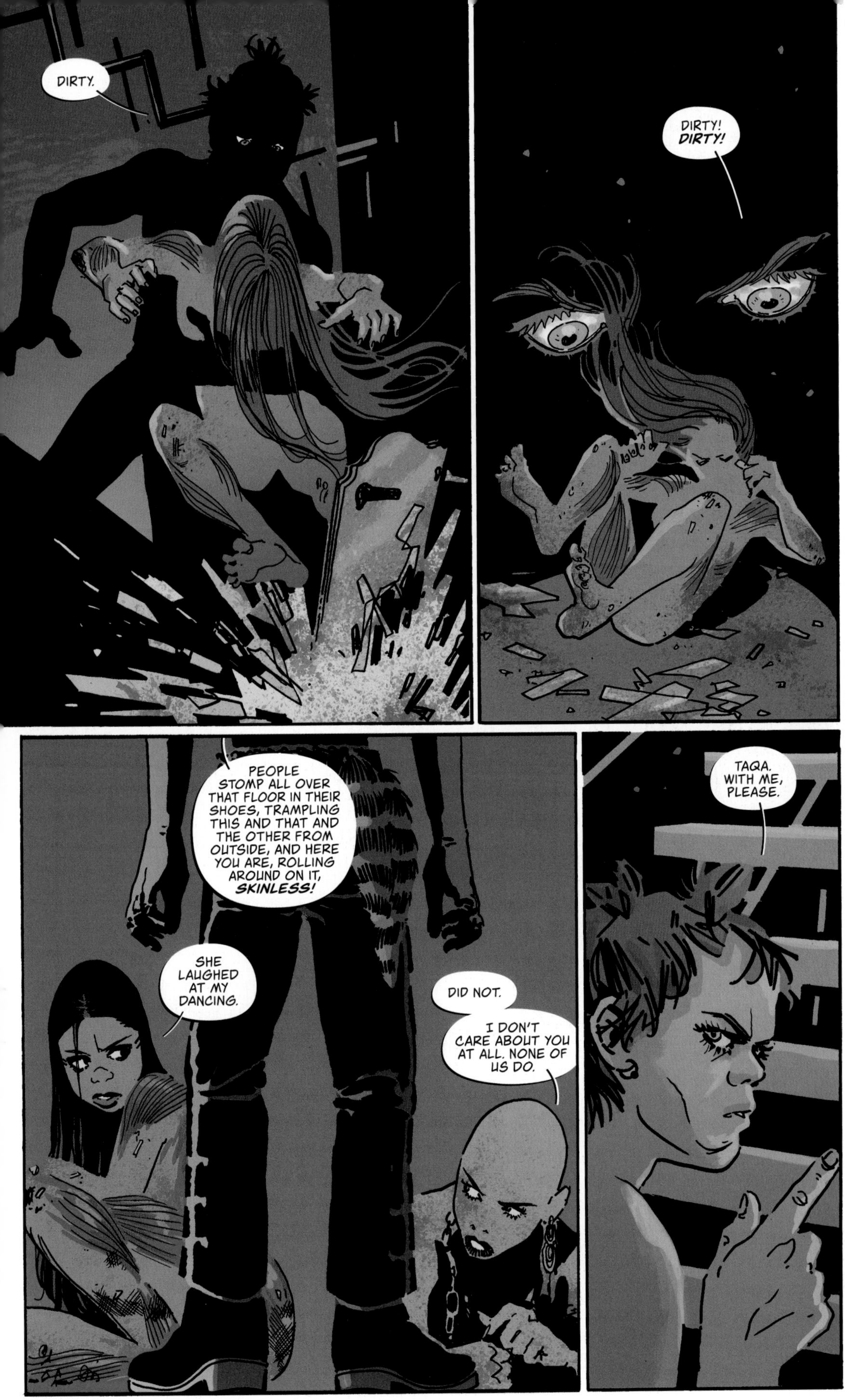
DIRTY.
DIRTY! DIRTY!
PEOPLE STOMP ALL OVER THAT FLOOR IN THEIR SHOES, TRAMPLING THIS AND THAT AND THE OTHER FROM OUTSIDE, AND HERE YOU ARE, ROLLING AROUND ON IT, SKINLESS!
SHE LAUGHED AT MY DANCING.
DID NOT.
I DON'T CARE ABOUT YOU AT ALL. NONE OF US DO.
TAQA. WITH ME, PLEASE.

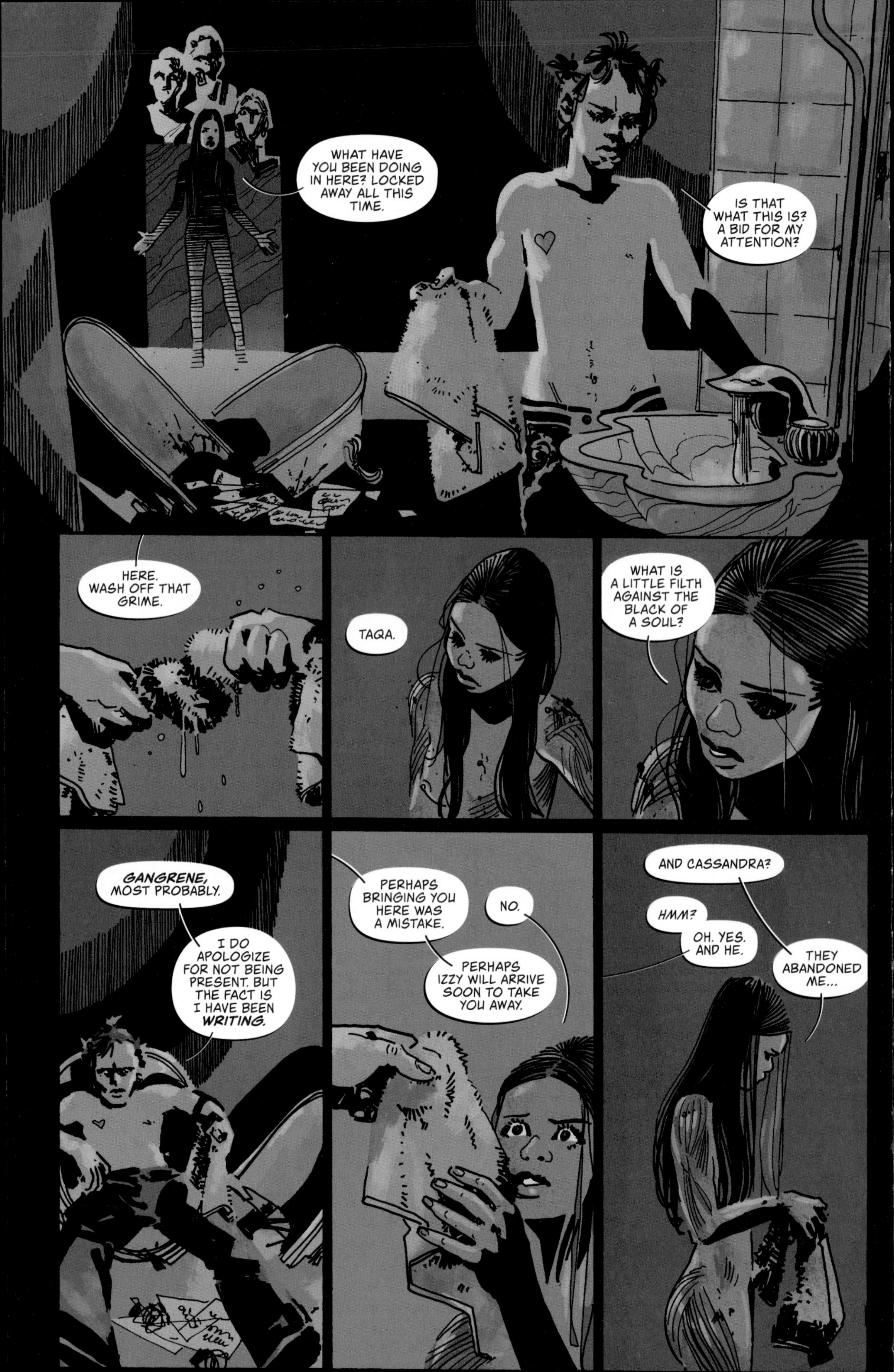
WHAT HAVE YOU BEEN DOING IN HERE? LOCKED AWAY ALL THIS TIME.
IS THAT WHAT THIS IS? A BID FOR MY ATTENTION?
HERE. WASH OFF THAT GRIME.
TAQA.
WHAT IS A LITTLE FILTH AGAINST THE BLACK OF A SOUL?
GANGRENE, MOST PROBABLY.
I DO APOLOGIZE FOR NOT BEING PRESENT. BUT THE FACT IS I HAVE BEEN WRITING.
PERHAPS BRINGING YOU HERE WAS A MISTAKE.
NO.
PERHAPS IZZY WILL ARRIVE SOON TO TAKE YOU AWAY.
AND CASSANDRA?
HMM?
OH. YES. AND HE.
THEY ABANDONED ME...

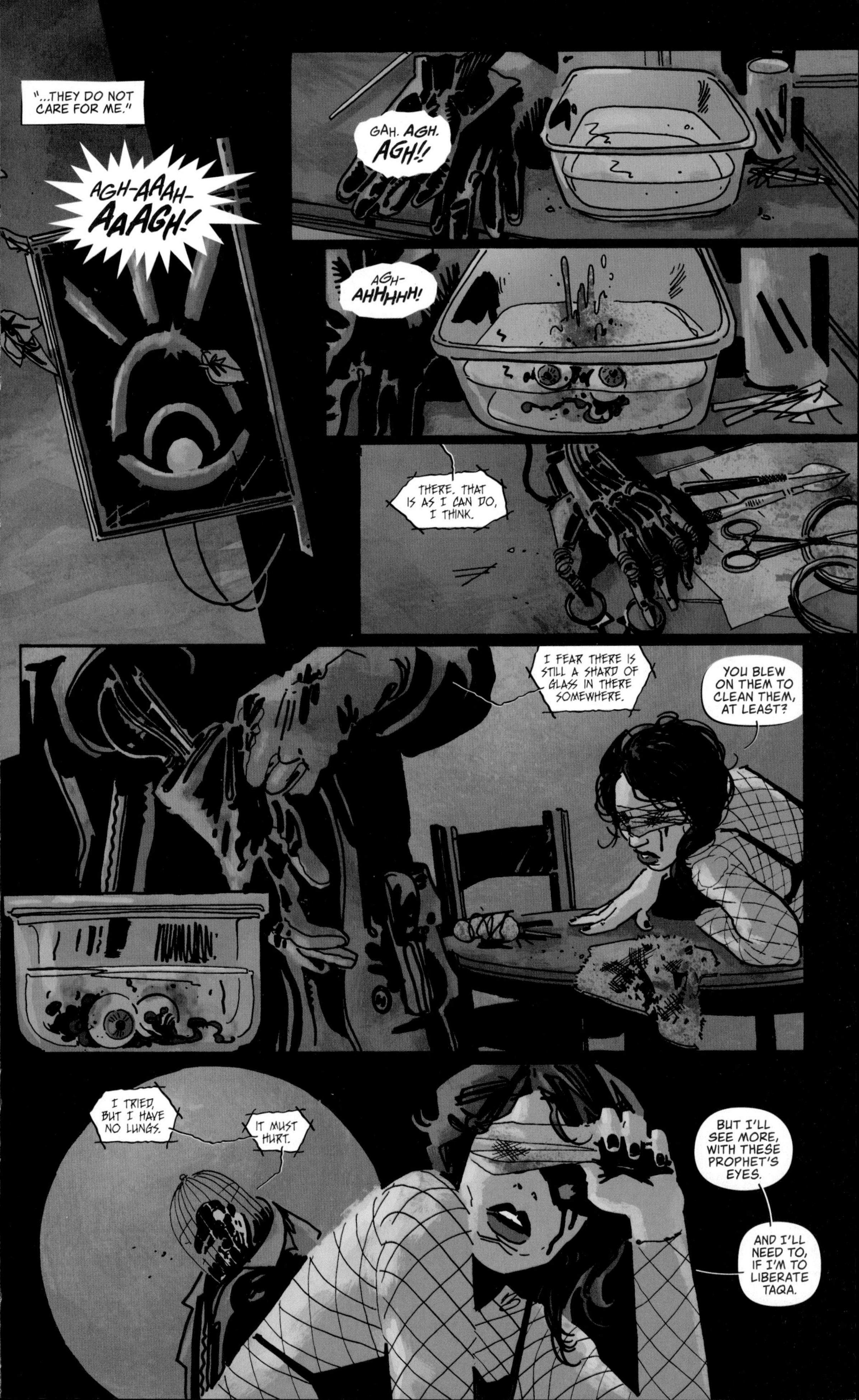
"...THEY DO NOT CARE FOR ME."
AGH-AAAH-AAAGH!
GAH. AGH. AGH!!
AGH-AHHHHH!
THERE. THAT IS AS I CAN DO, I THINK.
I FEAR THERE IS STILL A SHARD OF GLASS IN THERE SOMEWHERE.
YOU BLEW ON THEM TO CLEAN THEM, AT LEAST?
I TRIED, BUT I HAVE NO LUNGS.
IT MUST HURT.
BUT I'LL SEE MORE, WITH THESE PROPHET'S EYES.
AND I'LL NEED TO, IF I'M TO LIBERATE TAQA.

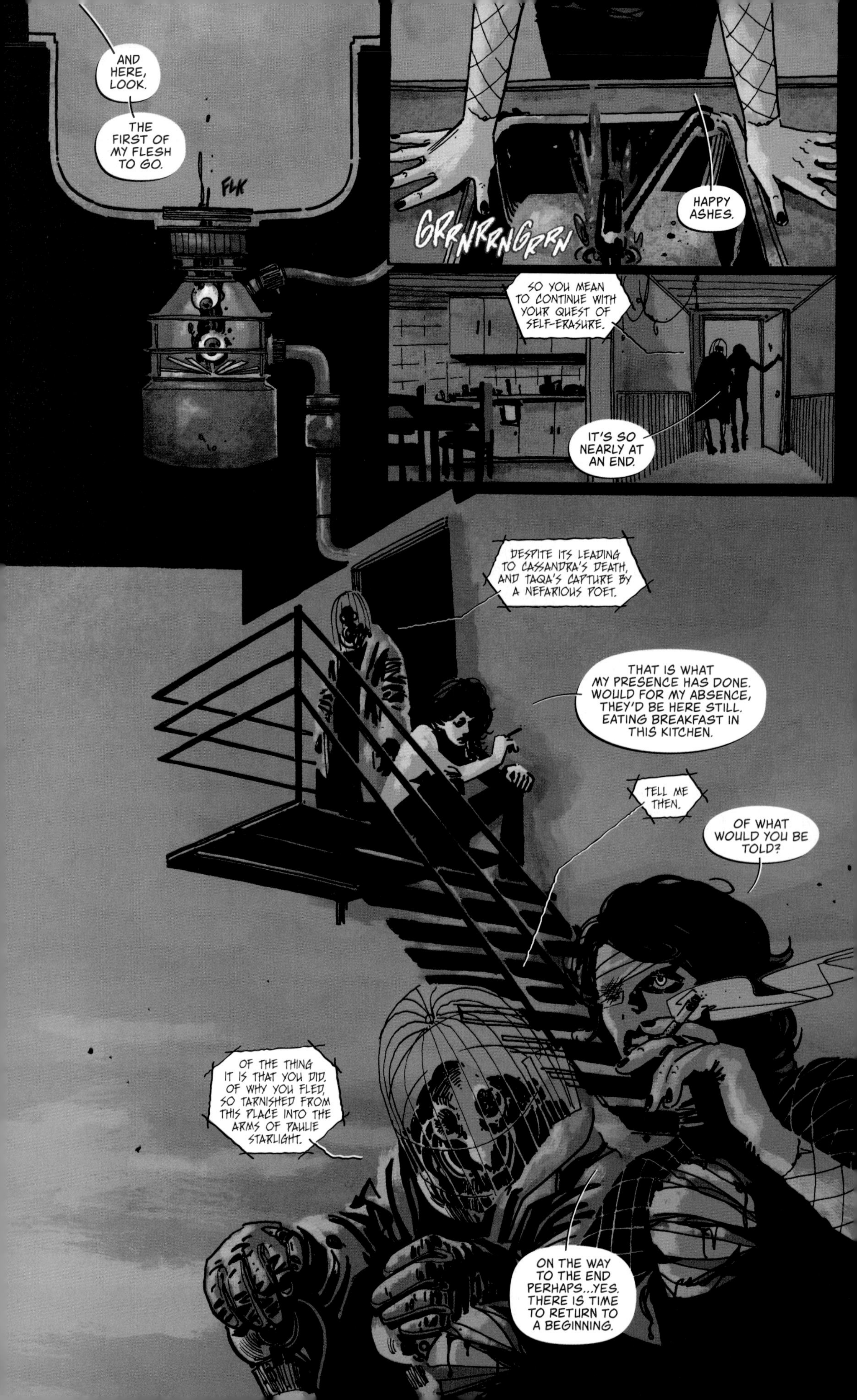
AND HERE, LOOK.
THE FIRST OF MY FLESH TO GO.
FLK
GRRNRRNGRRN
HAPPY ASHES.
SO YOU MEAN TO CONTINUE WITH YOUR QUEST OF SELF-ERASURE.
IT'S SO NEARLY AT AN END.
DESPITE ITS LEADING TO CASSANDRA'S DEATH, AND TAQA'S CAPTURE BY A NEFARIOUS POET.
THAT IS WHAT MY PRESENCE HAS DONE. WOULD FOR MY ABSENCE, THEY'D BE HERE STILL. EATING BREAKFAST IN THIS KITCHEN.
TELL ME THEN.
OF WHAT WOULD YOU BE TOLD?
OF THE THING IT IS THAT YOU DID. OF WHY YOU FLED, SO TARNISHED FROM THIS PLACE INTO THE ARMS OF PAULIE STARLIGHT.
ON THE WAY TO THE END PERHAPS...YES. THERE IS TIME TO RETURN TO A BEGINNING.

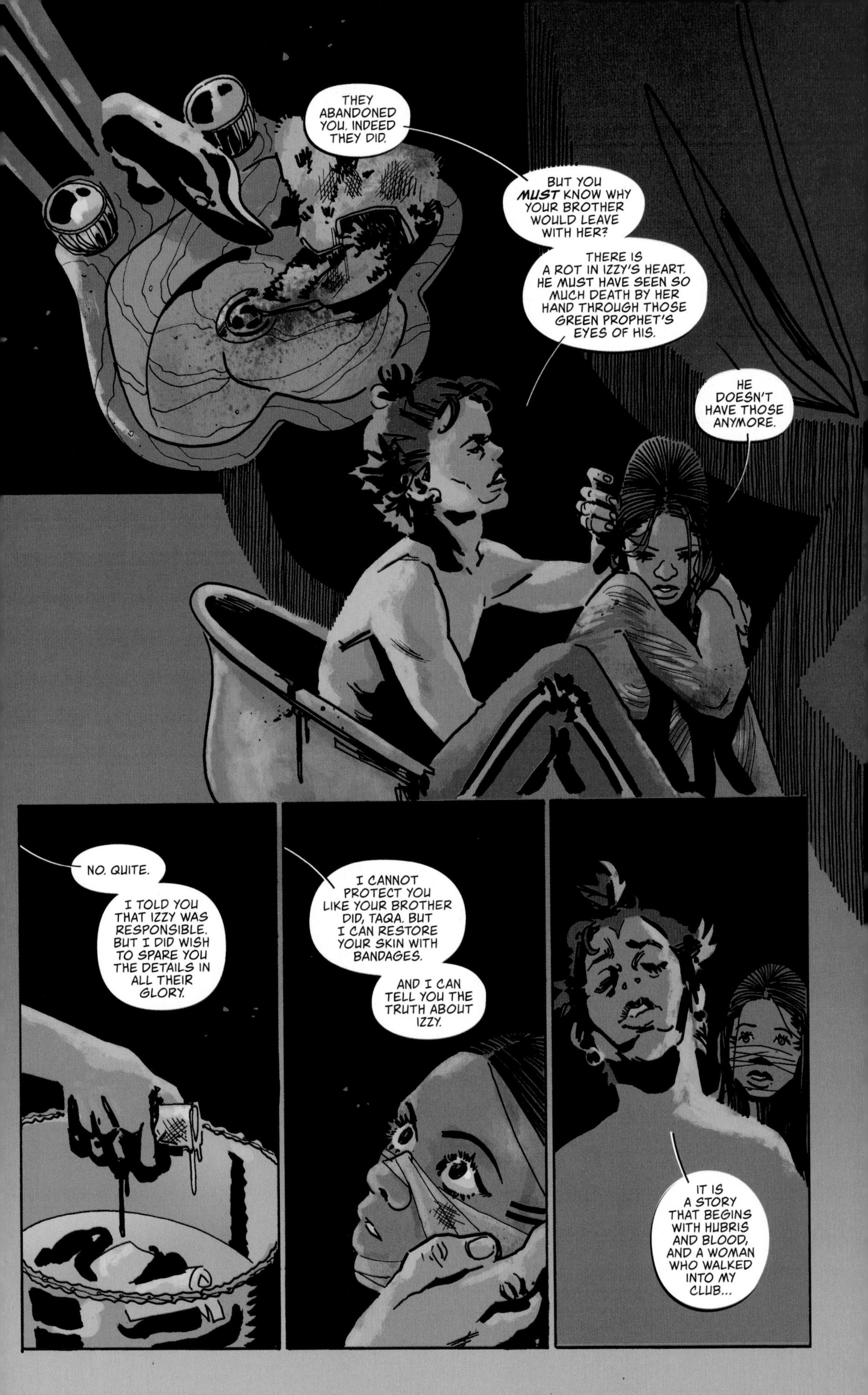
THEY ABANDONED YOU. INDEED THEY DID.
BUT YOU MUST KNOW WHY YOUR BROTHER WOULD LEAVE WITH HER?
THERE IS A ROT IN IZZY'S HEART. HE MUST HAVE SEEN SO MUCH DEATH BY HER HAND THROUGH THOSE GREEN PROPHET'S EYES OF HIS.
HE DOESN'T HAVE THOSE ANYMORE.
NO. QUITE.
I TOLD YOU THAT IZZY WAS RESPONSIBLE. BUT I DID WISH TO SPARE YOU THE DETAILS IN ALL THEIR GLORY.
I CANNOT PROTECT YOU LIKE YOUR BROTHER DID, TAQA. BUT I CAN RESTORE YOUR SKIN WITH BANDAGES.
AND I CAN TELL YOU THE TRUTH ABOUT IZZY.
IT IS A STORY THAT BEGINS WITH HUBRIS AND BLOOD, AND A WOMAN WHO WALKED INTO MY CLUB...

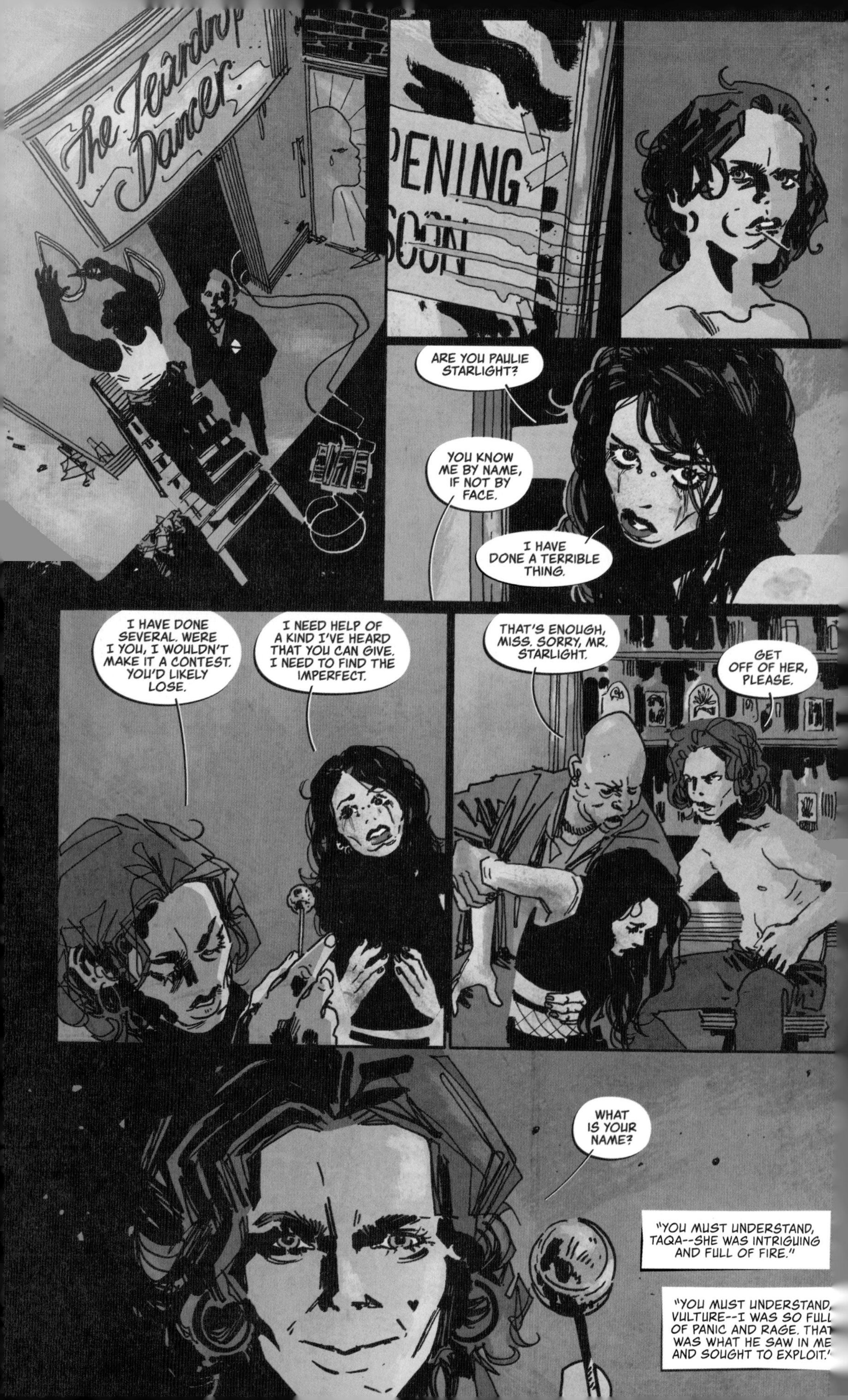

The Teardrop Dancer
PENING
SOON
ARE YOU PAULIE STARLIGHT?
YOU KNOW ME BY NAME, IF NOT BY FACE.
I HAVE DONE A TERRIBLE THING.
I HAVE DONE SEVERAL. WERE I YOU, I WOULDN'T MAKE IT A CONTEST. YOU'D LIKELY LOSE.
I NEED HELP OF A KIND I'VE HEARD THAT YOU CAN GIVE. I NEED TO FIND THE IMPERFECT.
THAT'S ENOUGH, MISS. SORRY, MR. STARLIGHT.
GET OFF OF HER, PLEASE.
WHAT IS YOUR NAME?
"YOU MUST UNDERSTAND, TAQA--SHE WAS INTRIGUING AND FULL OF FIRE."
"YOU MUST UNDERSTAND, VULTURE--I WAS SO FULL OF PANIC AND RAGE. THAT WAS WHAT HE SAW IN ME AND SOUGHT TO EXPLOIT."

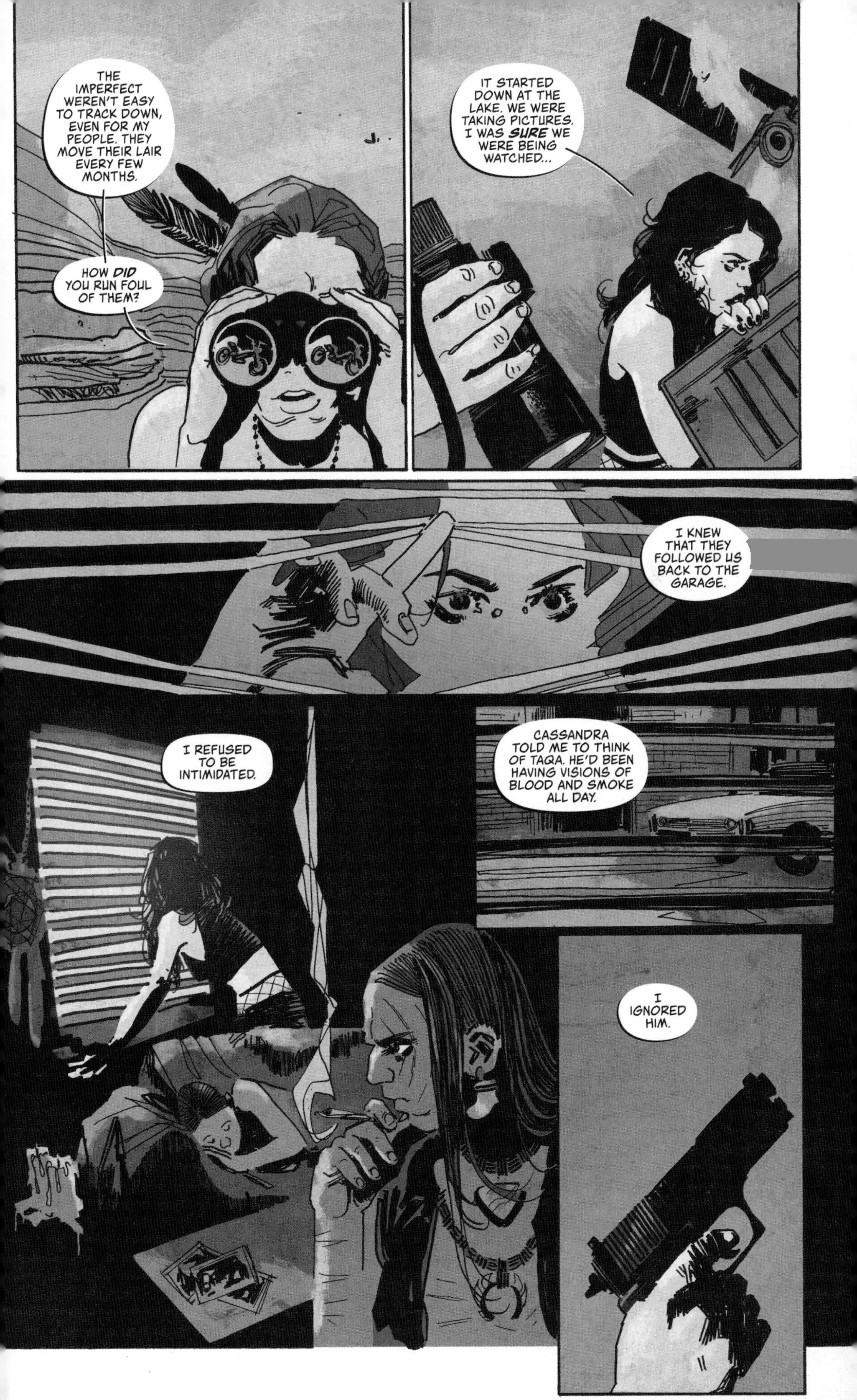
THE IMPERFECT WEREN'T EASY TO TRACK DOWN, EVEN FOR MY PEOPLE. THEY MOVE THEIR LAIR EVERY FEW MONTHS.
HOW *DID* YOU RUN FOUL OF THEM?
IT STARTED DOWN AT THE LAKE. WE WERE TAKING PICTURES. I WAS *SURE* WE WERE BEING WATCHED...
I KNEW THAT THEY FOLLOWED US BACK TO THE GARAGE.
I REFUSED TO BE INTIMIDATED.
CASSANDRA TOLD ME TO THINK OF TAQA. HE'D BEEN HAVING VISIONS OF BLOOD AND SMOKE ALL DAY.
I IGNORED HIM.

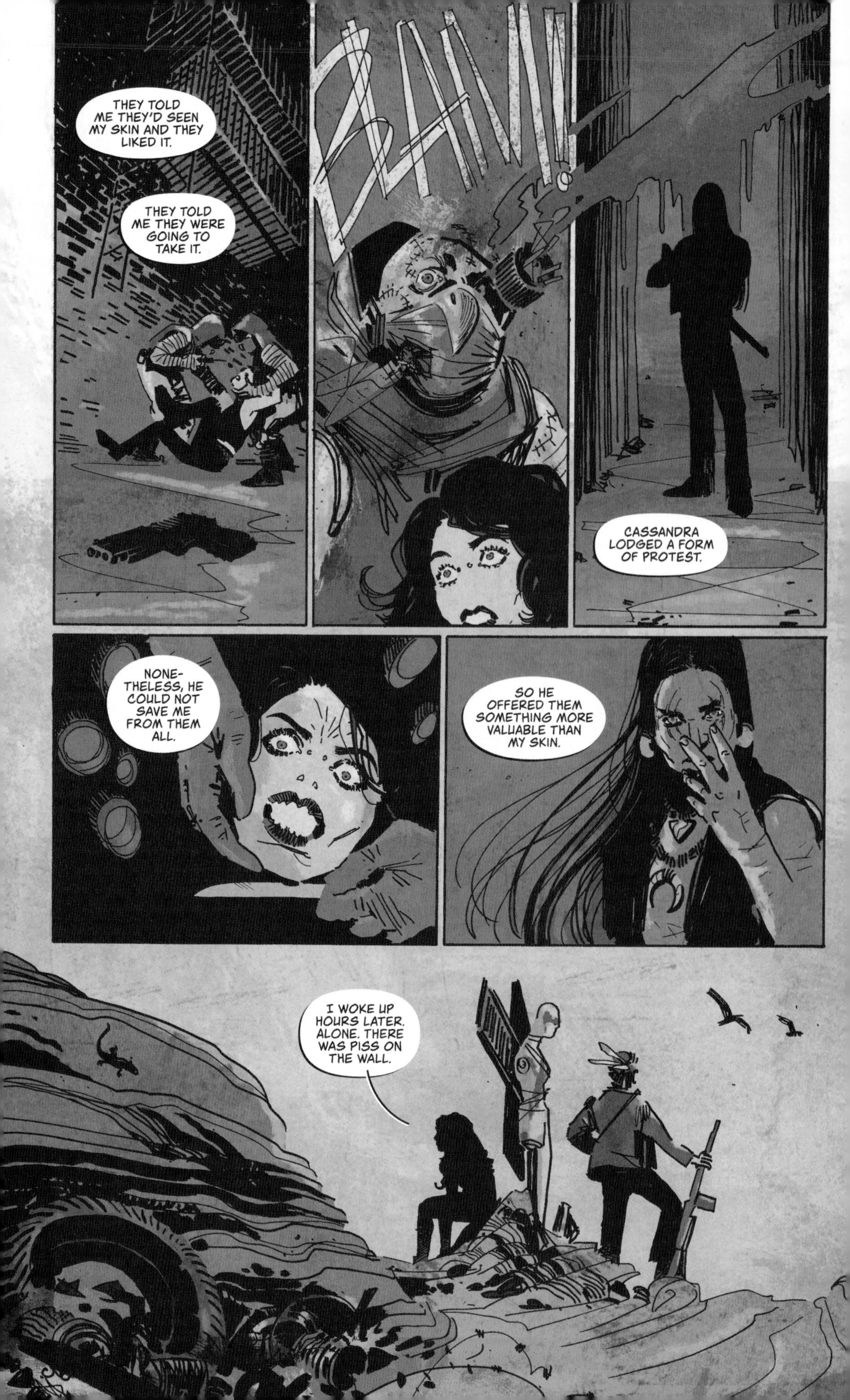
THEY TOLD ME THEY'D SEEN MY SKIN AND THEY LIKED IT.
THEY TOLD ME THEY WERE GOING TO TAKE IT.
BLAM!!
CASSANDRA LODGED A FORM OF PROTEST.
NONE-THELESS, HE COULD NOT SAVE ME FROM THEM ALL.
SO HE OFFERED THEM SOMETHING MORE VALUABLE THAN MY SKIN.
I WOKE UP HOURS LATER. ALONE. THERE WAS PISS ON THE WALL.

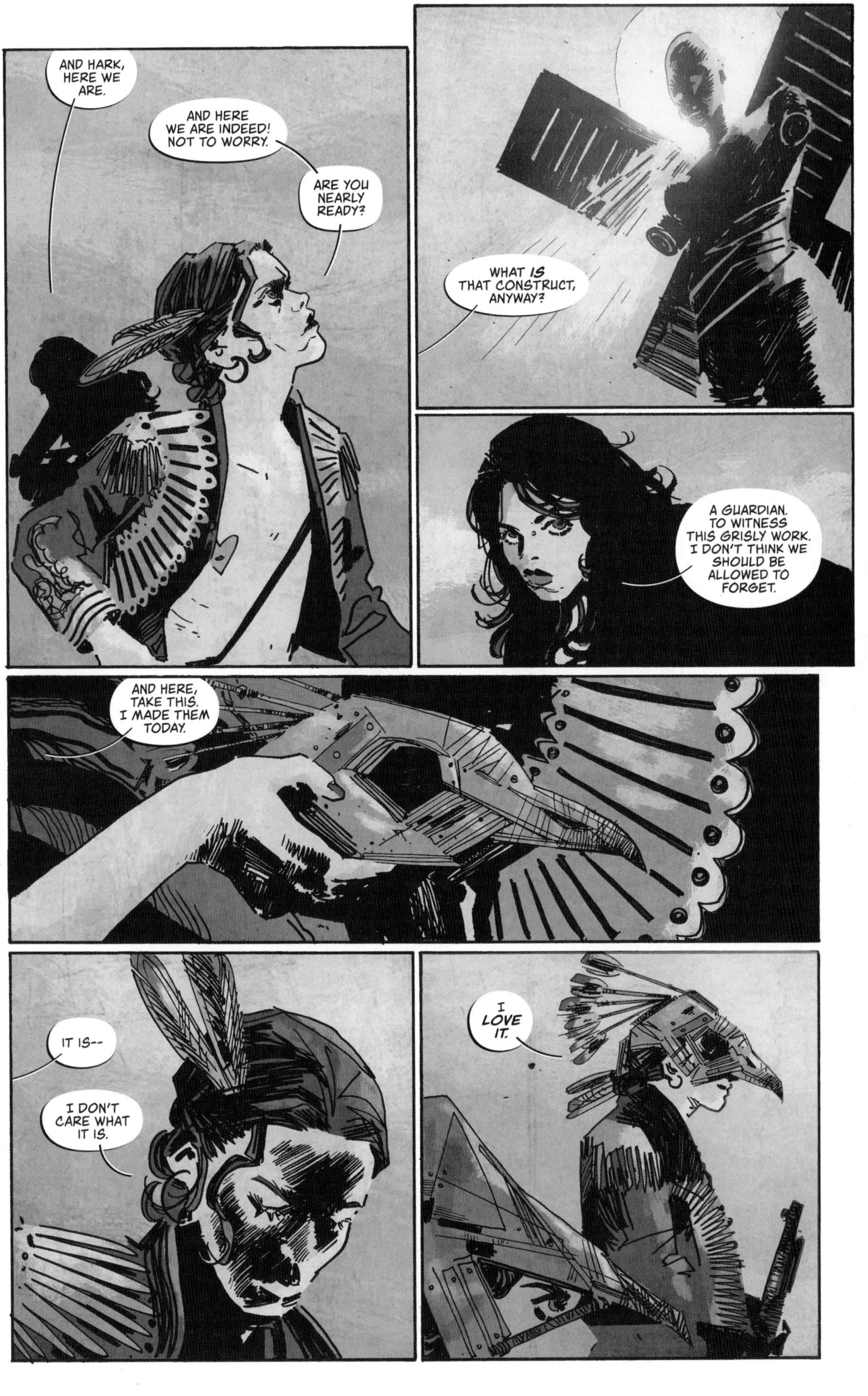
AND HARK, HERE WE ARE.
AND HERE WE ARE INDEED! NOT TO WORRY.
ARE YOU NEARLY READY?
WHAT IS THAT CONSTRUCT, ANYWAY?
A GUARDIAN. TO WITNESS THIS GRISLY WORK. I DON'T THINK WE SHOULD BE ALLOWED TO FORGET.
AND HERE, TAKE THIS. I MADE THEM TODAY.
IT IS--
I DON'T CARE WHAT IT IS.
I LOVE IT.

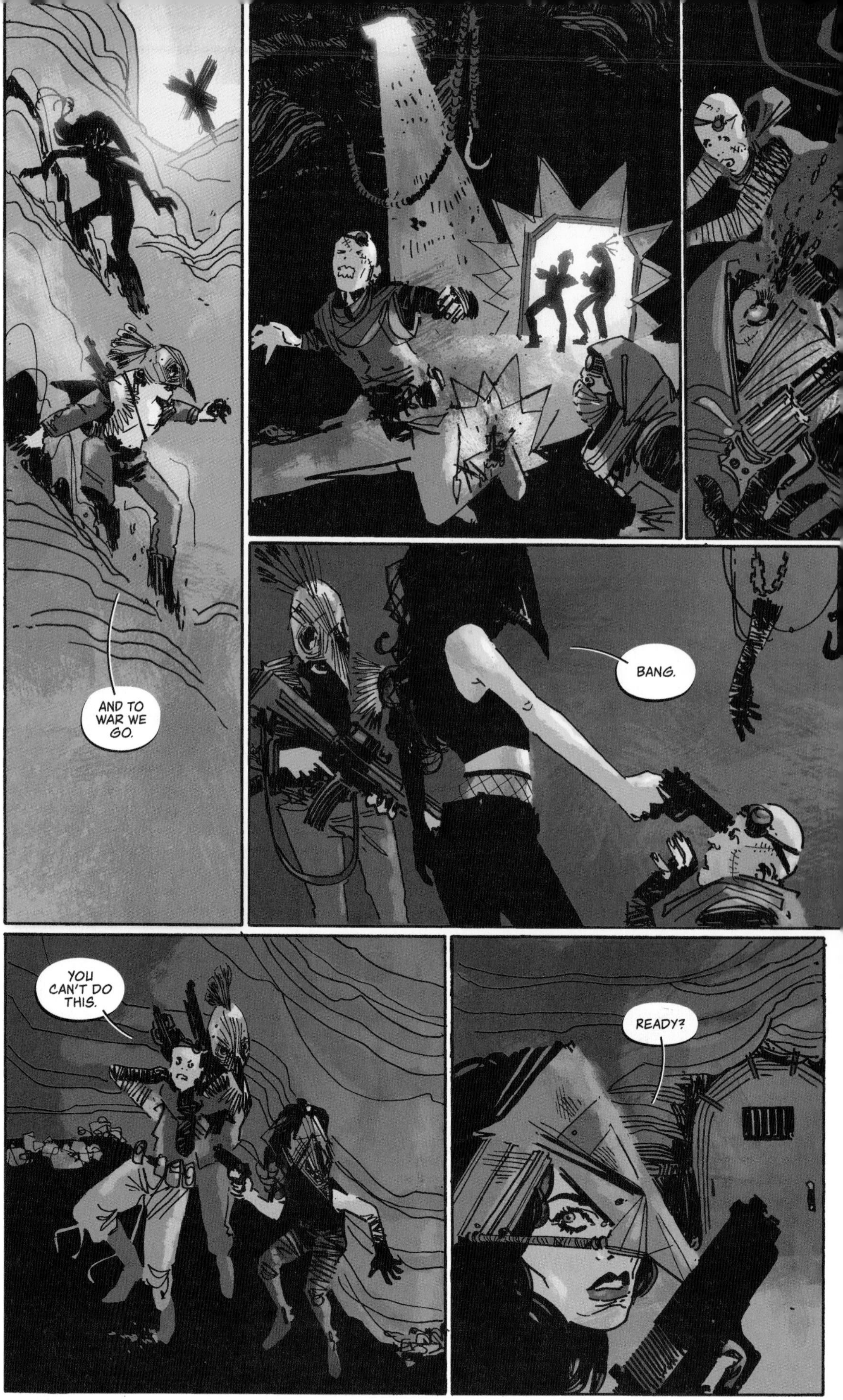
AND TO WAR WE GO.
BANG.
YOU CAN'T DO THIS.
READY?

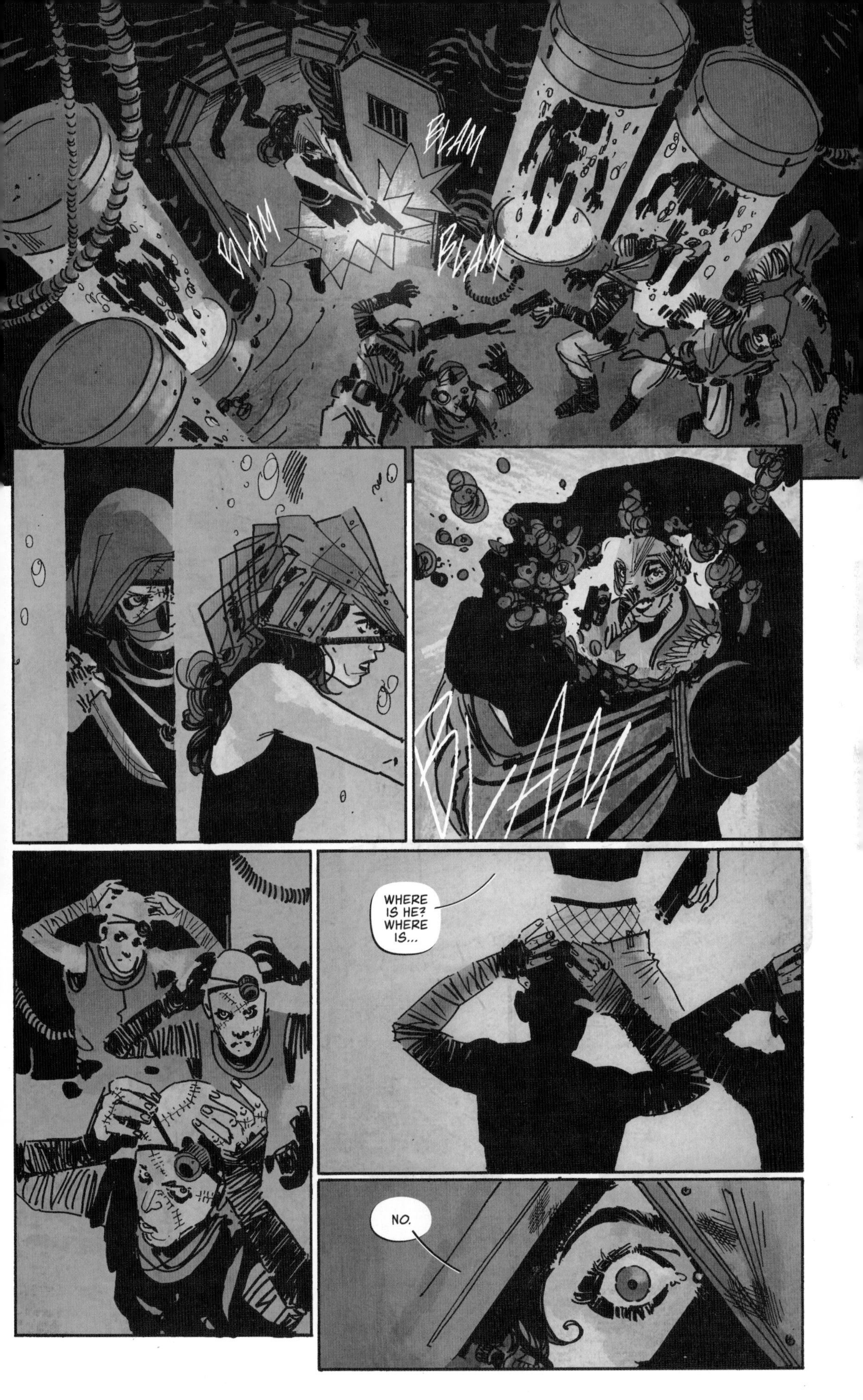
BLAM
BLAM
BLAM
BLAM
WHERE IS HE? WHERE IS...
NO.

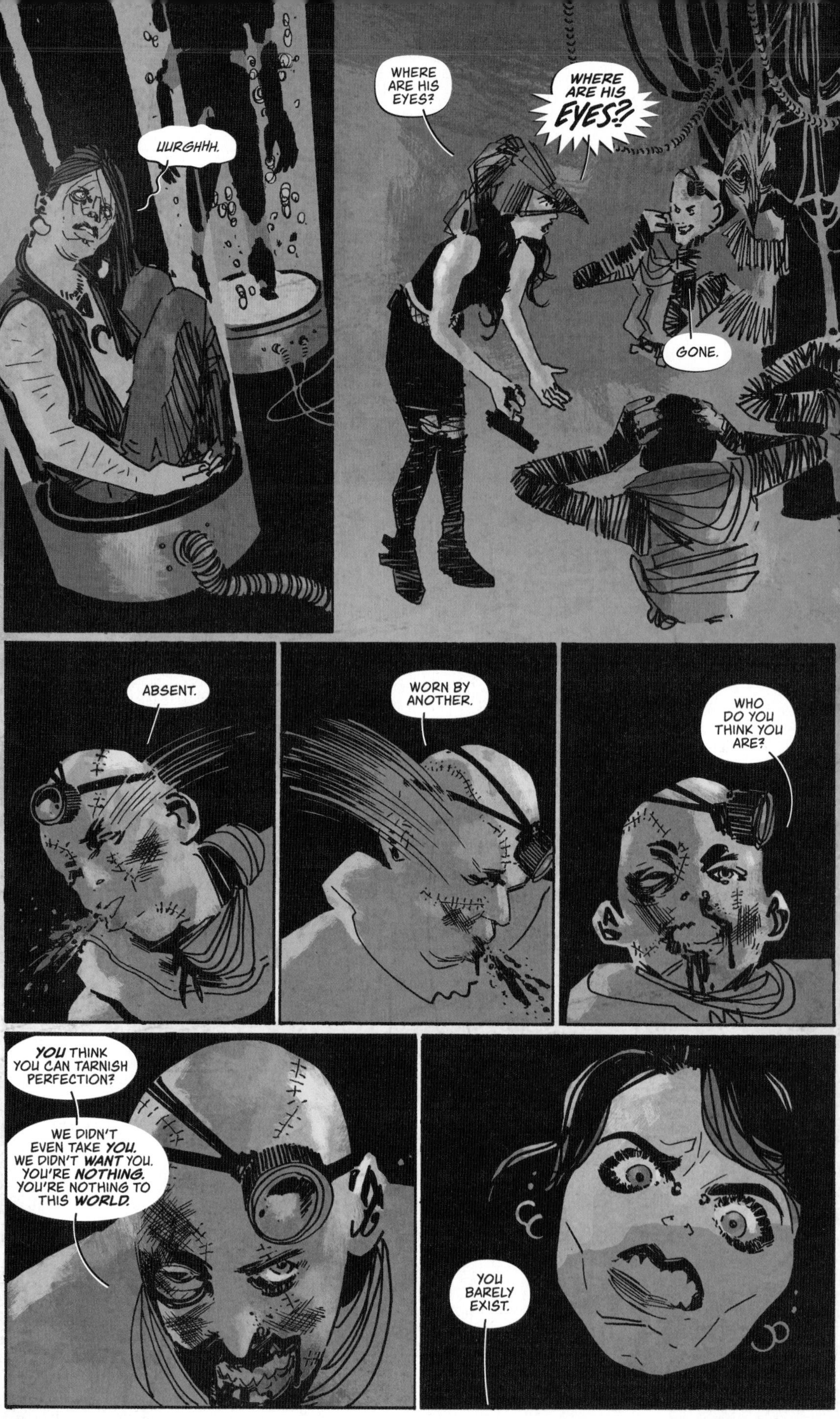
UURGHHH.
WHERE ARE HIS EYES?
WHERE ARE HIS EYES?!
GONE.
ABSENT.
WORN BY ANOTHER.
WHO DO YOU THINK YOU ARE?
YOU THINK YOU CAN TARNISH PERFECTION?
WE DIDN'T EVEN TAKE YOU. WE DIDN'T WANT YOU. YOU'RE NOTHING. YOU'RE NOTHING TO THIS WORLD.
YOU BARELY EXIST.

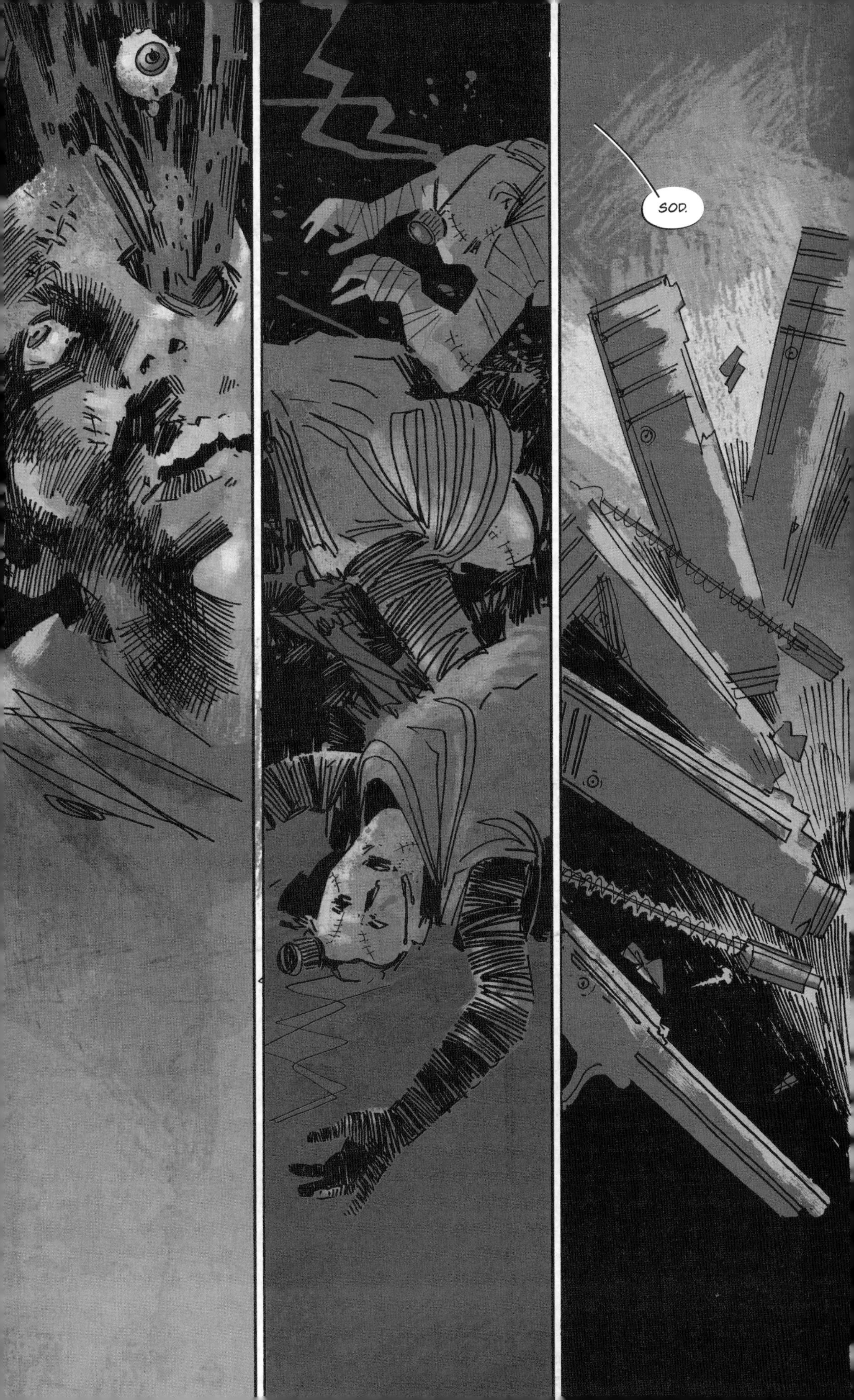
SOD.

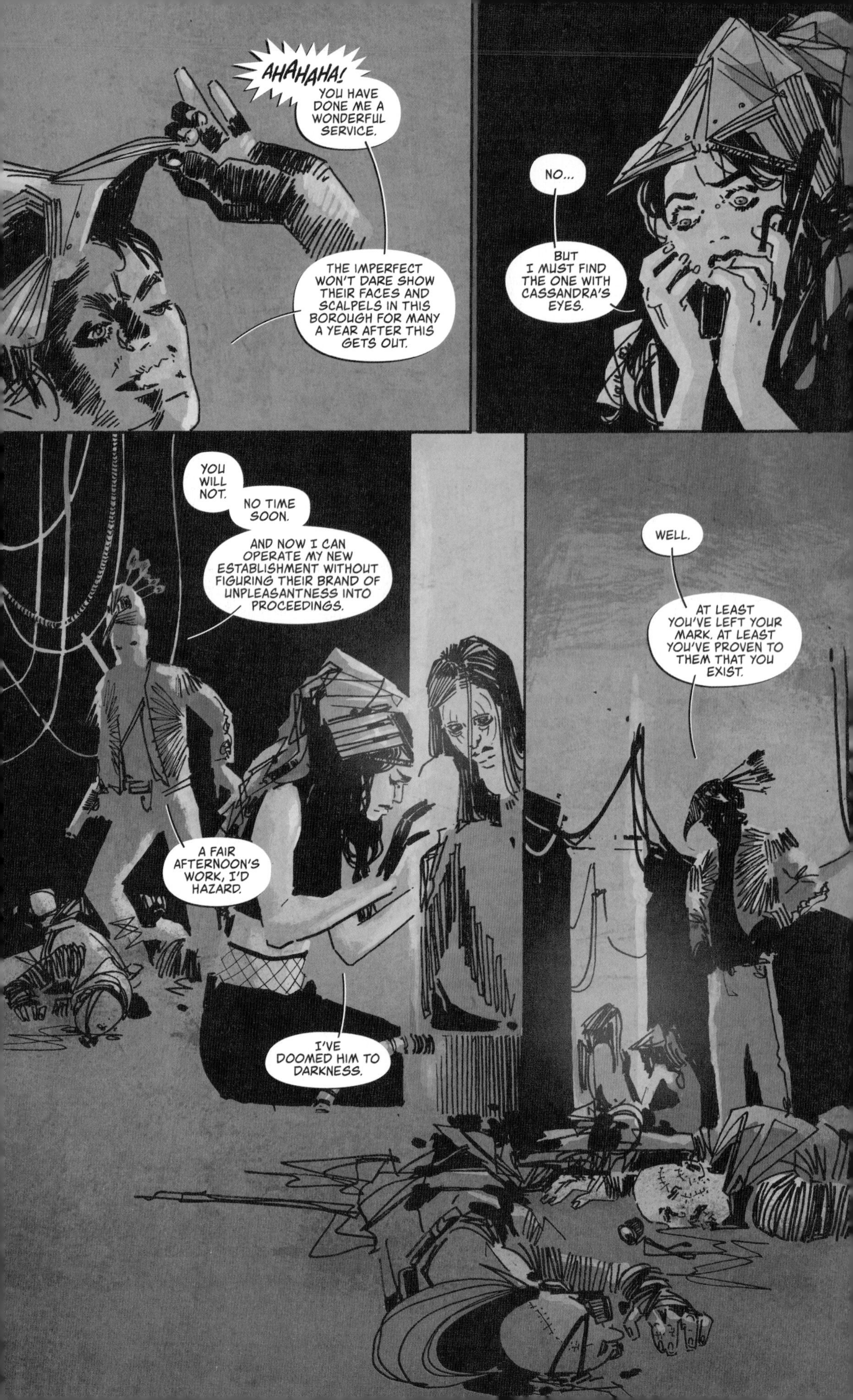
AHAHAHA!
YOU HAVE DONE ME A WONDERFUL SERVICE.
THE IMPERFECT WON'T DARE SHOW THEIR FACES AND SCALPELS IN THIS BOROUGH FOR MANY A YEAR AFTER THIS GETS OUT.
NO...
BUT I MUST FIND THE ONE WITH CASSANDRA'S EYES.
YOU WILL NOT.
NO TIME SOON.
AND NOW I CAN OPERATE MY NEW ESTABLISHMENT WITHOUT FIGURING THEIR BRAND OF UNPLEASANTNESS INTO PROCEEDINGS.
A FAIR AFTERNOON'S WORK, I'D HAZARD.
I'VE DOOMED HIM TO DARKNESS.
WELL.
AT LEAST YOU'VE LEFT YOUR MARK. AT LEAST YOU'VE PROVEN TO THEM THAT YOU EXIST.

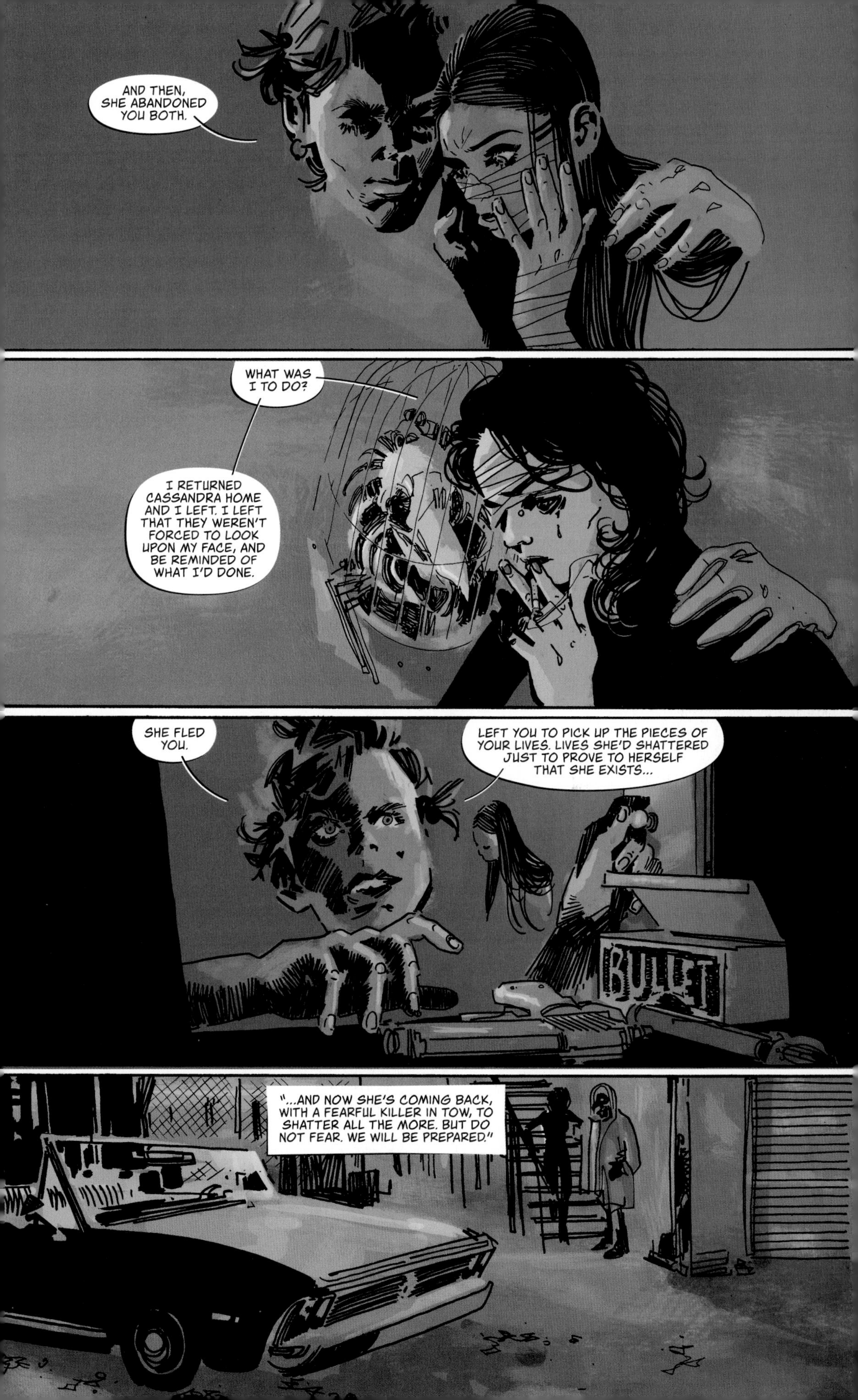
AND THEN, SHE ABANDONED YOU BOTH.
WHAT WAS I TO DO?
I RETURNED CASSANDRA HOME AND I LEFT. I LEFT THAT THEY WEREN'T FORCED TO LOOK UPON MY FACE, AND BE REMINDED OF WHAT I'D DONE.
SHE FLED YOU.
LEFT YOU TO PICK UP THE PIECES OF YOUR LIVES. LIVES SHE'D SHATTERED JUST TO PROVE TO HERSELF THAT SHE EXISTS...
BULLET
"...AND NOW SHE'S COMING BACK, WITH A FEARFUL KILLER IN TOW, TO SHATTER ALL THE MORE. BUT DO NOT FEAR. WE WILL BE PREPARED."

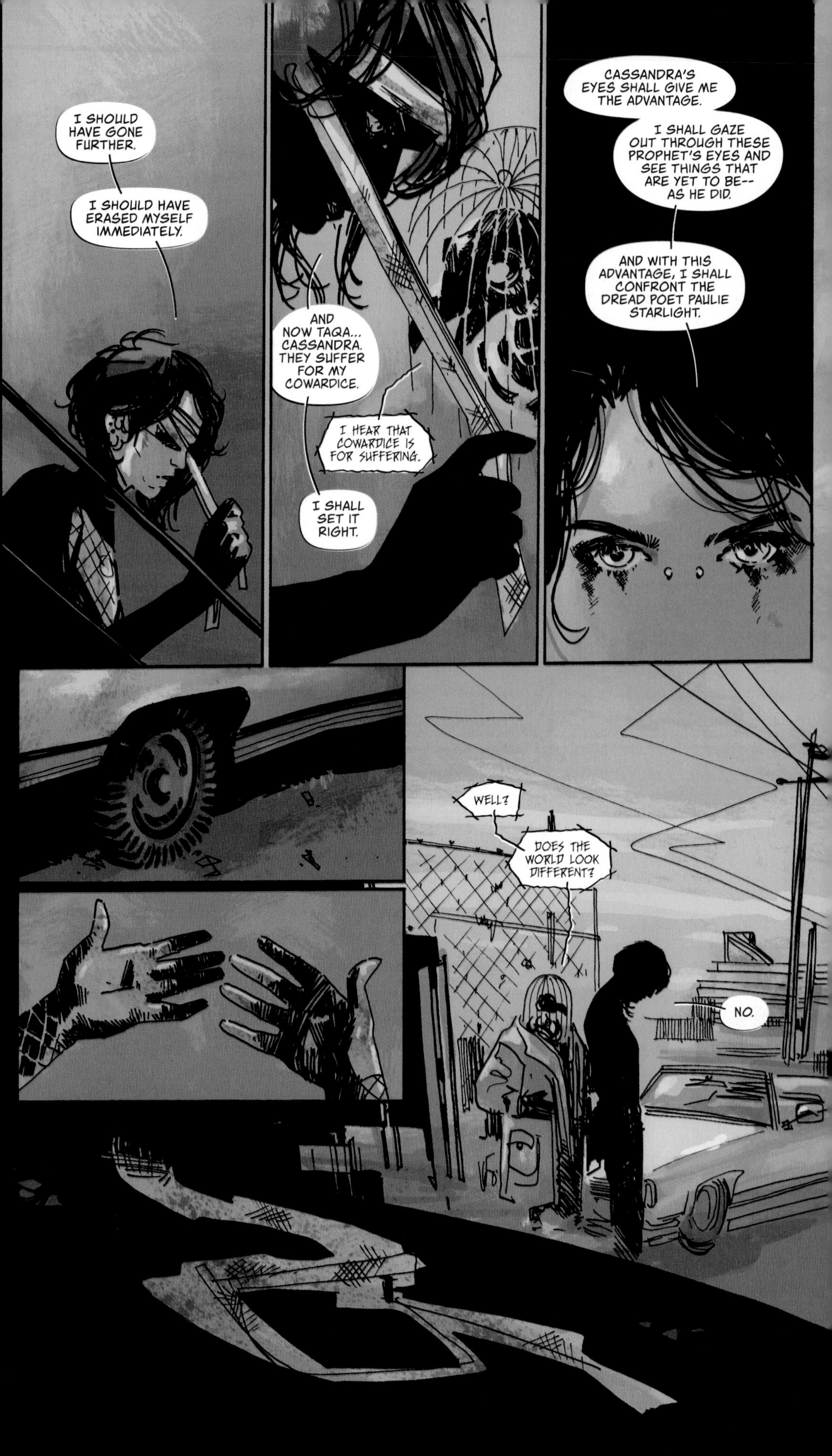
I SHOULD HAVE GONE FURTHER.
I SHOULD HAVE ERASED MYSELF IMMEDIATELY.
AND NOW TAQA... CASSANDRA. THEY SUFFER FOR MY COWARDICE.
I HEAR THAT COWARDICE IS FOR SUFFERING.
I SHALL SET IT RIGHT.
CASSANDRA'S EYES SHALL GIVE ME THE ADVANTAGE.
I SHALL GAZE OUT THROUGH THESE PROPHET'S EYES AND SEE THINGS THAT ARE YET TO BE-- AS HE DID.
AND WITH THIS ADVANTAGE, I SHALL CONFRONT THE DREAD POET PAULIE STARLIGHT.
WELL?
DOES THE WORLD LOOK DIFFERENT?
NO.

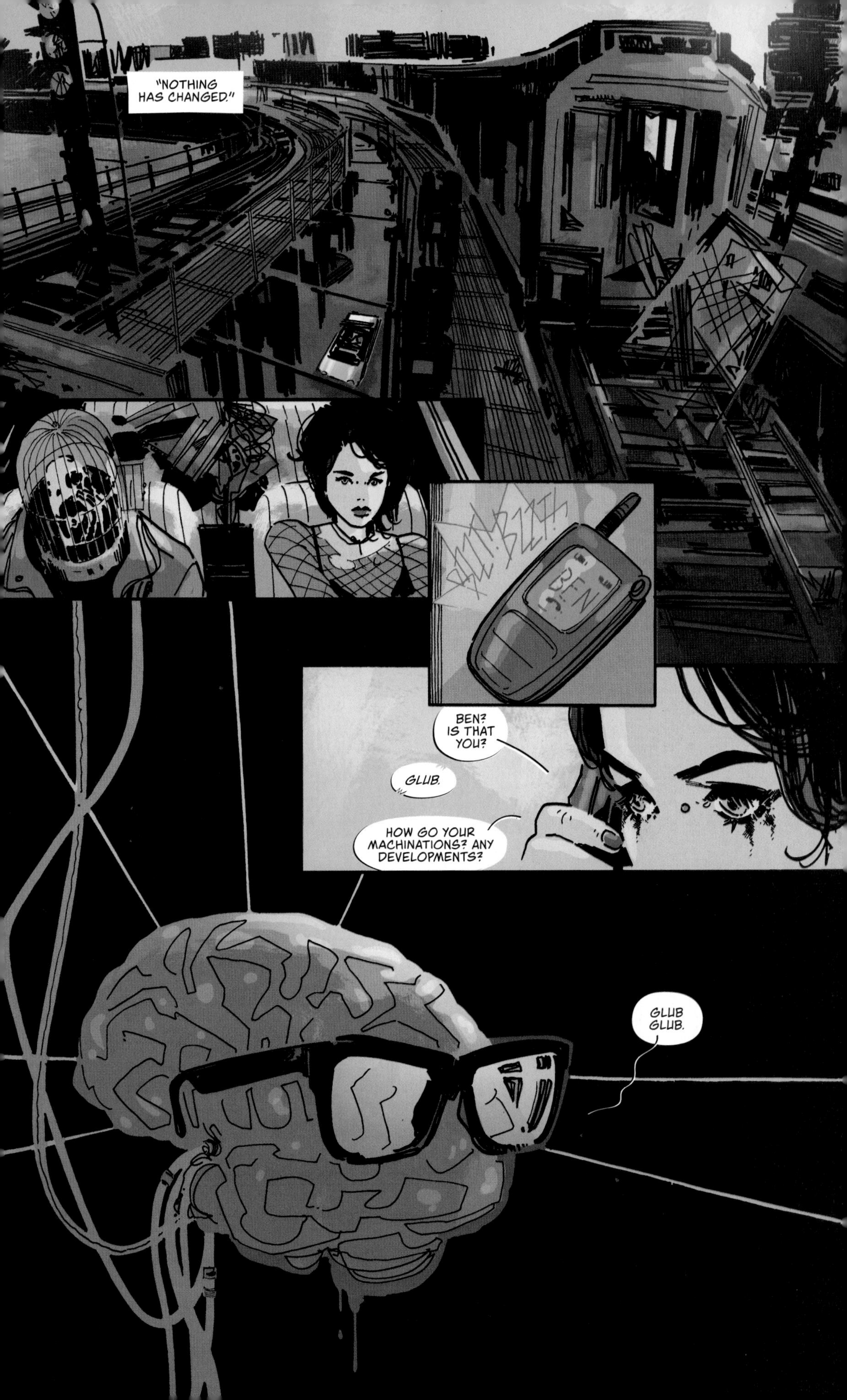
"NOTHING HAS CHANGED."
BEN
BEN? IS THAT YOU?
GLUB.
HOW GO YOUR MACHINATIONS? ANY DEVELOPMENTS?
GLUB GLUB.

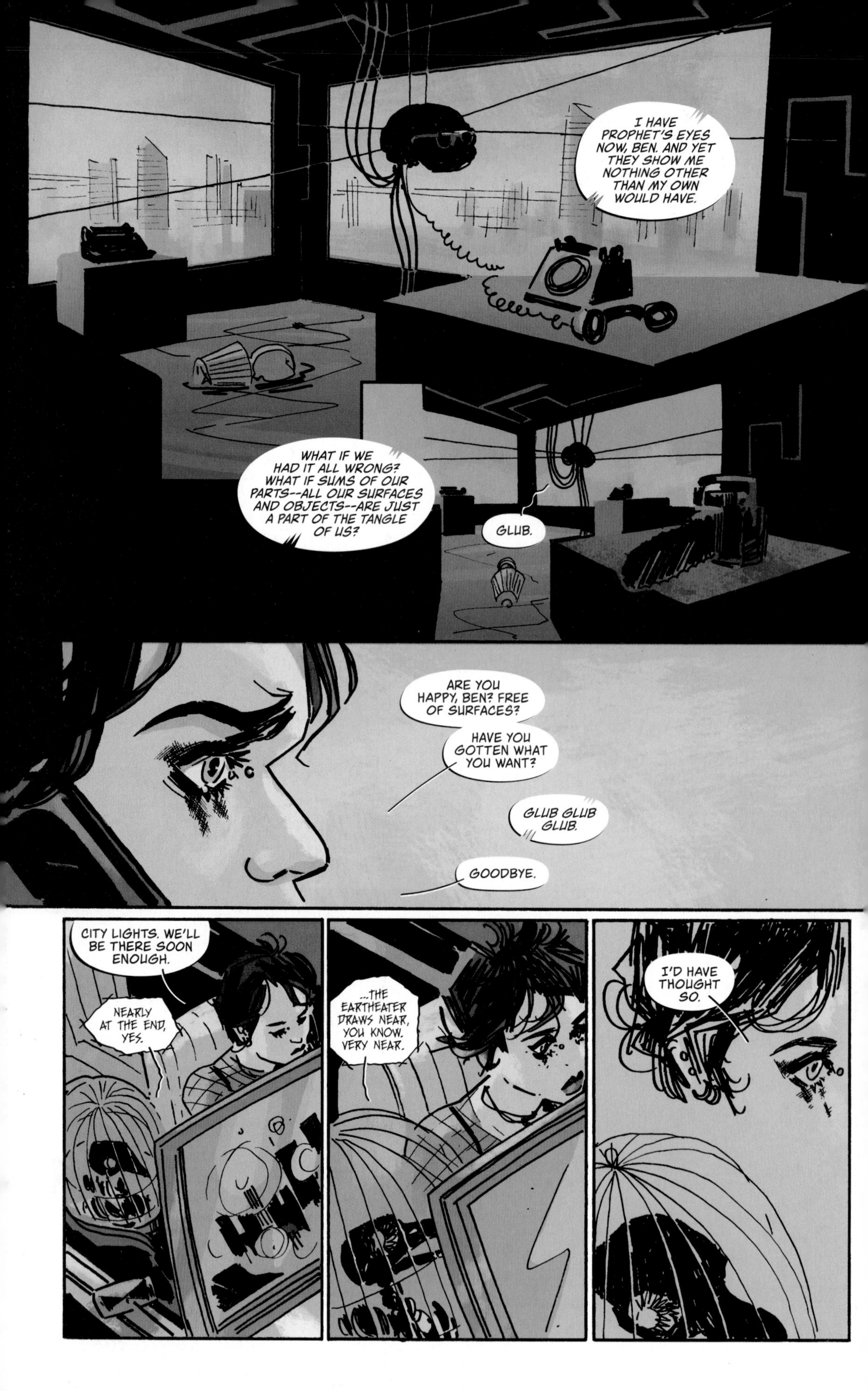
I HAVE PROPHET'S EYES NOW, BEN. AND YET THEY SHOW ME NOTHING OTHER THAN MY OWN WOULD HAVE.
WHAT IF WE HAD IT ALL WRONG? WHAT IF SUMS OF OUR PARTS--ALL OUR SURFACES AND OBJECTS--ARE JUST A PART OF THE TANGLE OF US?
GLUB.
ARE YOU HAPPY, BEN? FREE OF SURFACES?
HAVE YOU GOTTEN WHAT YOU WANT?
GLUB GLUB GLUB.
GOODBYE.
CITY LIGHTS. WE'LL BE THERE SOON ENOUGH.
NEARLY AT THE END, YES.
...THE EARTHEATER DRAWS NEAR, YOU KNOW. VERY NEAR.
I'D HAVE THOUGHT SO.

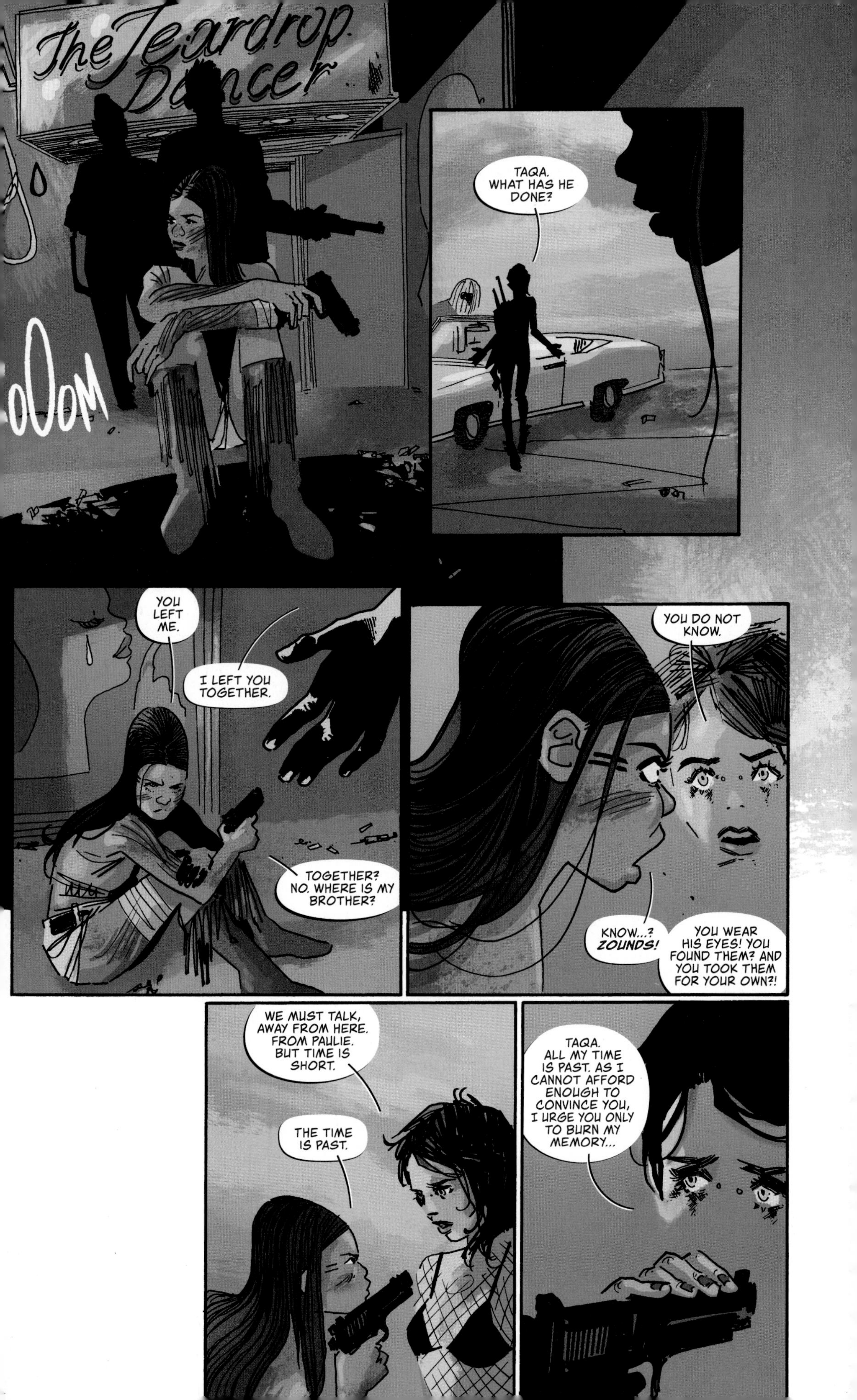
The Teardrop Dancer
OOOM
TAQA. WHAT HAS HE DONE?
YOU LEFT ME.
I LEFT YOU TOGETHER.
TOGETHER? NO. WHERE IS MY BROTHER?
YOU DO NOT KNOW.
KNOW...? ZOUNDS!
YOU WEAR HIS EYES! YOU FOUND THEM? AND YOU TOOK THEM FOR YOUR OWN?!
WE MUST TALK, AWAY FROM HERE. FROM PAULIE. BUT TIME IS SHORT.
THE TIME IS PAST.
TAQA. ALL MY TIME IS PAST. AS I CANNOT AFFORD ENOUGH TO CONVINCE YOU, I URGE YOU ONLY TO BURN MY MEMORY...

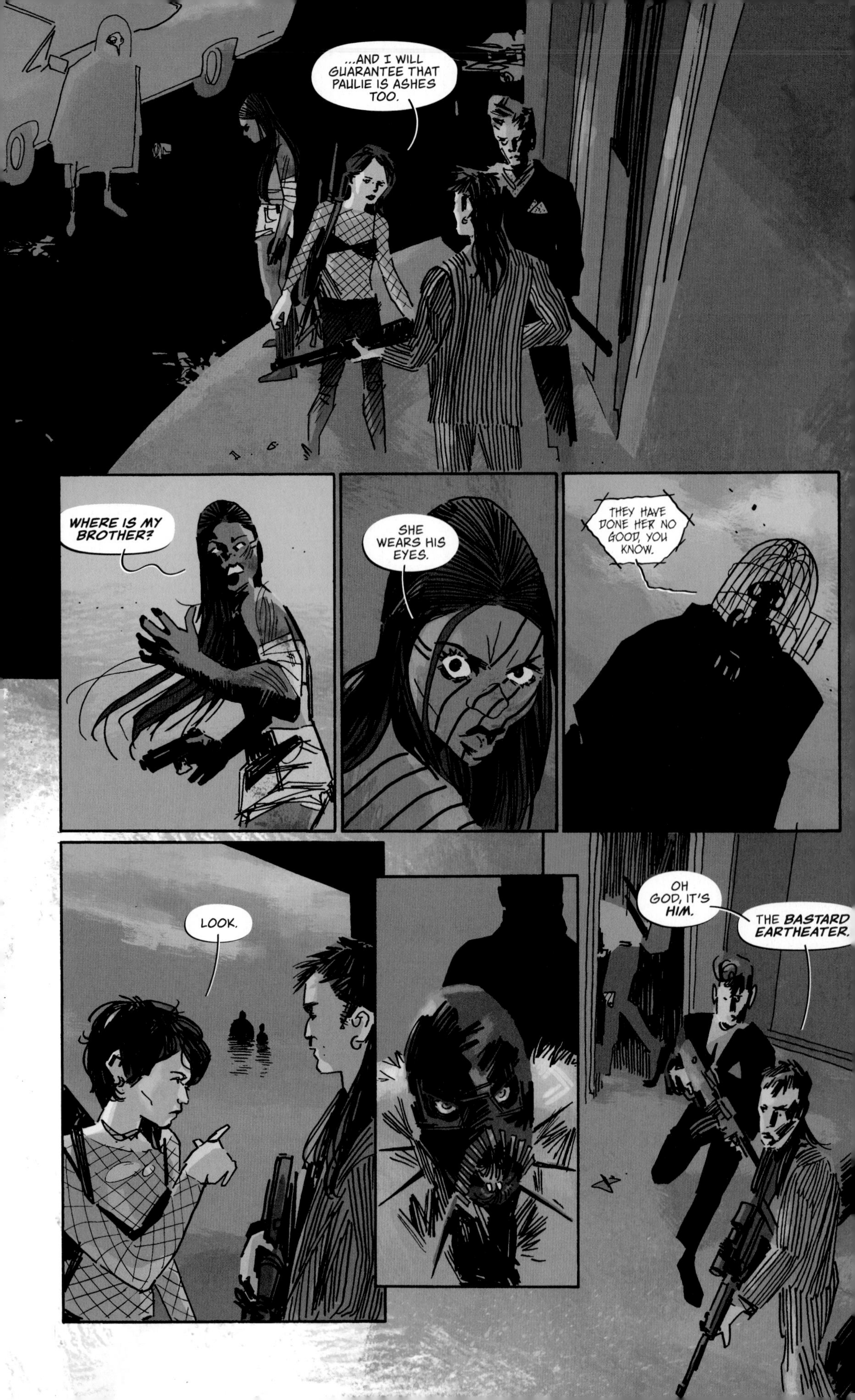
...AND I WILL GUARANTEE THAT PAULIE IS ASHES TOO.
WHERE IS MY BROTHER?
SHE WEARS HIS EYES.
THEY HAVE DONE HER NO GOOD, YOU KNOW.
LOOK.
OH GOD, IT'S HIM.
THE BASTARD EARTHEATER.

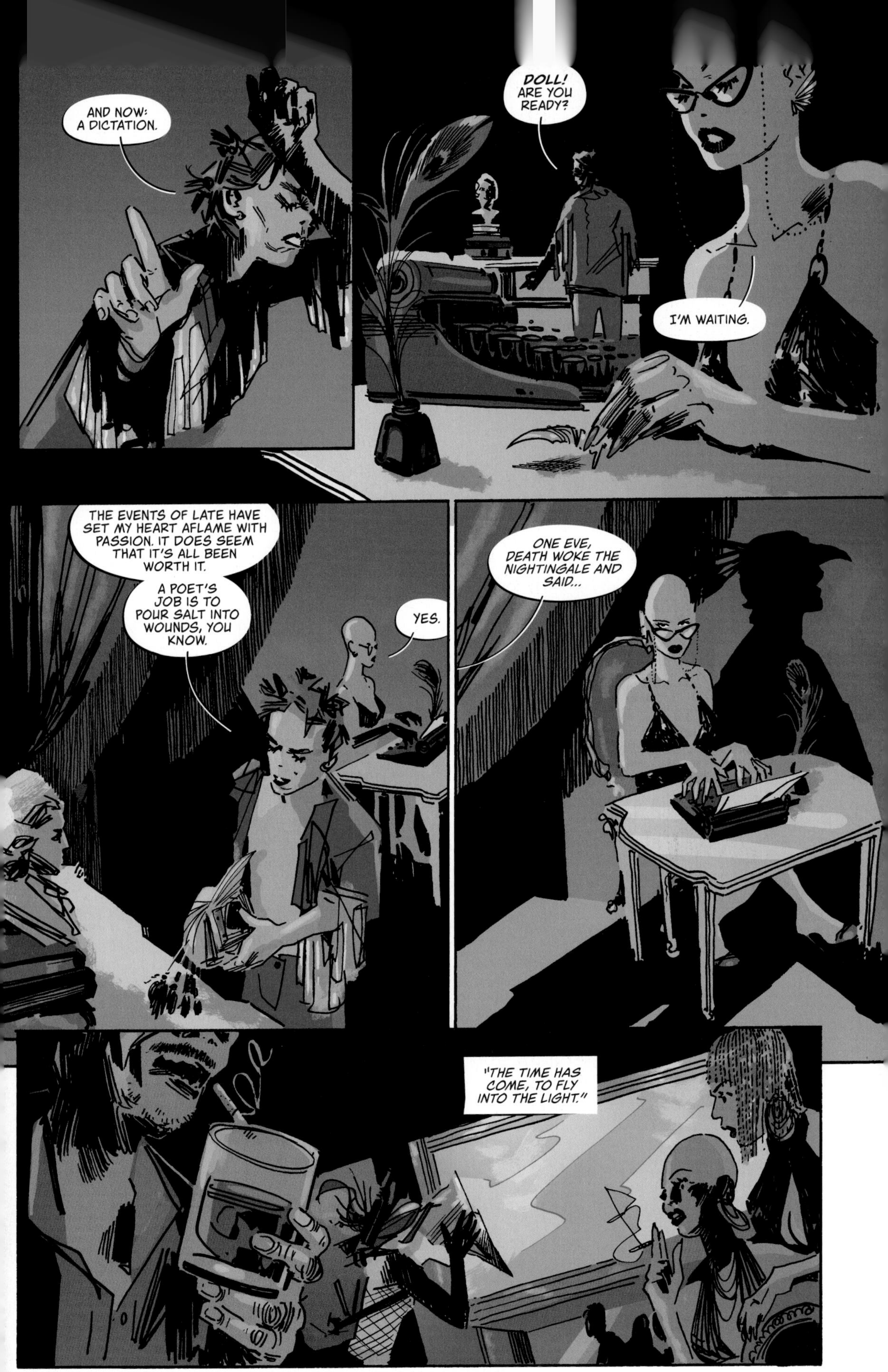
AND NOW: A DICTATION.
DOLL! ARE YOU READY?
I'M WAITING.
THE EVENTS OF LATE HAVE SET MY HEART AFLAME WITH PASSION. IT DOES SEEM THAT IT'S ALL BEEN WORTH IT.
A POET'S JOB IS TO POUR SALT INTO WOUNDS, YOU KNOW.
YES.
ONE EVE, DEATH WOKE THE NIGHTINGALE AND SAID...
"THE TIME HAS COME, TO FLY INTO THE LIGHT."

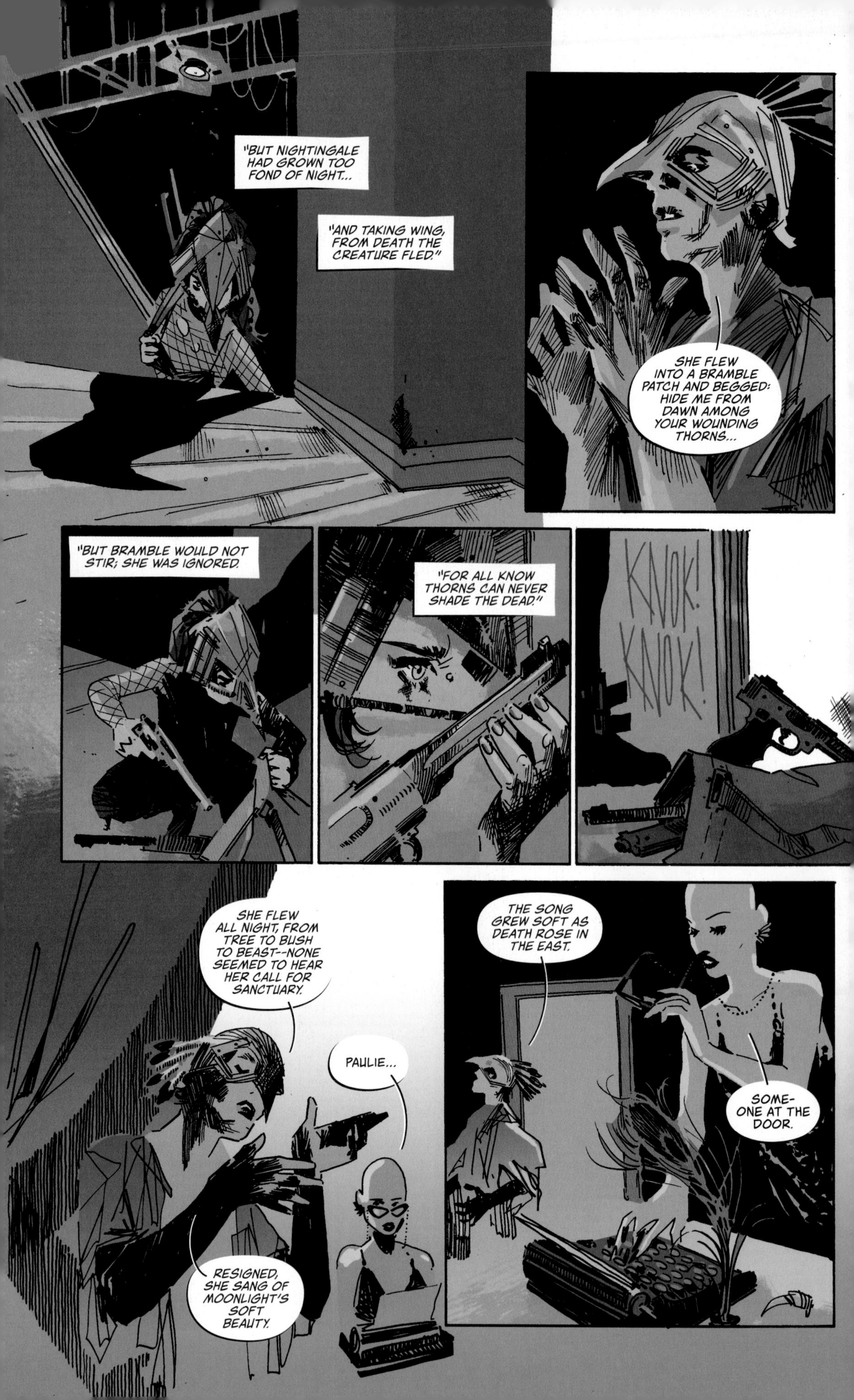
"BUT NIGHTINGALE HAD GROWN TOO FOND OF NIGHT...
"AND TAKING WING, FROM DEATH THE CREATURE FLED."
SHE FLEW INTO A BRAMBLE PATCH AND BEGGED: HIDE ME FROM DAWN AMONG YOUR WOUNDING THORNS...
"BUT BRAMBLE WOULD NOT STIR; SHE WAS IGNORED.
"FOR ALL KNOW THORNS CAN NEVER SHADE THE DEAD."
KNOK! KNOK!
SHE FLEW ALL NIGHT, FROM TREE TO BUSH TO BEAST--NONE SEEMED TO HEAR HER CALL FOR SANCTUARY.
RESIGNED, SHE SANG OF MOONLIGHT'S SOFT BEAUTY.
PAULIE...
THE SONG GREW SOFT AS DEATH ROSE IN THE EAST.
SOME-ONE AT THE DOOR.

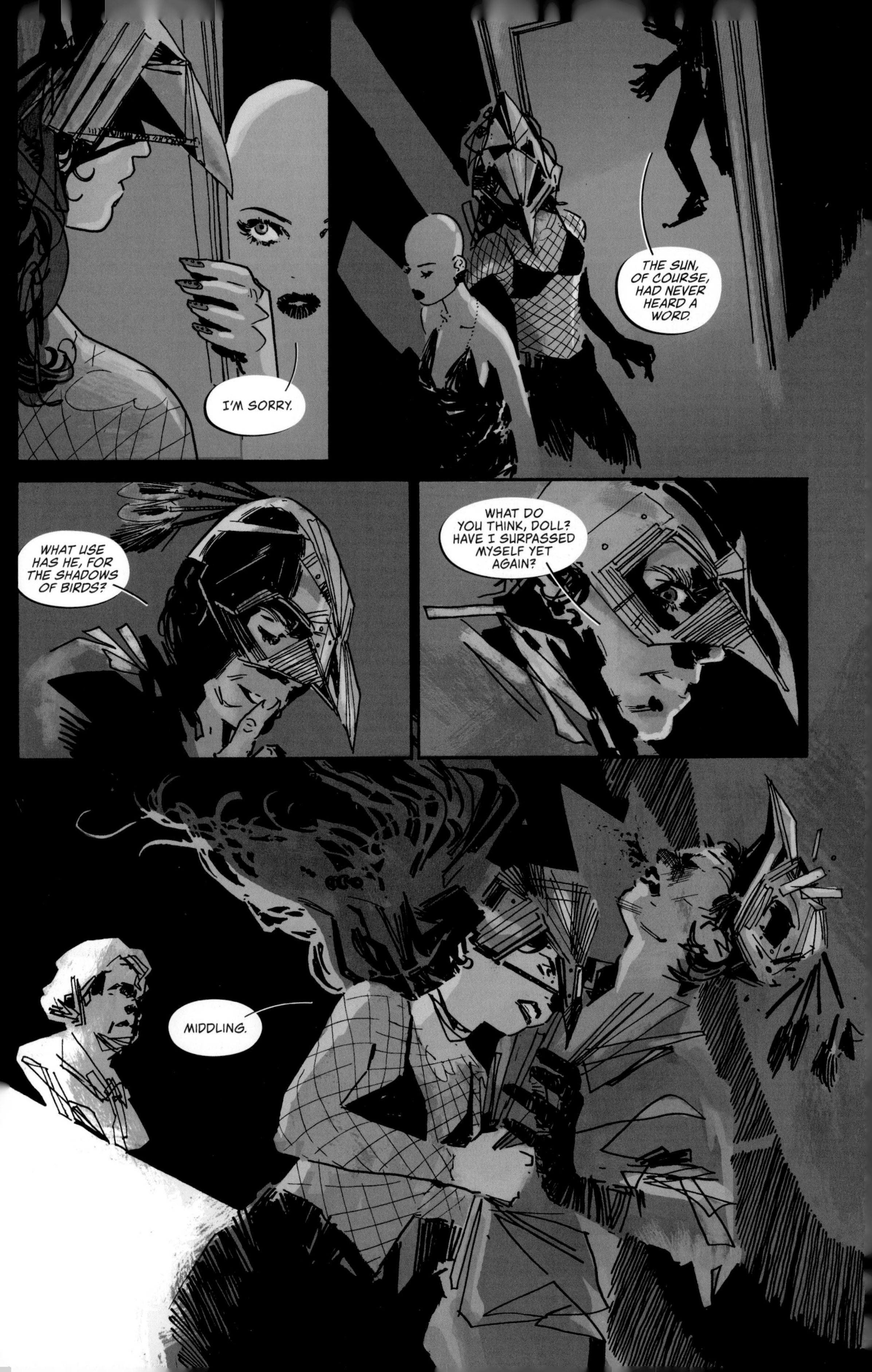
I'M SORRY.
THE SUN, OF COURSE, HAD NEVER HEARD A WORD.
WHAT USE HAS HE, FOR THE SHADOWS OF BIRDS?
WHAT DO YOU THINK, DOLL? HAVE I SURPASSED MYSELF YET AGAIN?
MIDDLING.

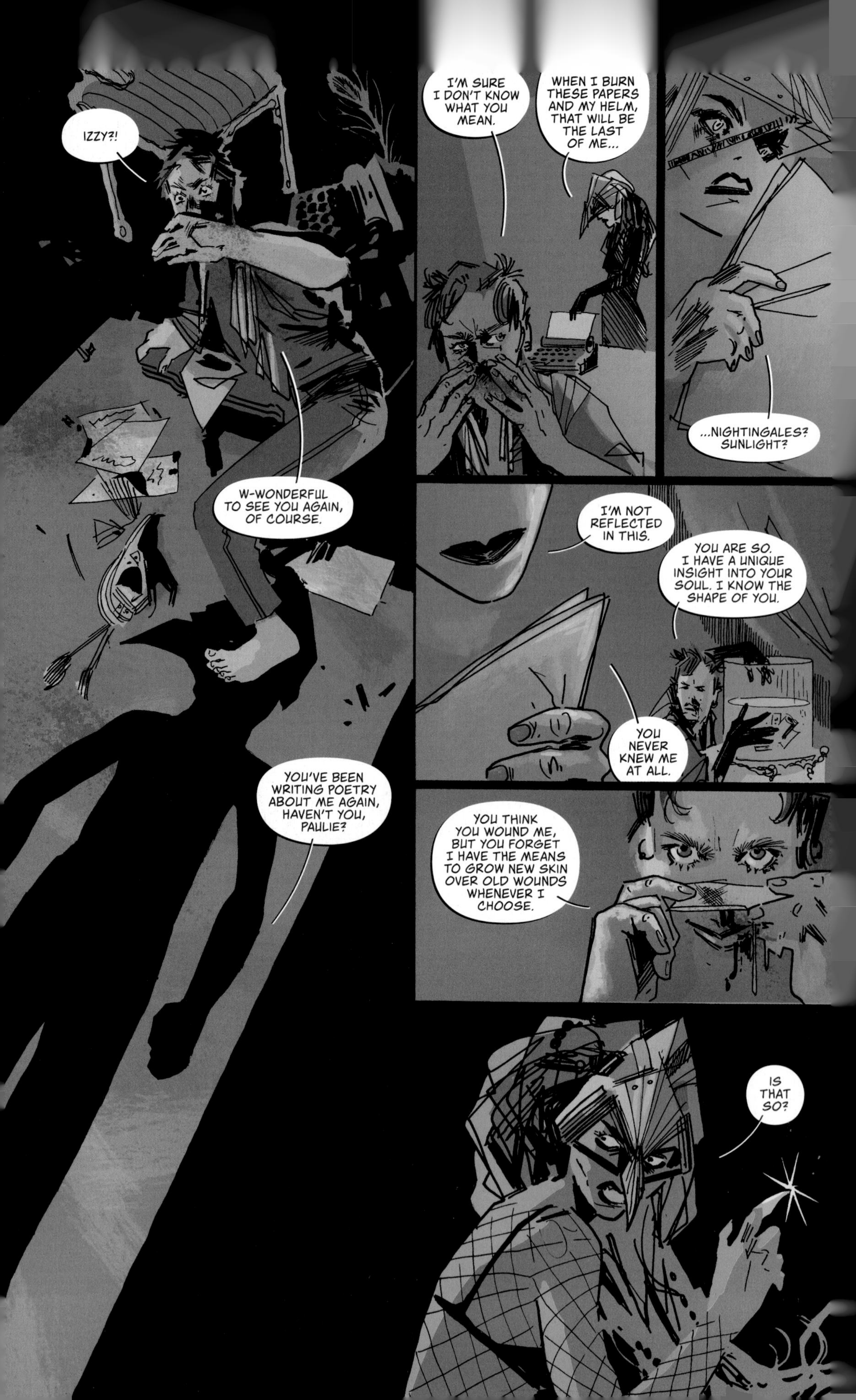
IZZY?!
W-WONDERFUL TO SEE YOU AGAIN, OF COURSE.
YOU'VE BEEN WRITING POETRY ABOUT ME AGAIN, HAVEN'T YOU, PAULIE?
I'M SURE I DON'T KNOW WHAT YOU MEAN.
WHEN I BURN THESE PAPERS AND MY HELM, THAT WILL BE THE LAST OF ME...
...NIGHTINGALES? SUNLIGHT?
I'M NOT REFLECTED IN THIS.
YOU ARE SO. I HAVE A UNIQUE INSIGHT INTO YOUR SOUL. I KNOW THE SHAPE OF YOU.
YOU NEVER KNEW ME AT ALL.
YOU THINK YOU WOUND ME, BUT YOU FORGET I HAVE THE MEANS TO GROW NEW SKIN OVER OLD WOUNDS WHENEVER I CHOOSE.
IS THAT SO?

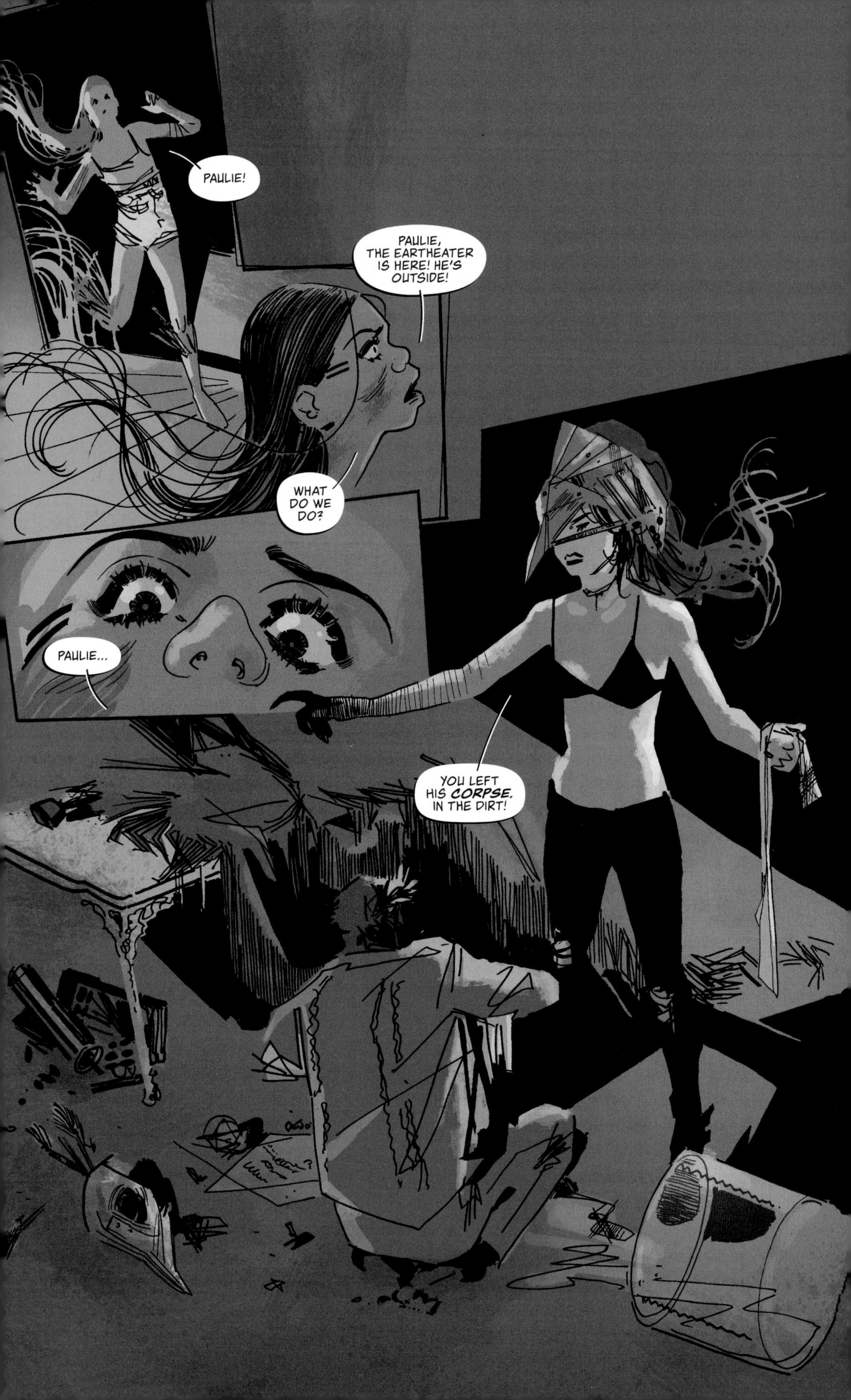
PAULIE!
PAULIE, THE EARTHEATER IS HERE! HE'S OUTSIDE!
WHAT DO WE DO?
PAULIE...
YOU LEFT HIS CORPSE. IN THE DIRT!

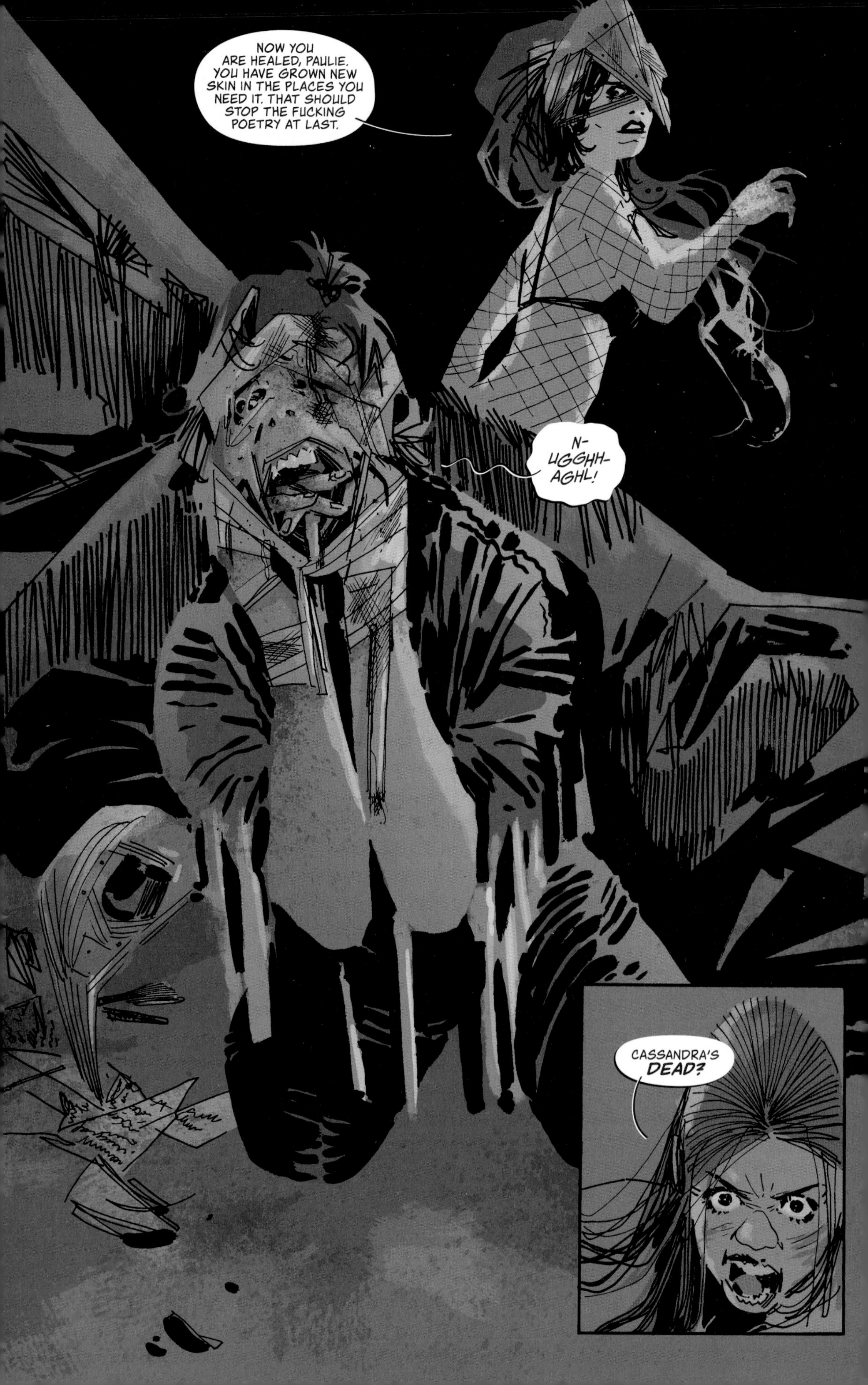
NOW YOU ARE HEALED, PAULIE. YOU HAVE GROWN NEW SKIN IN THE PLACES YOU NEED IT. THAT SHOULD STOP THE FUCKING POETRY AT LAST.
N- UGGHH- AGHL!
CASSANDRA'S DEAD?

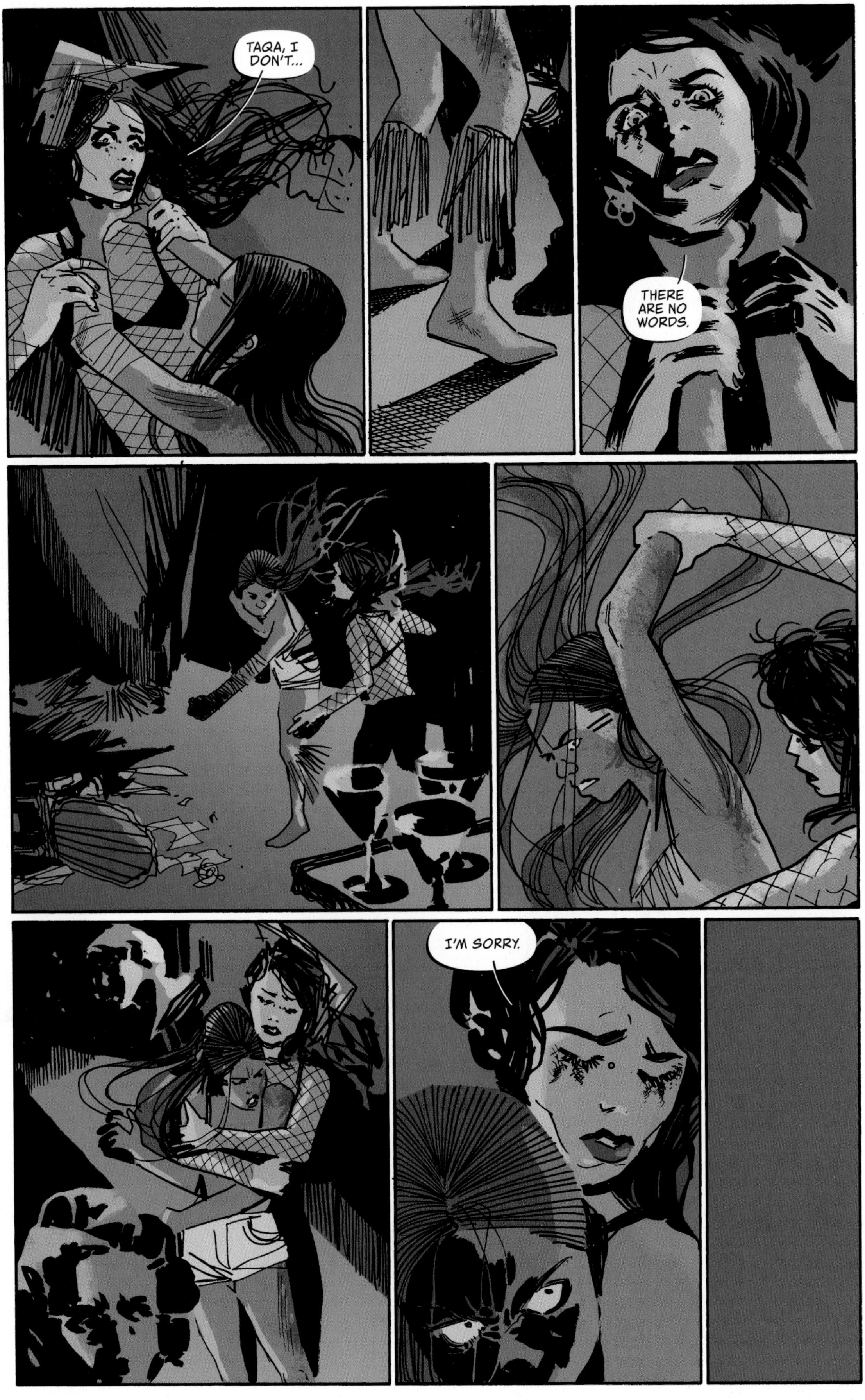
TAQA, I DON'T...
THERE ARE NO WORDS.
I'M SORRY.

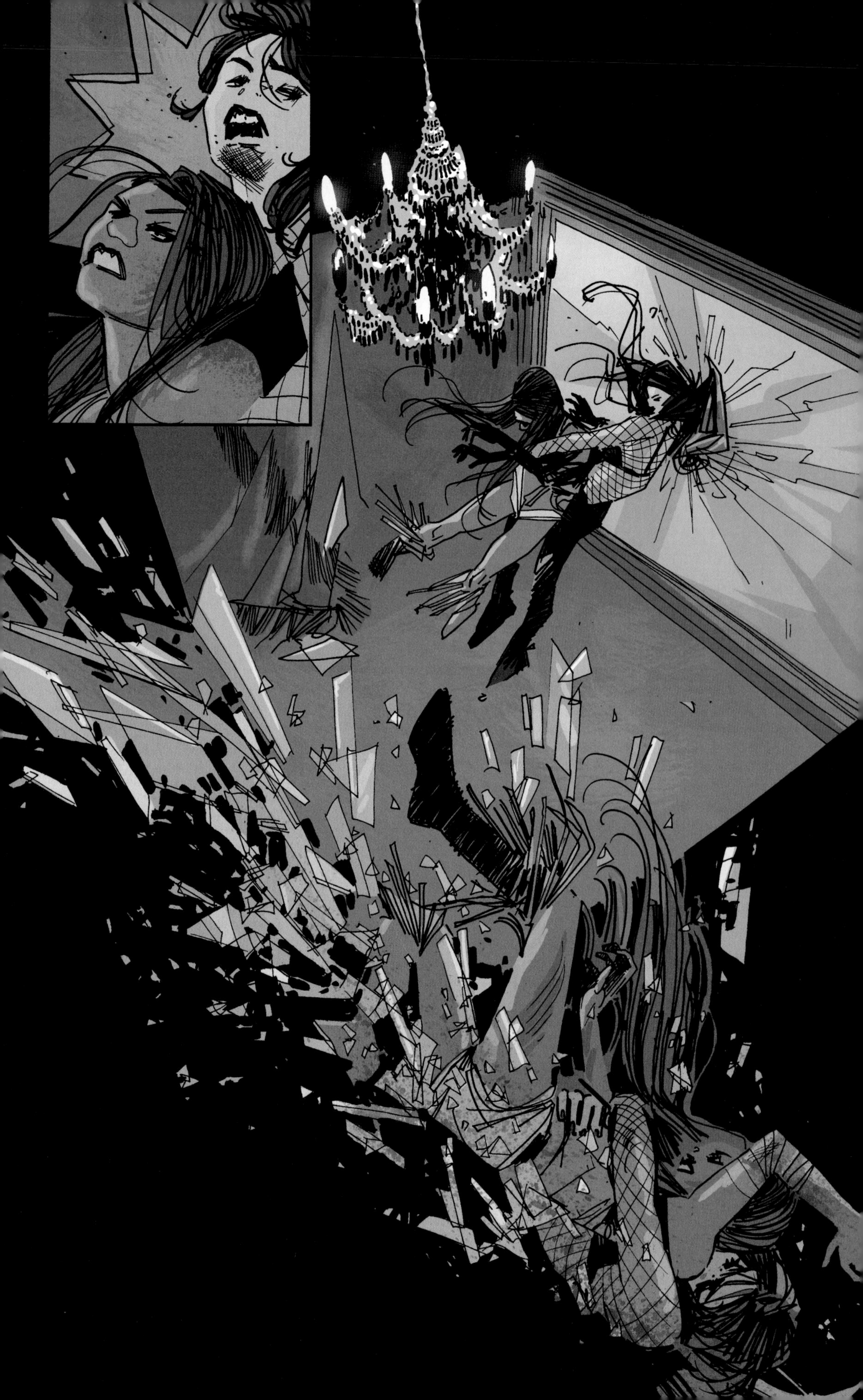

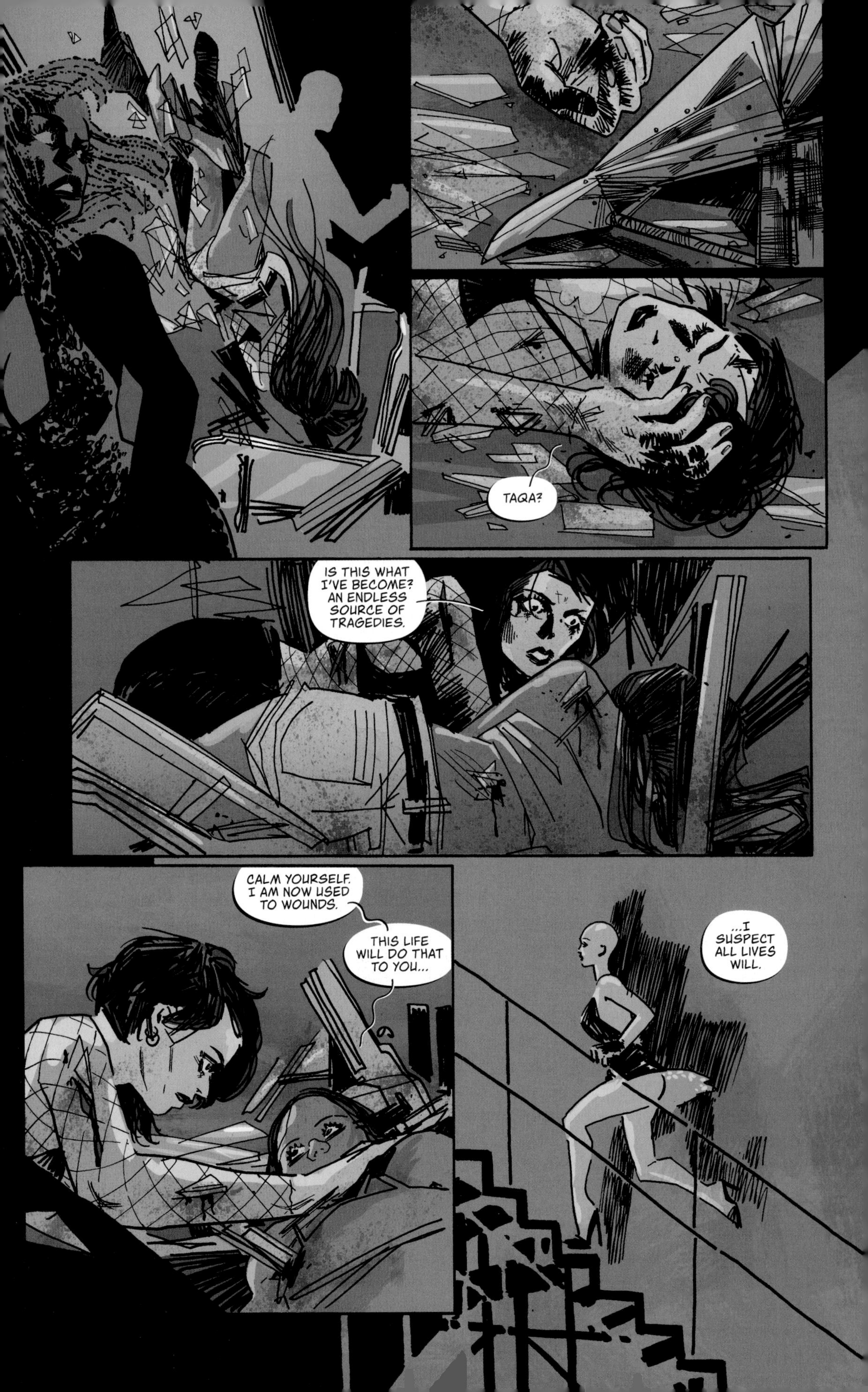
TAQA?
IS THIS WHAT I'VE BECOME? AN ENDLESS SOURCE OF TRAGEDIES.
CALM YOURSELF. I AM NOW USED TO WOUNDS.
THIS LIFE WILL DO THAT TO YOU...
...I SUSPECT ALL LIVES WILL.

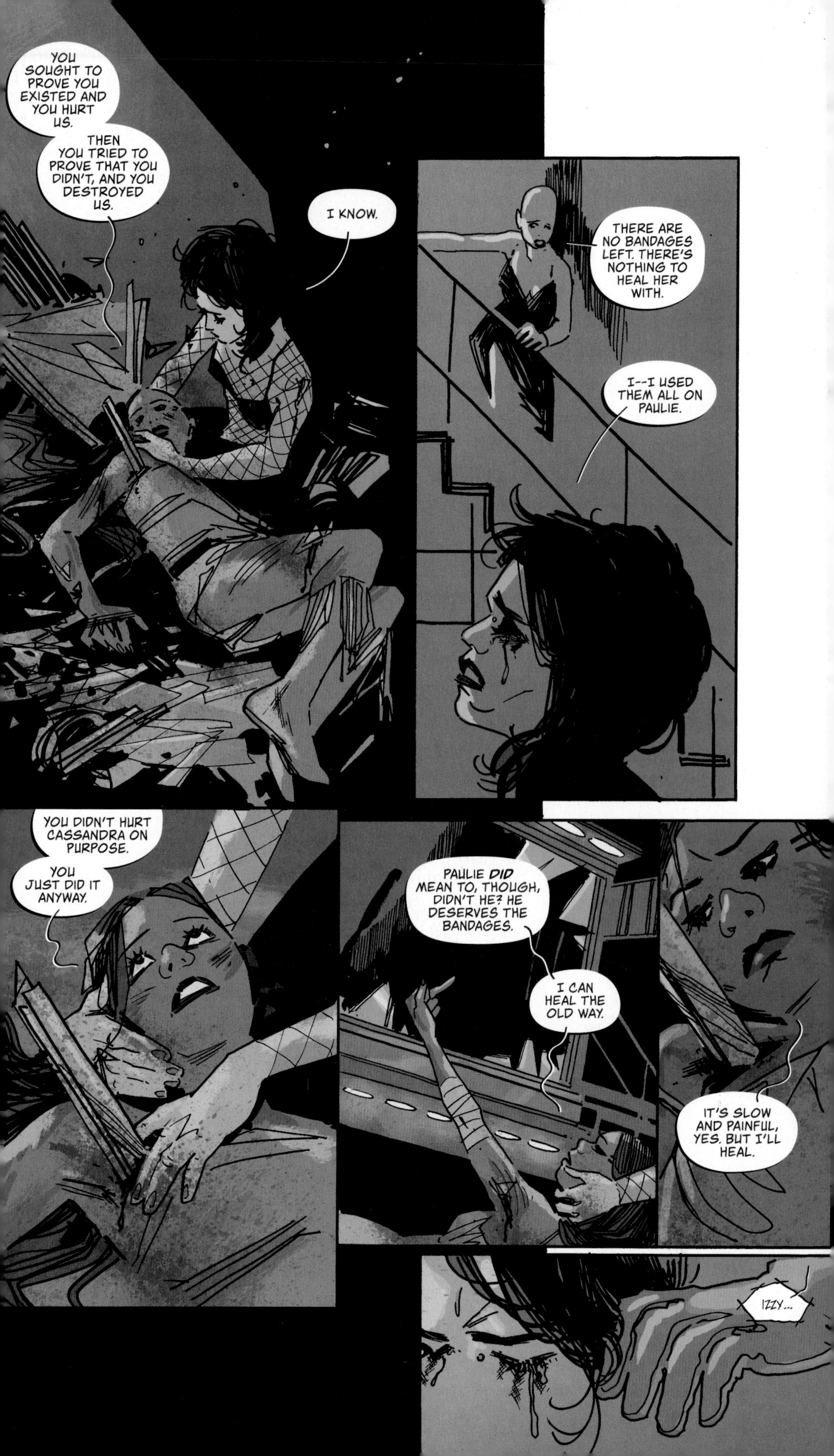
YOU SOUGHT TO PROVE YOU EXISTED AND YOU HURT US.
THEN YOU TRIED TO PROVE THAT YOU DIDN'T, AND YOU DESTROYED US.
I KNOW.
THERE ARE NO BANDAGES LEFT. THERE'S NOTHING TO HEAL HER WITH.
I--I USED THEM ALL ON PAULIE.
YOU DIDN'T HURT CASSANDRA ON PURPOSE.
YOU JUST DID IT ANYWAY.
PAULIE *DID* MEAN TO, THOUGH, DIDN'T HE? HE DESERVES THE BANDAGES.
I CAN HEAL THE OLD WAY.
IT'S SLOW AND PAINFUL, YES. BUT I'LL HEAL.
IZZY...

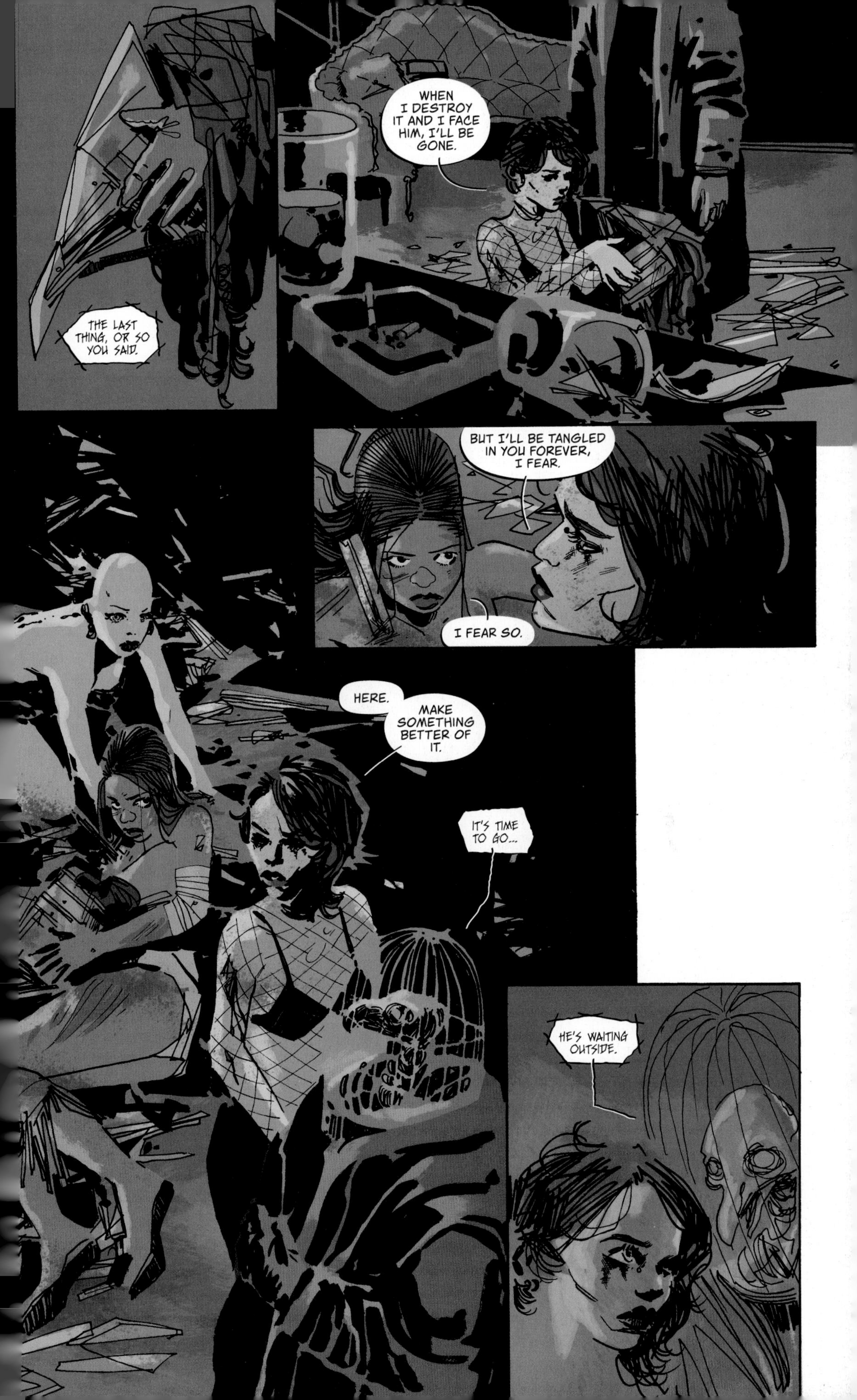
THE LAST THING, OR SO YOU SAID.
WHEN I DESTROY IT AND I FACE HIM, I'LL BE GONE.
BUT I'LL BE TANGLED IN YOU FOREVER, I FEAR.
I FEAR SO.
HERE.
MAKE SOMETHING BETTER OF IT.
IT'S TIME TO GO...
HE'S WAITING OUTSIDE.

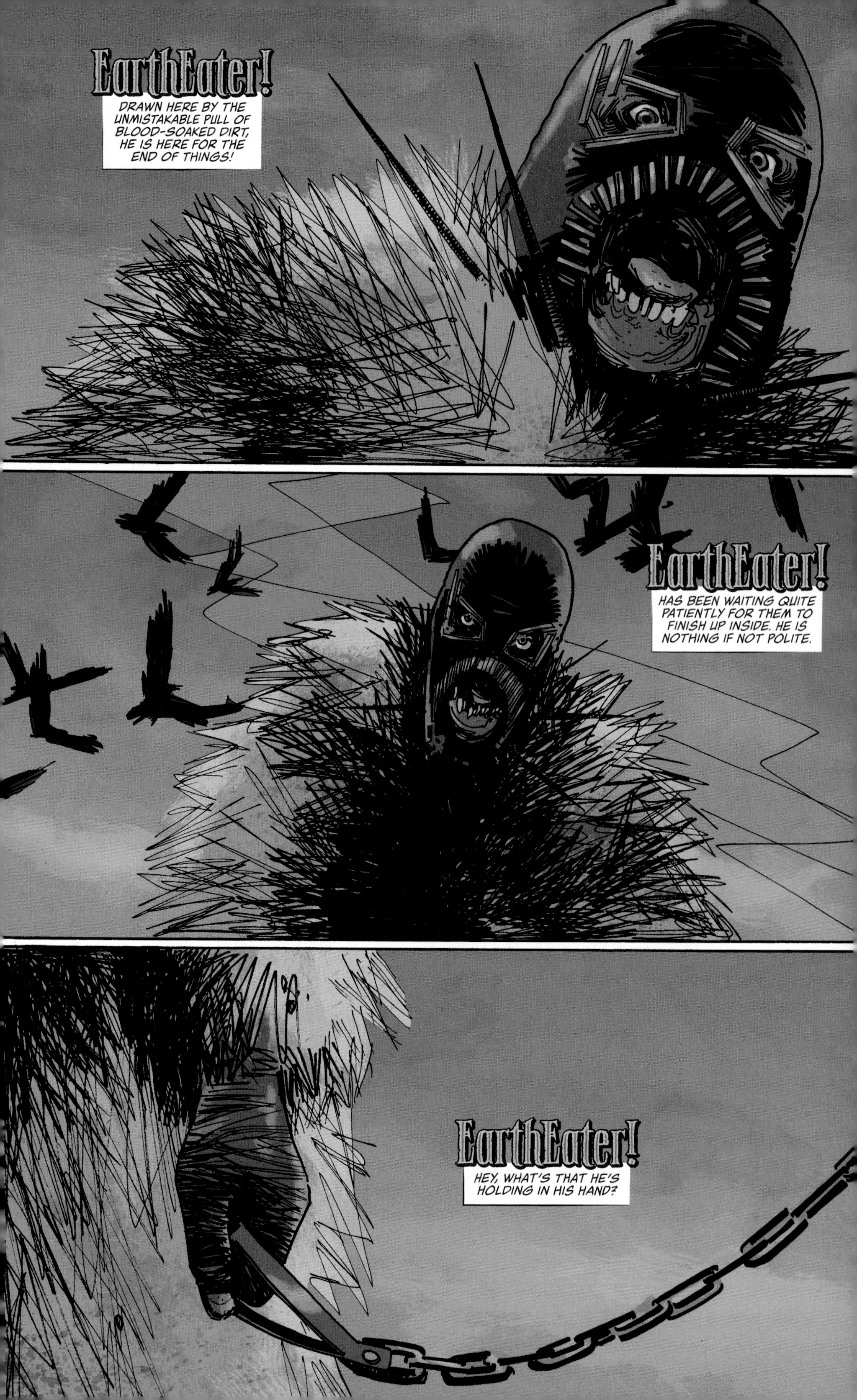
EarthEater!
DRAWN HERE BY THE UNMISTAKABLE PULL OF BLOOD-SOAKED DIRT, HE IS HERE FOR THE END OF THINGS!
EarthEater!
HAS BEEN WAITING QUITE PATIENTLY FOR THEM TO FINISH UP INSIDE. HE IS NOTHING IF NOT POLITE.
EarthEater!
HEY, WHAT'S THAT HE'S HOLDING IN HIS HAND?

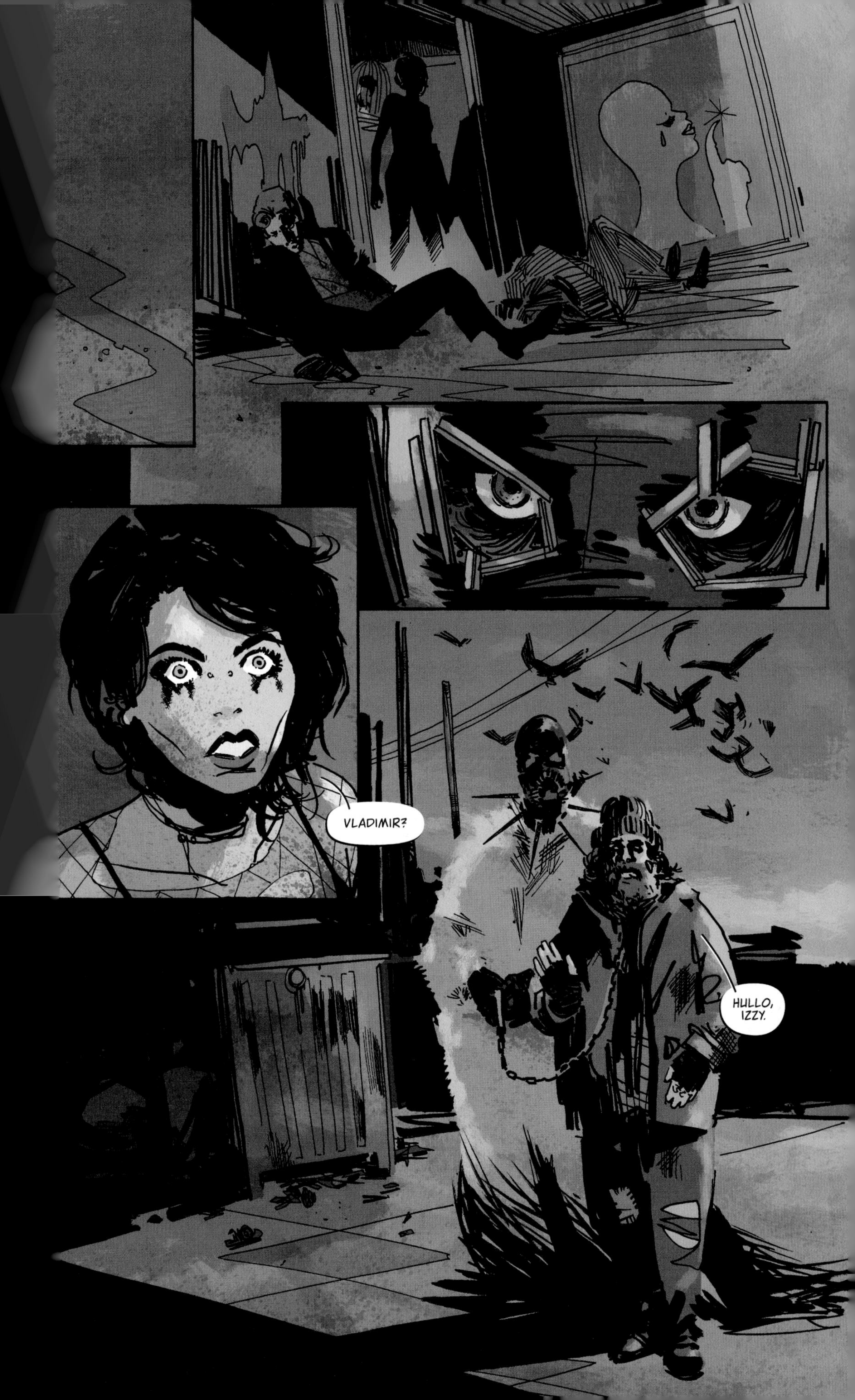
VLADIMIR?
HULLO, IZZY.

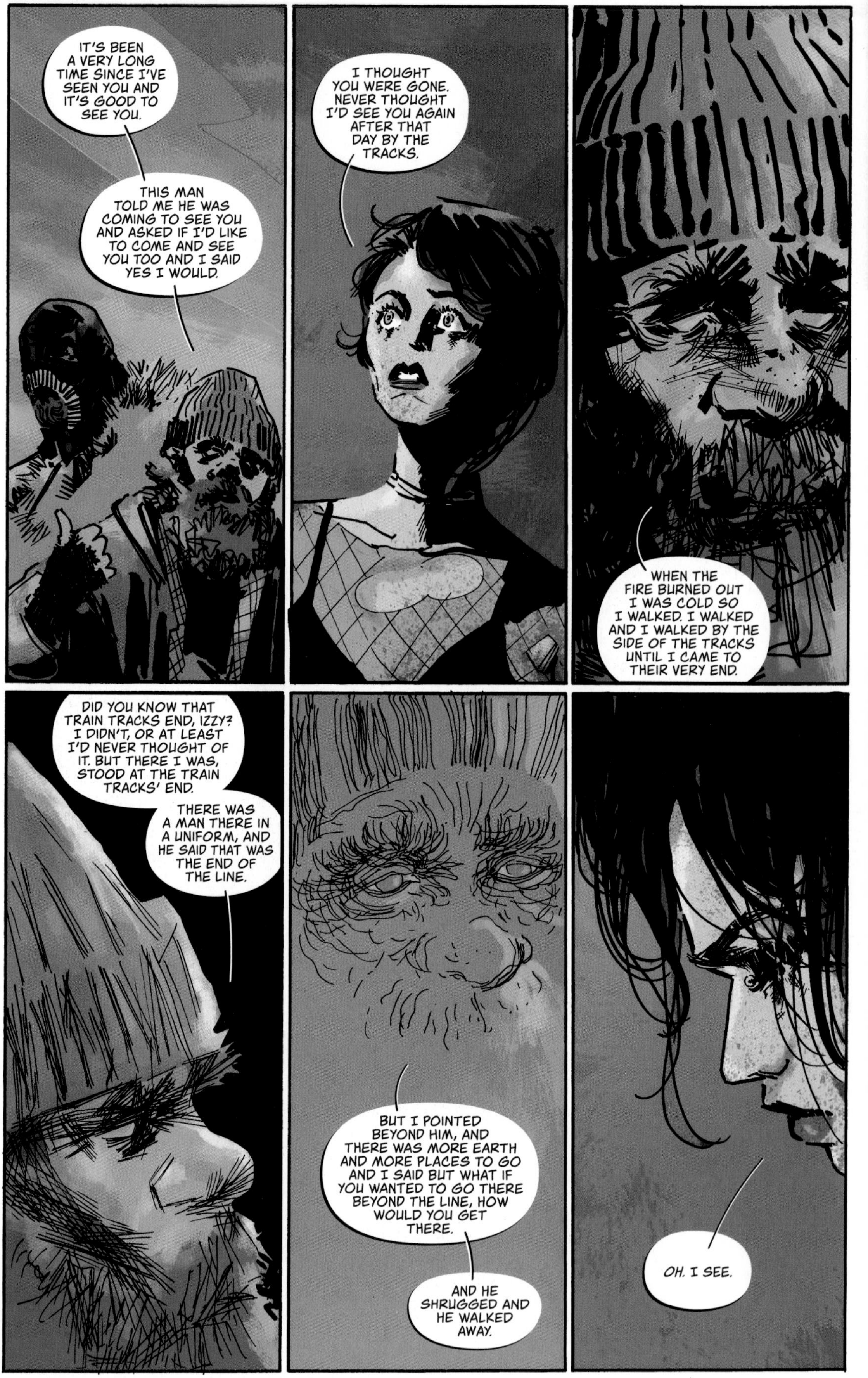
IT'S BEEN A VERY LONG TIME SINCE I'VE SEEN YOU AND IT'S GOOD TO SEE YOU.
THIS MAN TOLD ME HE WAS COMING TO SEE YOU AND ASKED IF I'D LIKE TO COME AND SEE YOU TOO AND I SAID YES I WOULD.
I THOUGHT YOU WERE GONE. NEVER THOUGHT I'D SEE YOU AGAIN AFTER THAT DAY BY THE TRACKS.
WHEN THE FIRE BURNED OUT I WAS COLD SO I WALKED. I WALKED AND I WALKED BY THE SIDE OF THE TRACKS UNTIL I CAME TO THEIR VERY END.
DID YOU KNOW THAT TRAIN TRACKS END, IZZY? I DIDN'T, OR AT LEAST I'D NEVER THOUGHT OF IT. BUT THERE I WAS, STOOD AT THE TRAIN TRACKS' END.
THERE WAS A MAN THERE IN A UNIFORM, AND HE SAID THAT WAS THE END OF THE LINE.
BUT I POINTED BEYOND HIM, AND THERE WAS MORE EARTH AND MORE PLACES TO GO AND I SAID BUT WHAT IF YOU WANTED TO GO THERE BEYOND THE LINE, HOW WOULD YOU GET THERE.
AND HE SHRUGGED AND HE WALKED AWAY.
OH. I SEE.

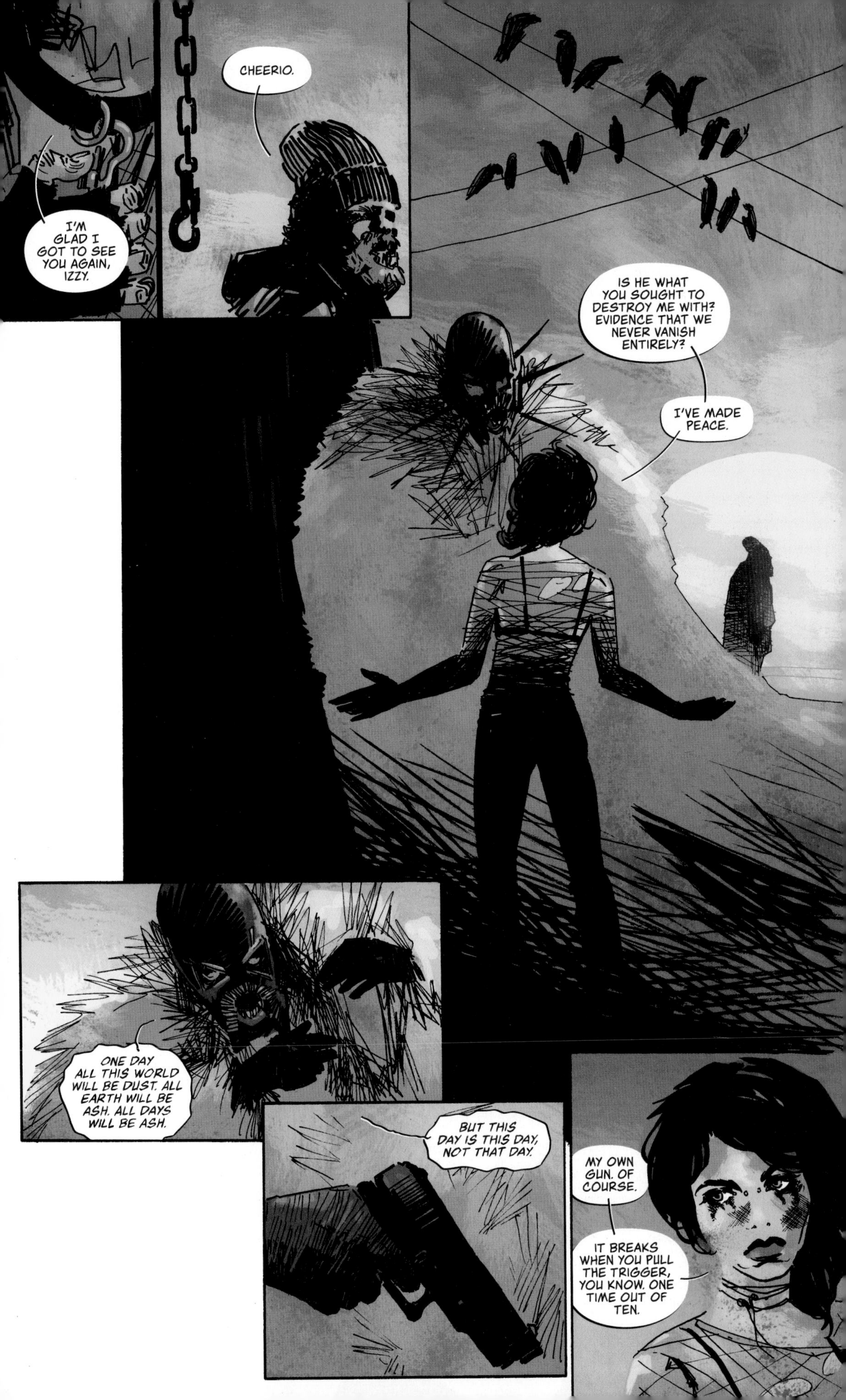
I'M GLAD I GOT TO SEE YOU AGAIN, IZZY.
CHEERIO.
IS HE WHAT YOU SOUGHT TO DESTROY ME WITH? EVIDENCE THAT WE NEVER VANISH ENTIRELY?
I'VE MADE PEACE.
ONE DAY ALL THIS WORLD WILL BE DUST. ALL EARTH WILL BE ASH. ALL DAYS WILL BE ASH.
BUT THIS DAY IS THIS DAY, NOT THAT DAY.
MY OWN GUN. OF COURSE.
IT BREAKS WHEN YOU PULL THE TRIGGER, YOU KNOW. ONE TIME OUT OF TEN.

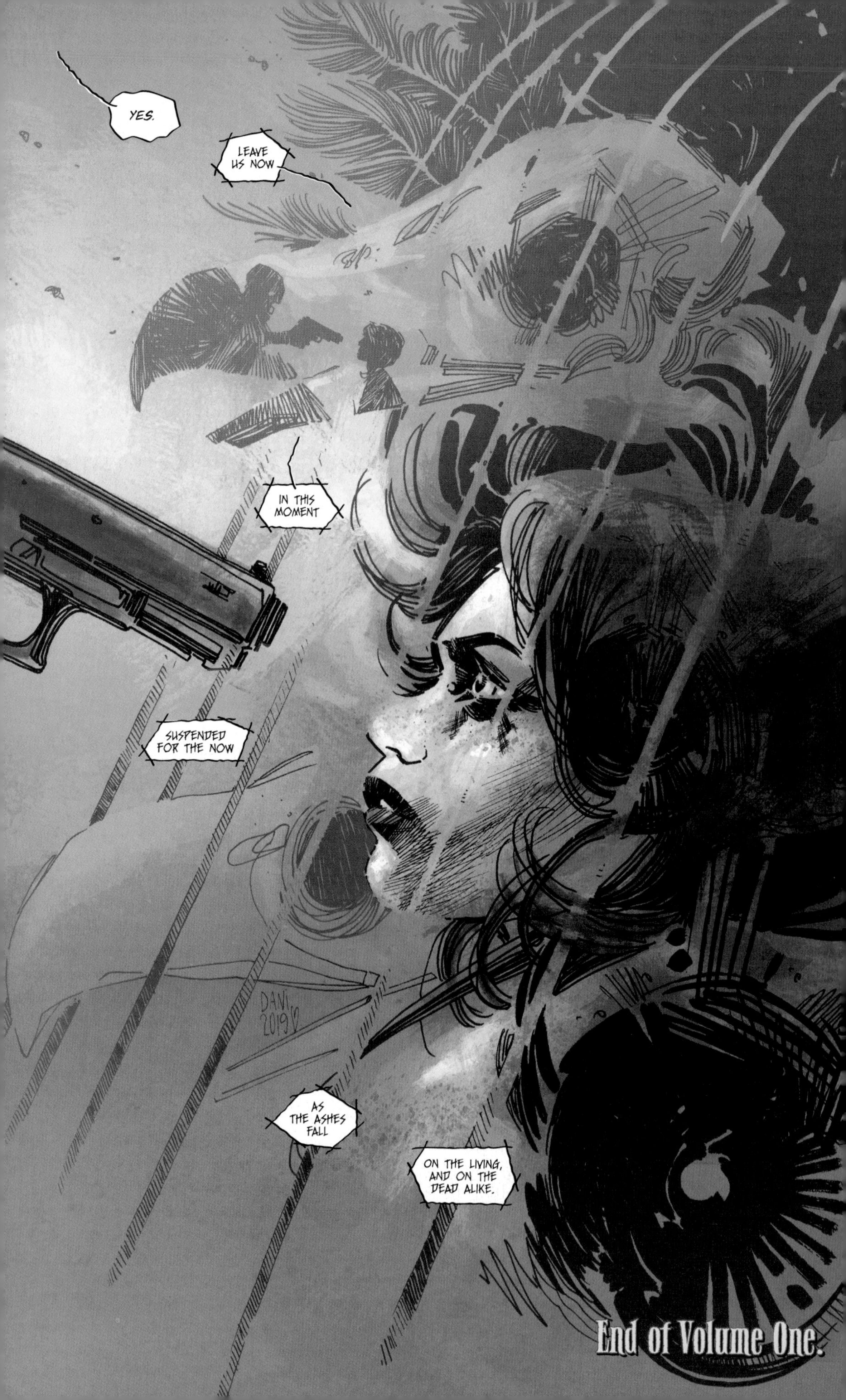
YES.
LEAVE US NOW
IN THIS MOMENT
SUSPENDED FOR THE NOW
AS THE ASHES FALL
ON THE LIVING, AND ON THE DEAD ALIKE.
DANI 2019
End of Volume One.

There follows a

GALLERY

#1 Inks: **DANI**, Colors: **BRAD SIMPSON**

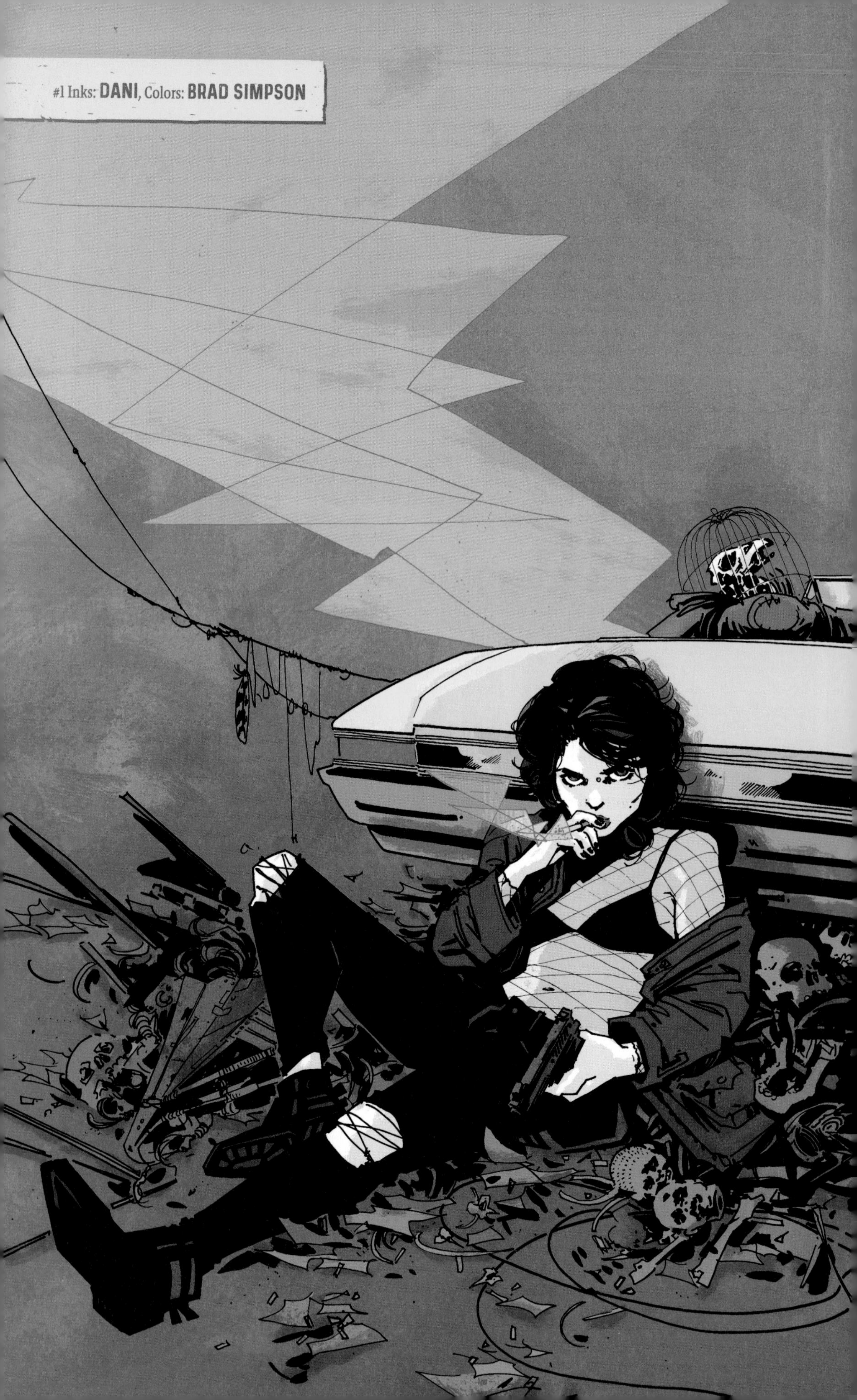

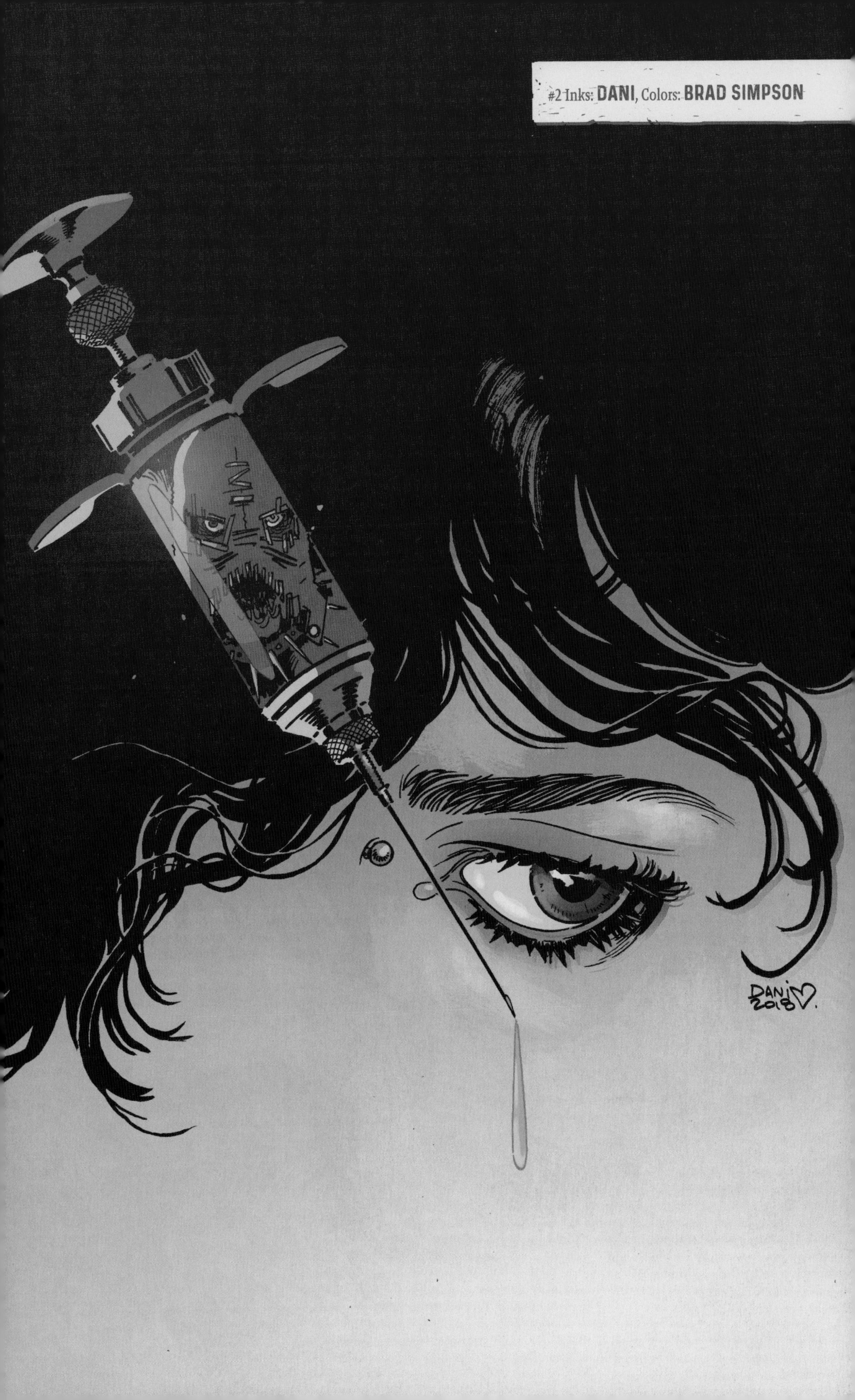
DANI 2018

#2 Inks: **DANI**, Colors: **BRAD SIMPSON**

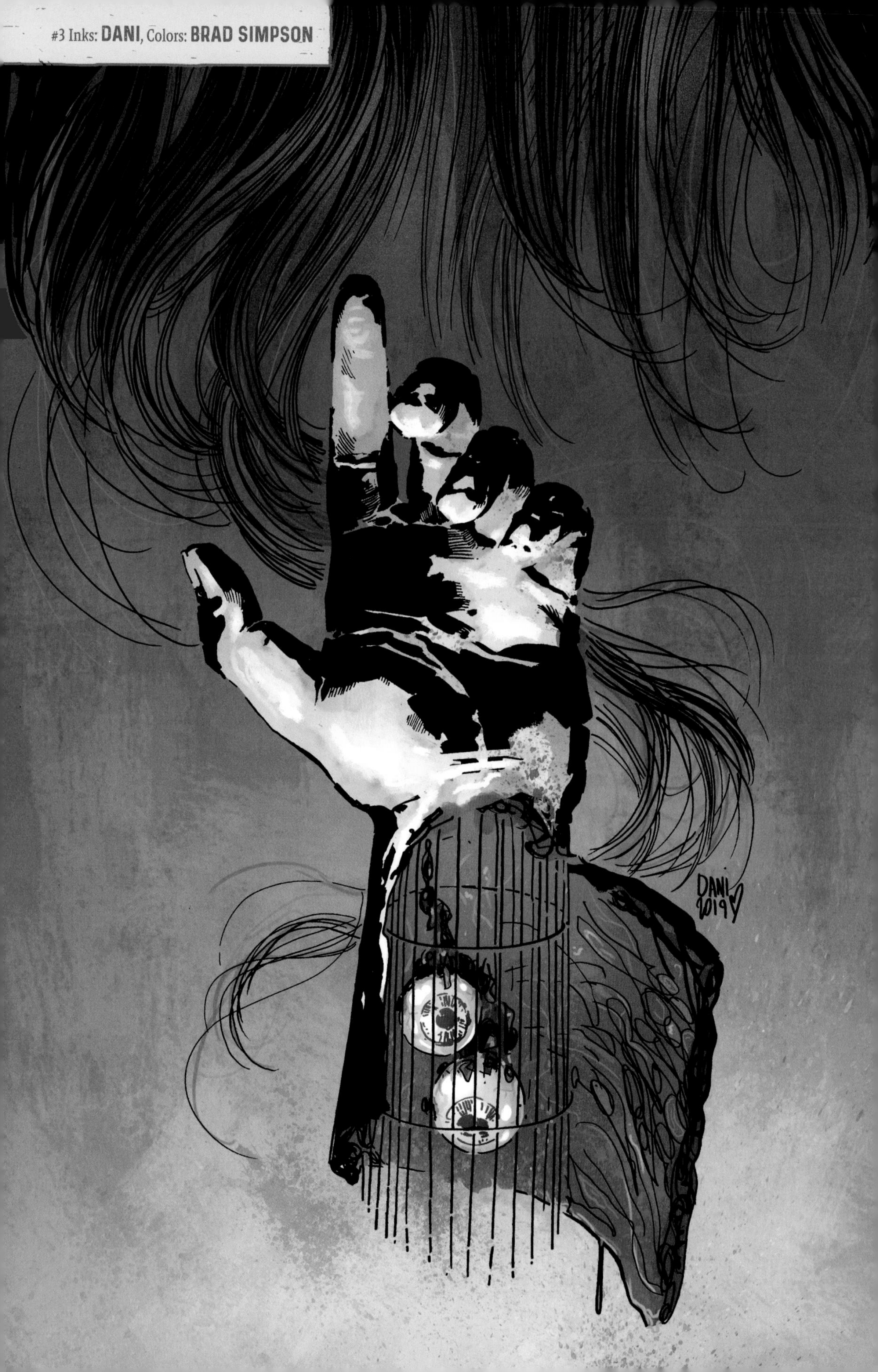
DANI
2019

#3 Inks: **DANI**, Colors: **BRAD SIMPSON**

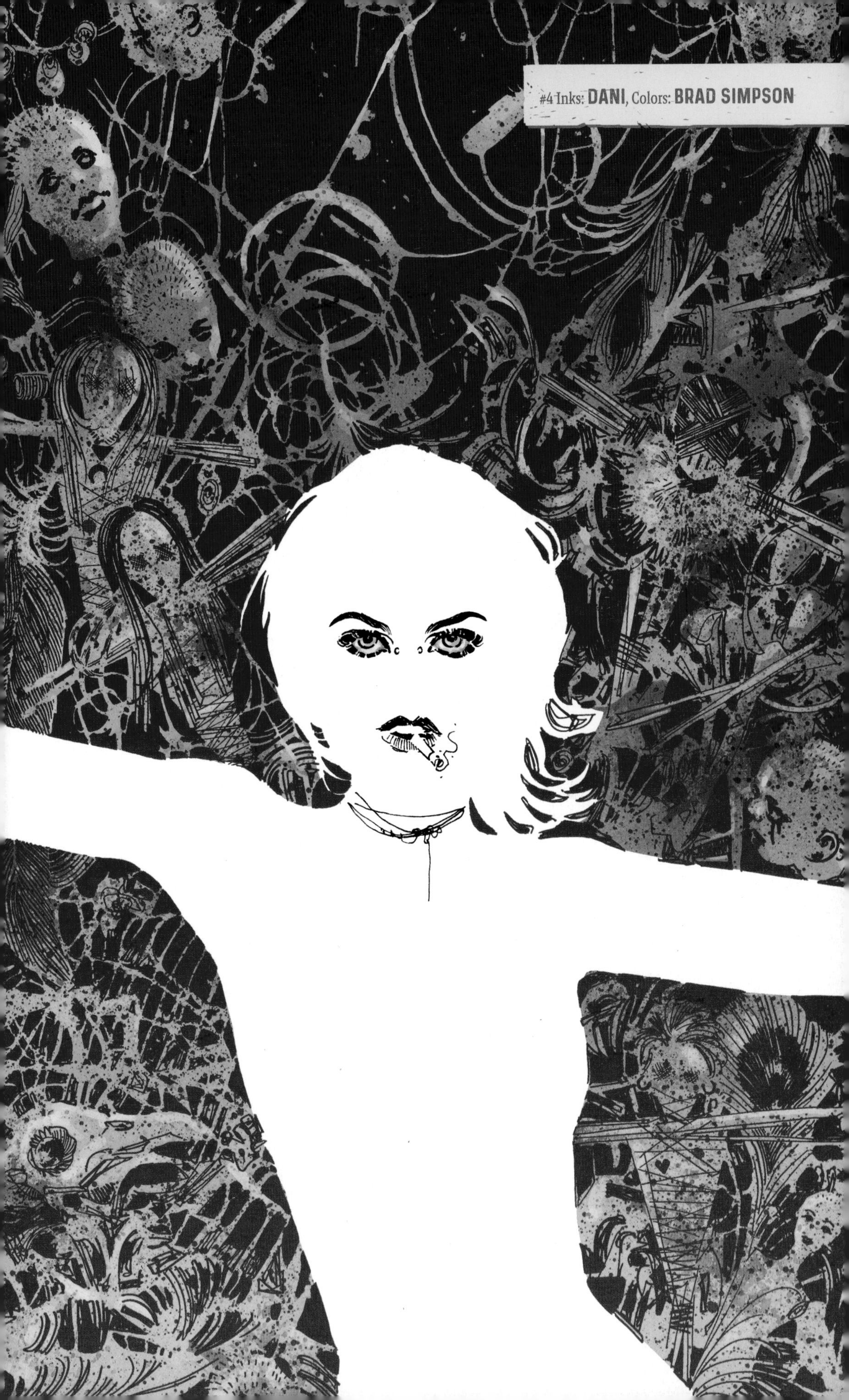

#4 Inks: **DANI**, Colors: **BRAD SIMPSON**

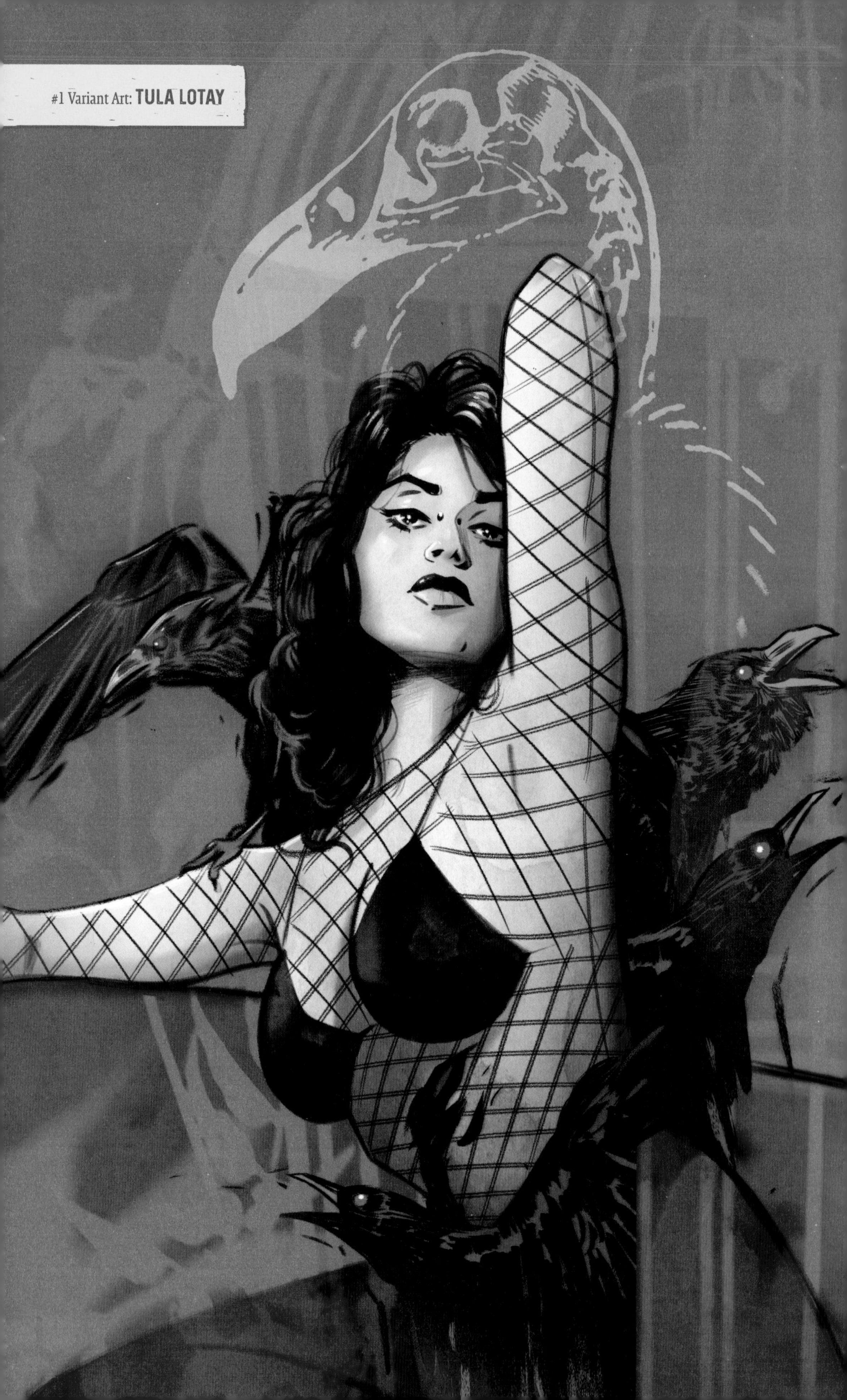

#1 Variant Art: **TULA LOTAY**

#1 Variant Art: **MIKE CHROME**

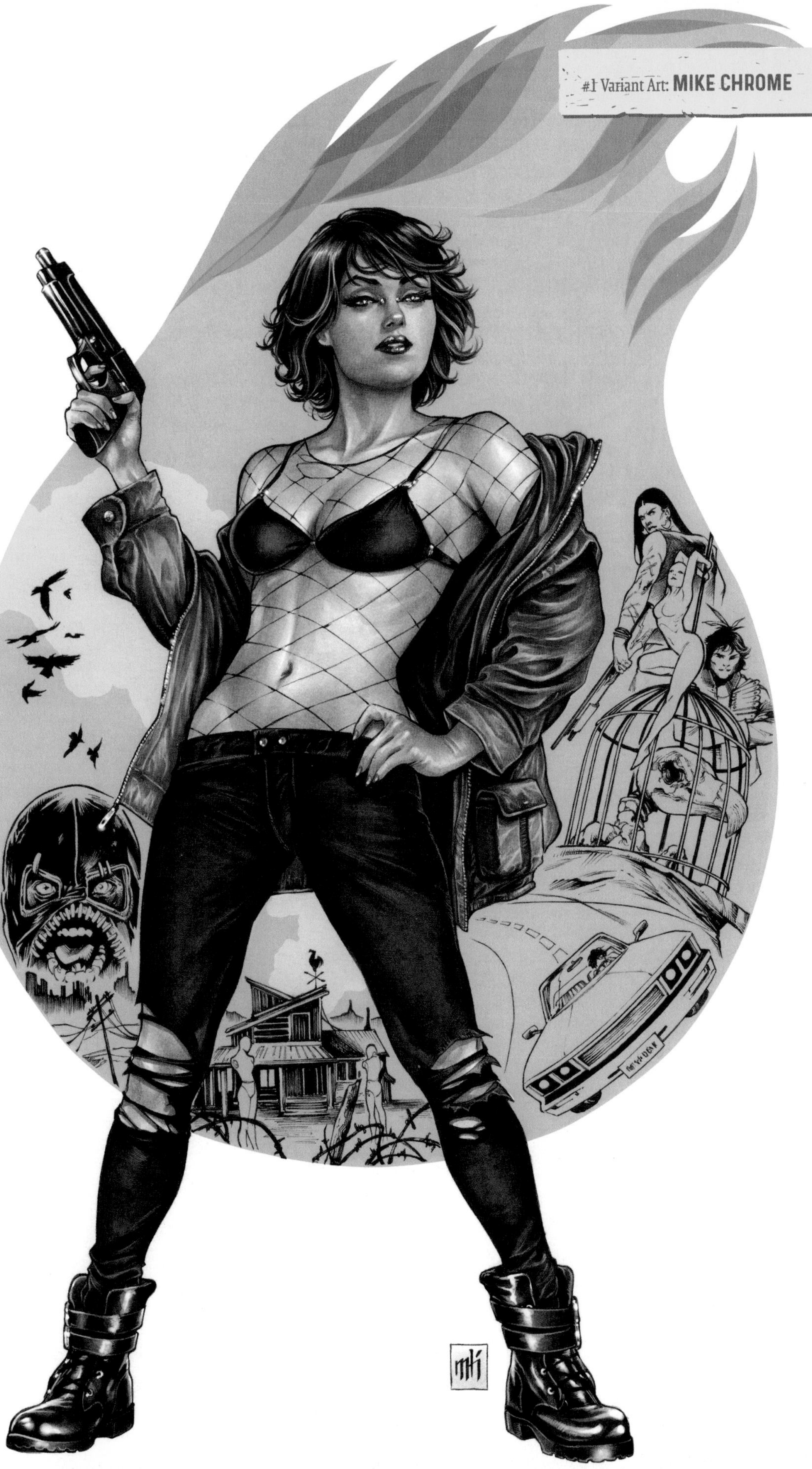

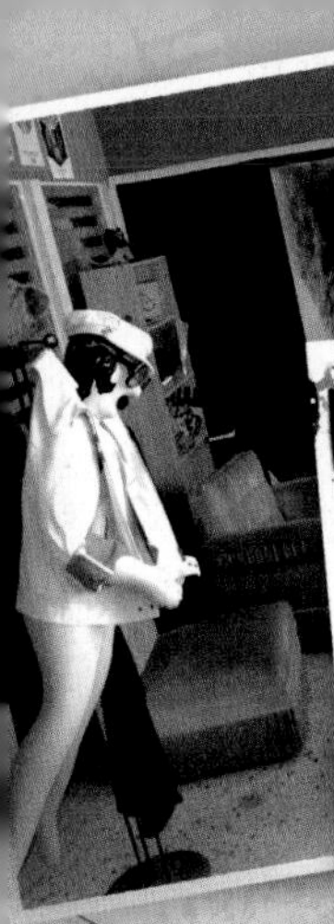

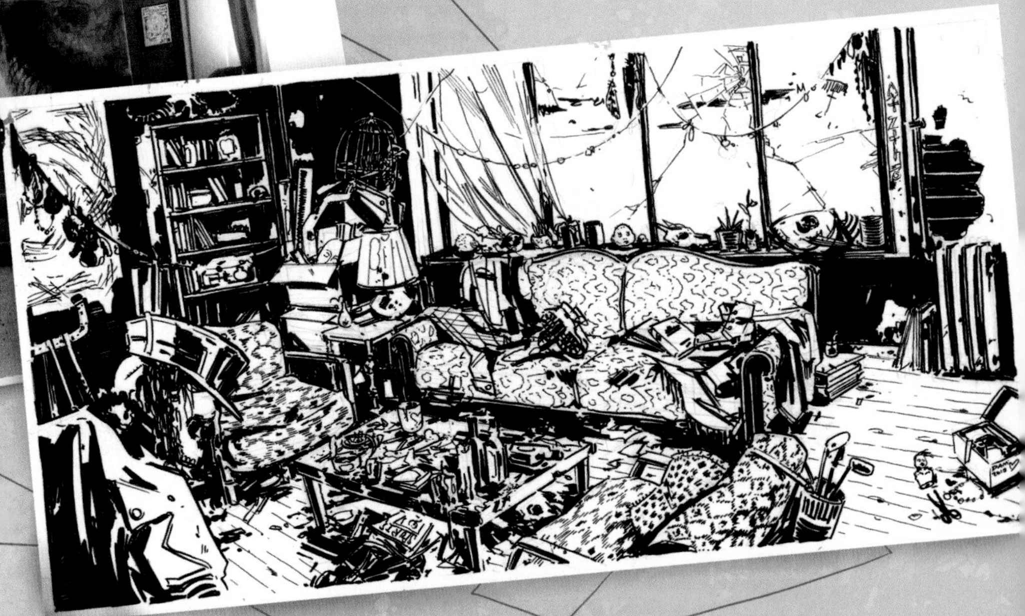

IZZY

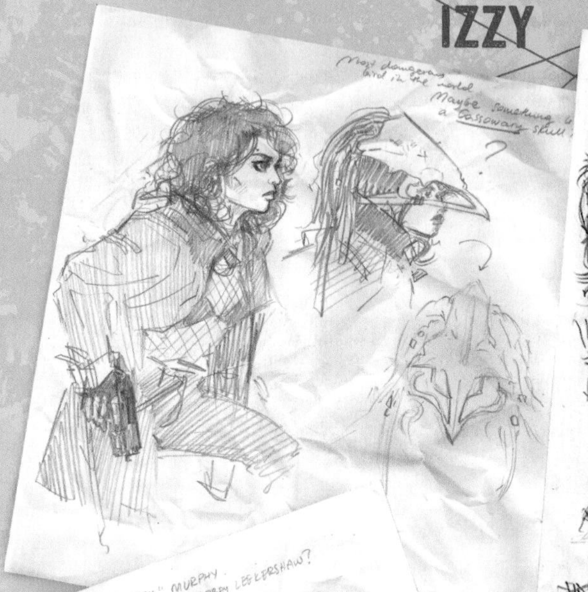
Most dangerous bird in the world
Maybe something like a Cassowary skull

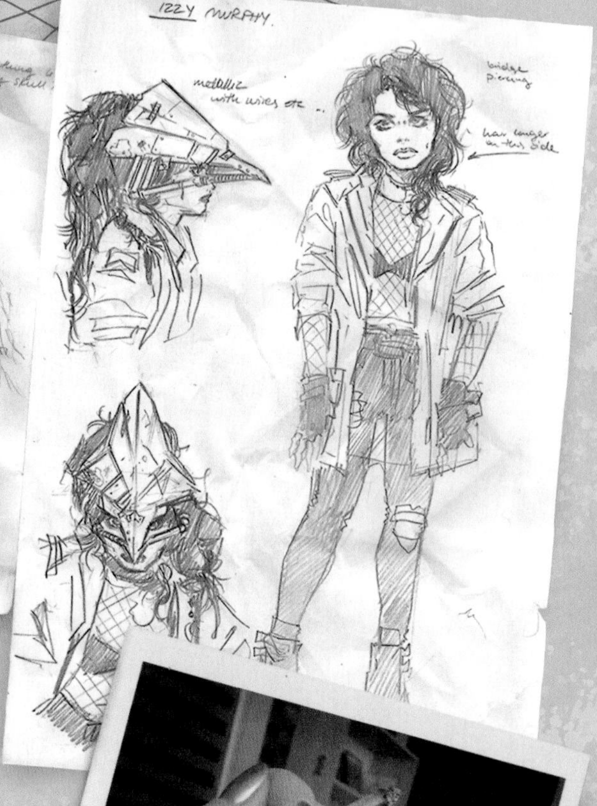
IZZY MURPHY.
metallic with wires etc..
bridge piercing
hair longer on this side

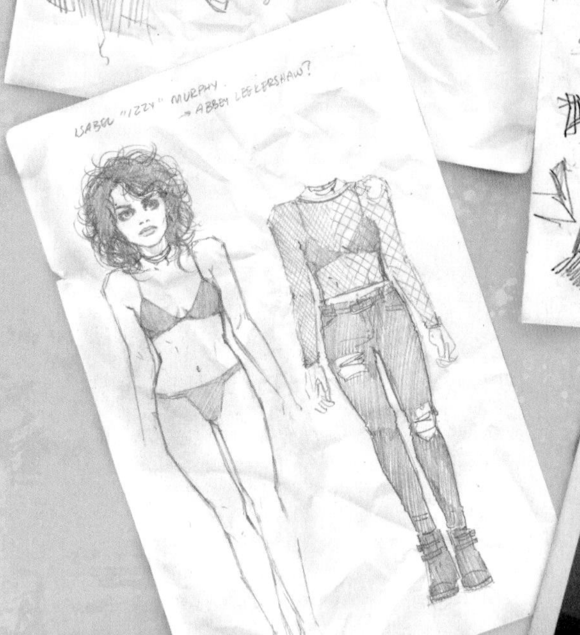
ISABEL "IZZY" MURPHY.
→ ABBEY LEEKERSHAW?

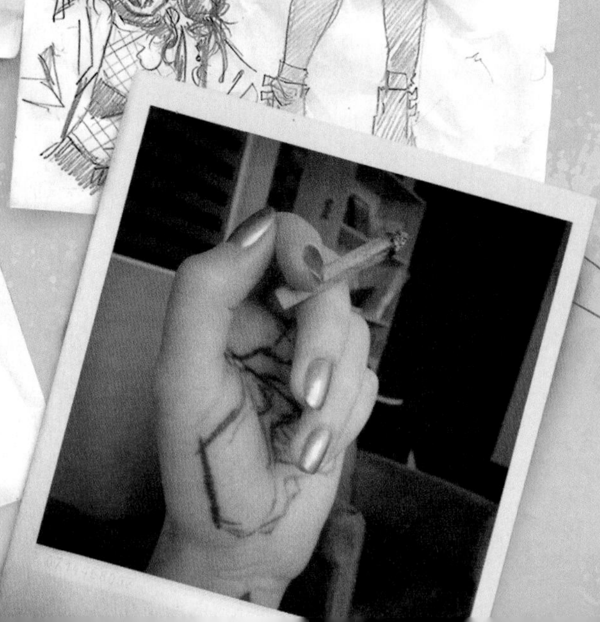

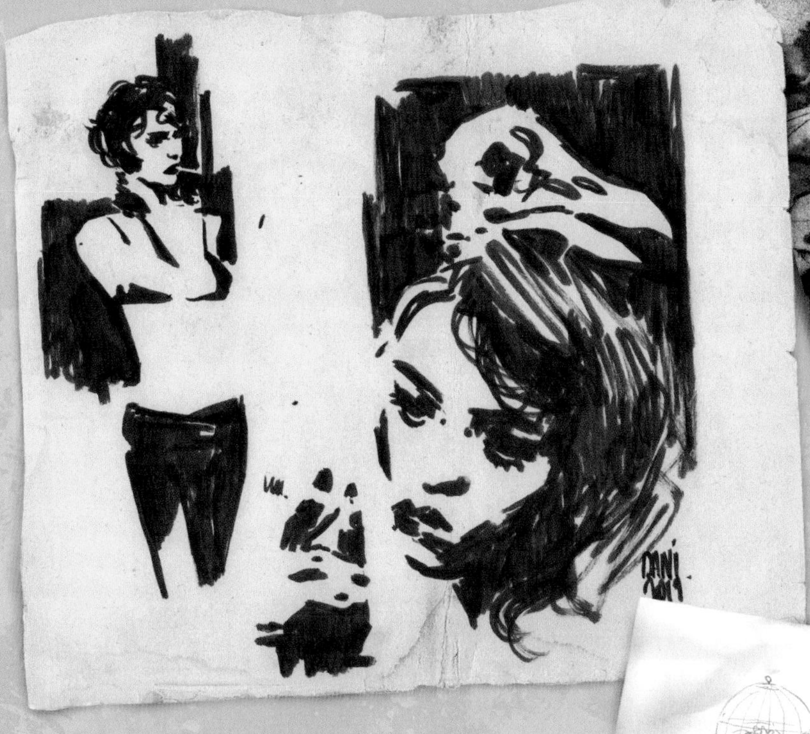

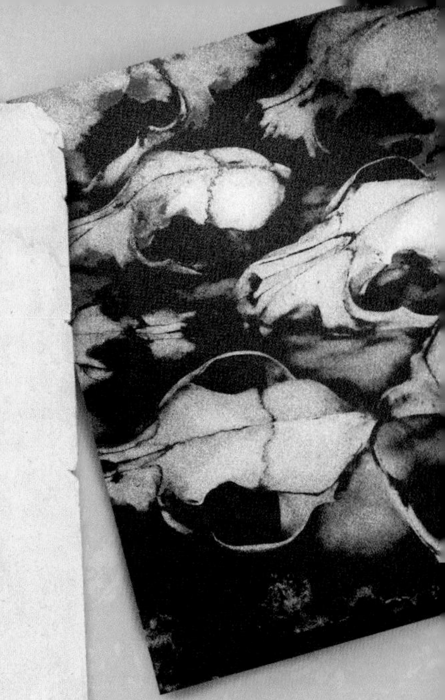

VULTURE

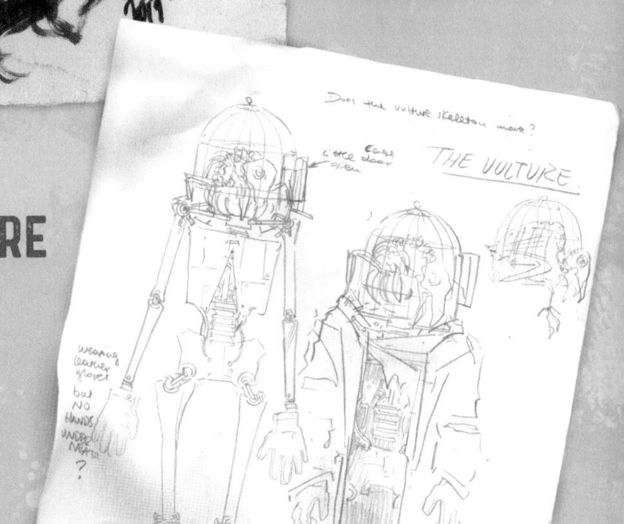
Does the vulture skeleton move?
THE VULTURE
Little cage door open
wearing leather gloves but NO HANDS underneath?
Joint broken?

CASSANDRA

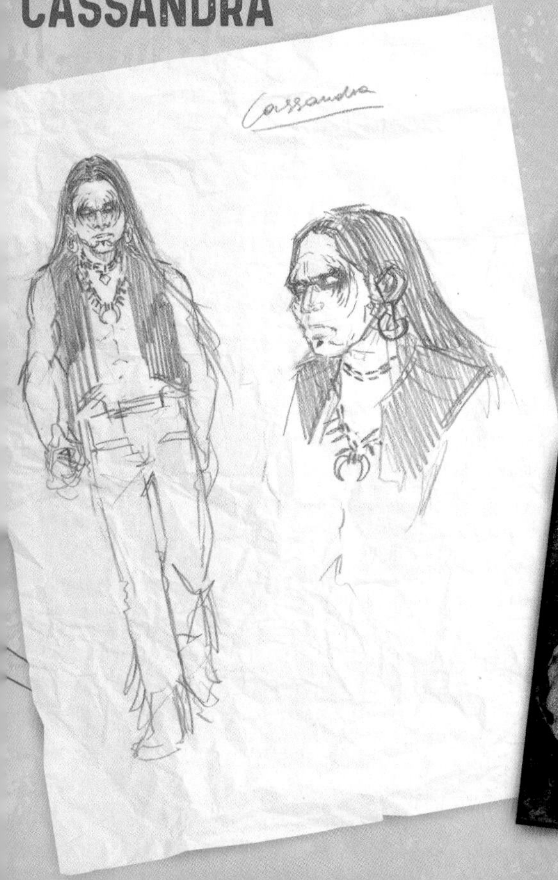
Cassandra

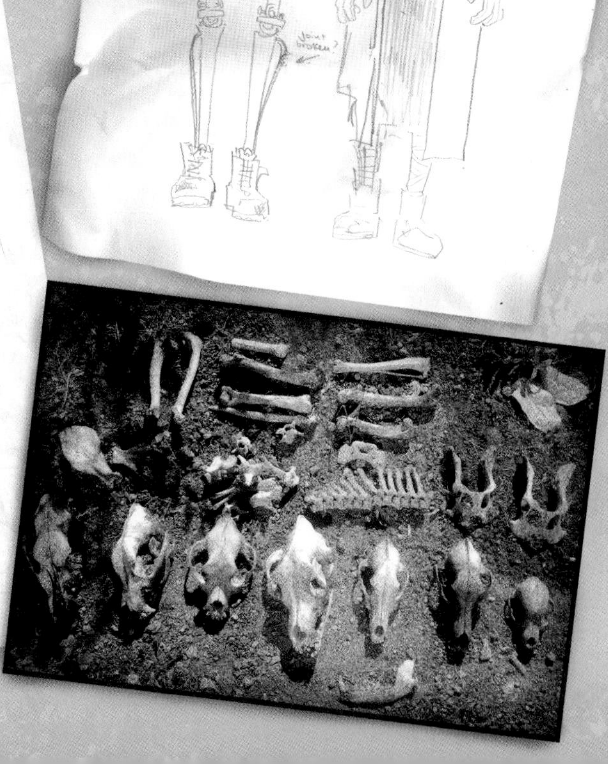

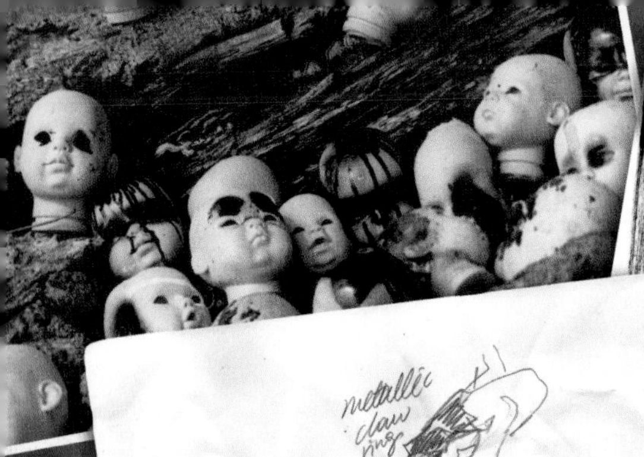

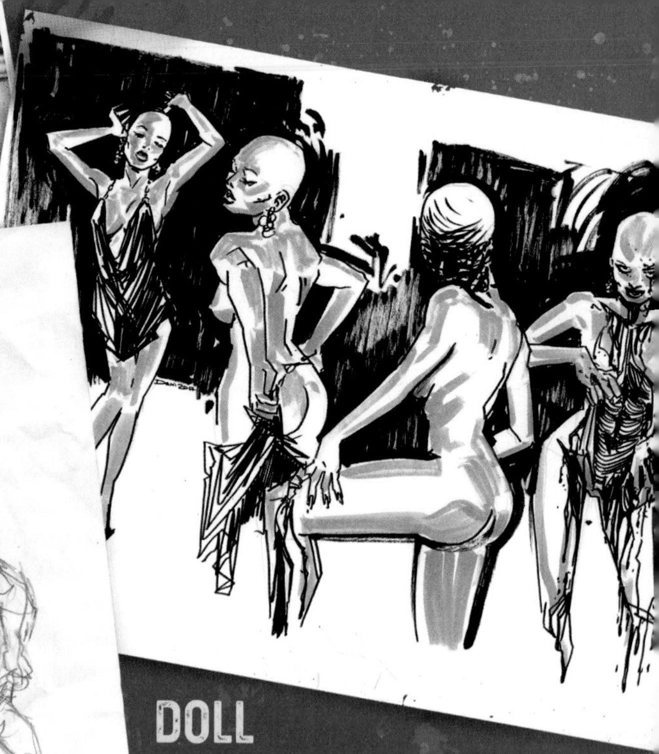

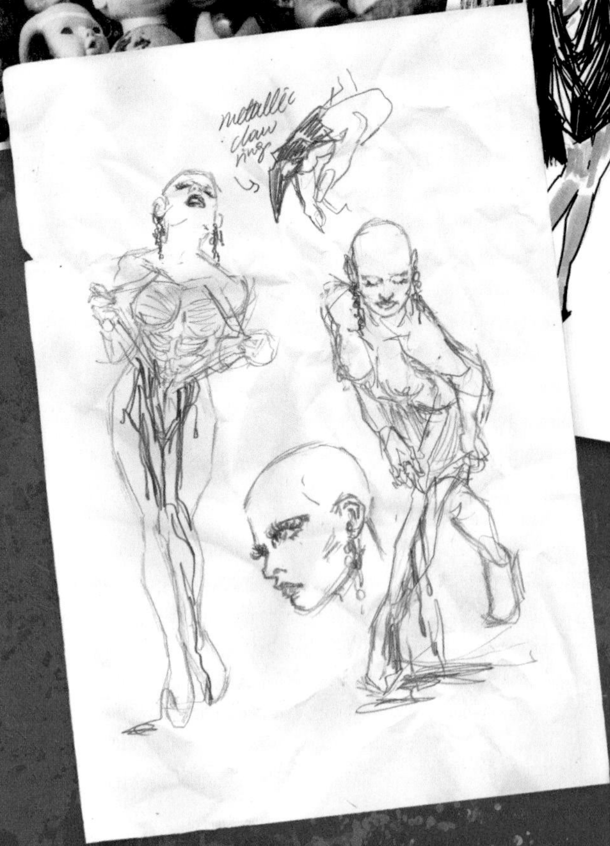
metallic claw rings

DOLL

TAQA

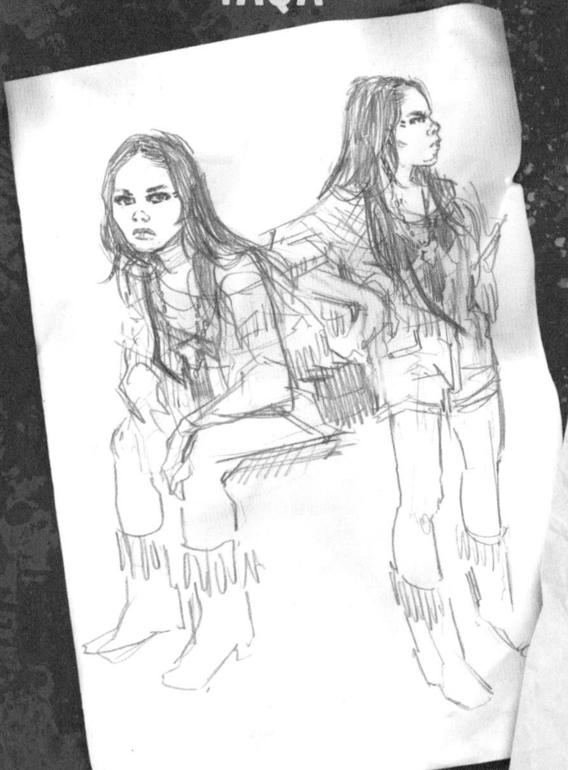

PAULIE

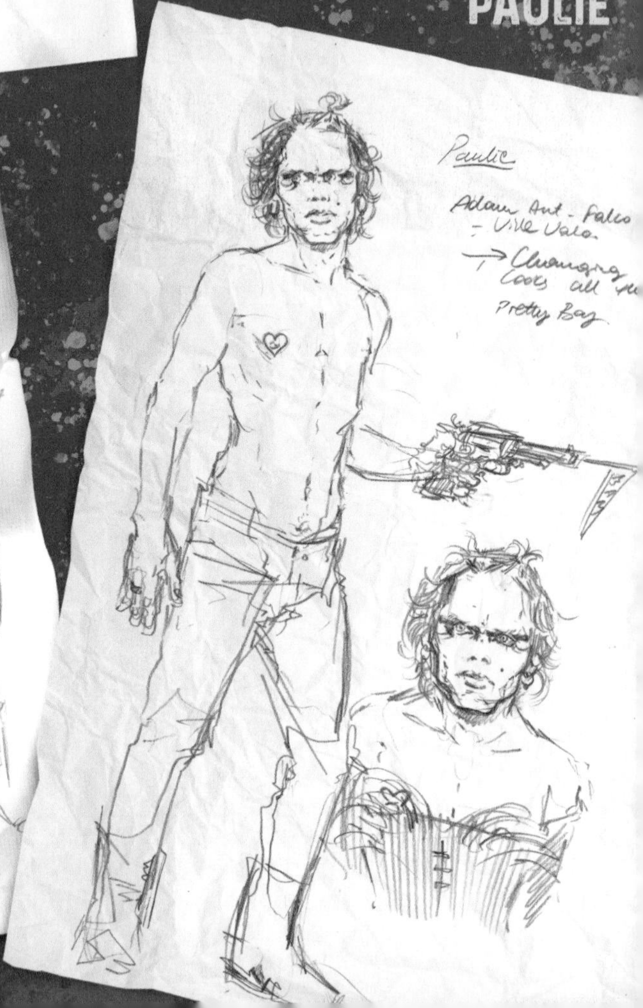
Paulie
Adam Ant - Falco
- Ville Valo.
→ Changing Looks all
Pretty Boy

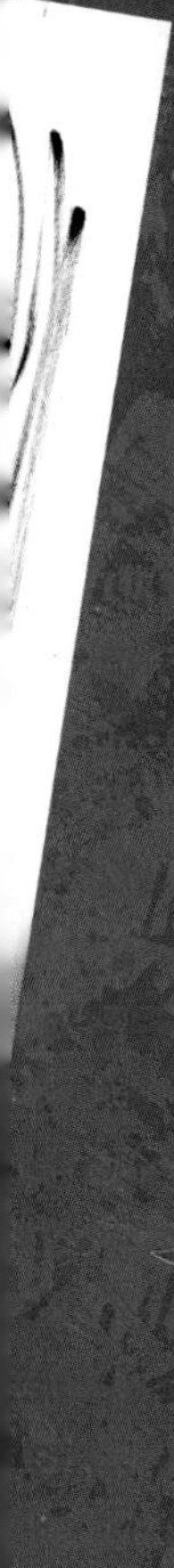

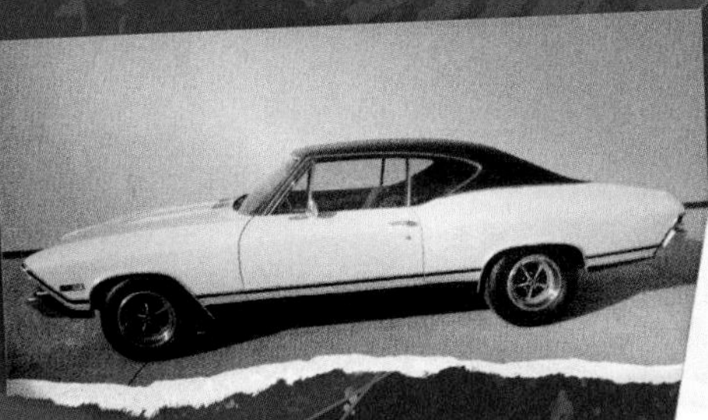

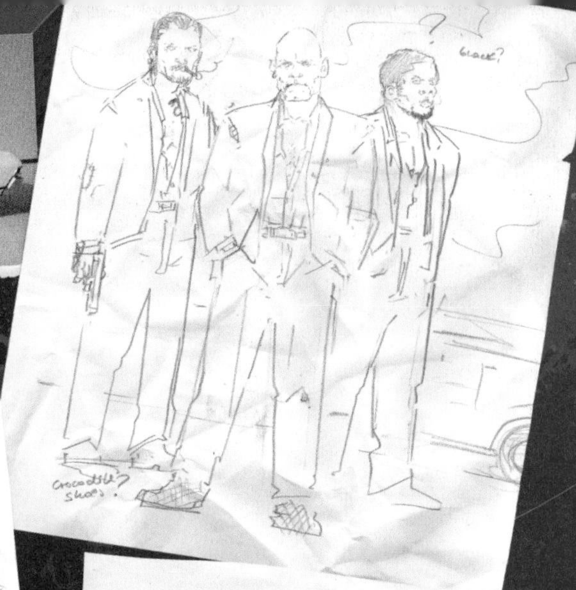

black?
crocodile? shoes?

PAULIE'S MEN

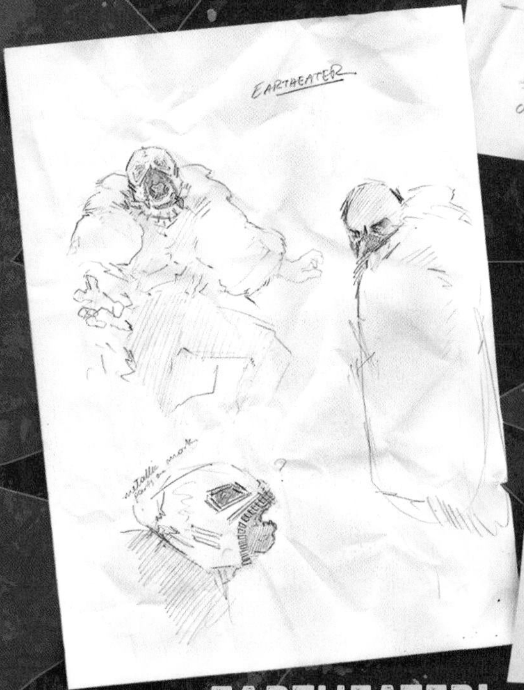

EARTHEATER
metallic parts on mask

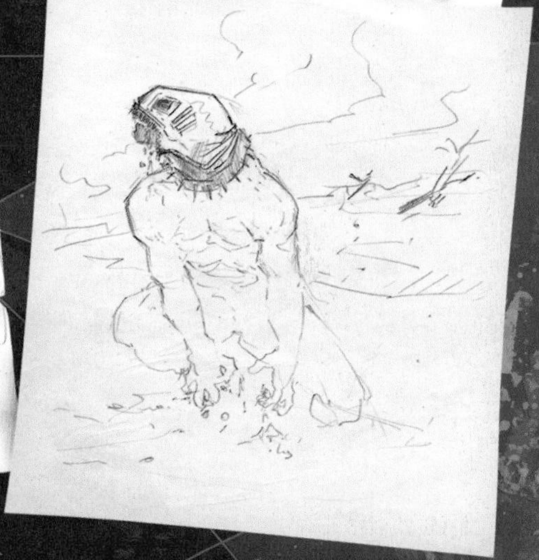

EARTHEATER!

IMPERFECTS

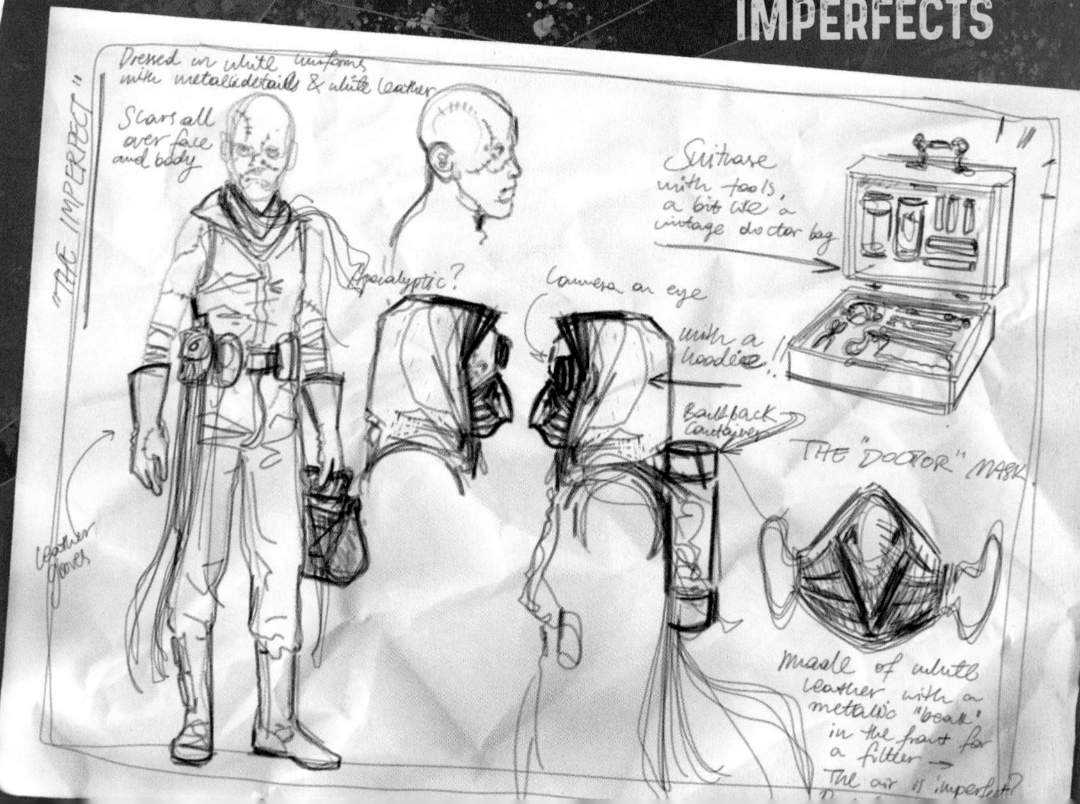

"THE IMPERFECT"
Dressed in white uniforms with metallic details & white leather
Scars all over face and body
Suitcase with tools, a bit like a vintage doctor bag
Apocalyptic?
Camera on eye
with a headset!
Backpack container
THE "DOCTOR" MASK
Leather gloves
Made of white leather with a metallic "beak" in the front for a filter →
The air is 'imperfect'?

Guest Art: **RAÚL ALLÉN**

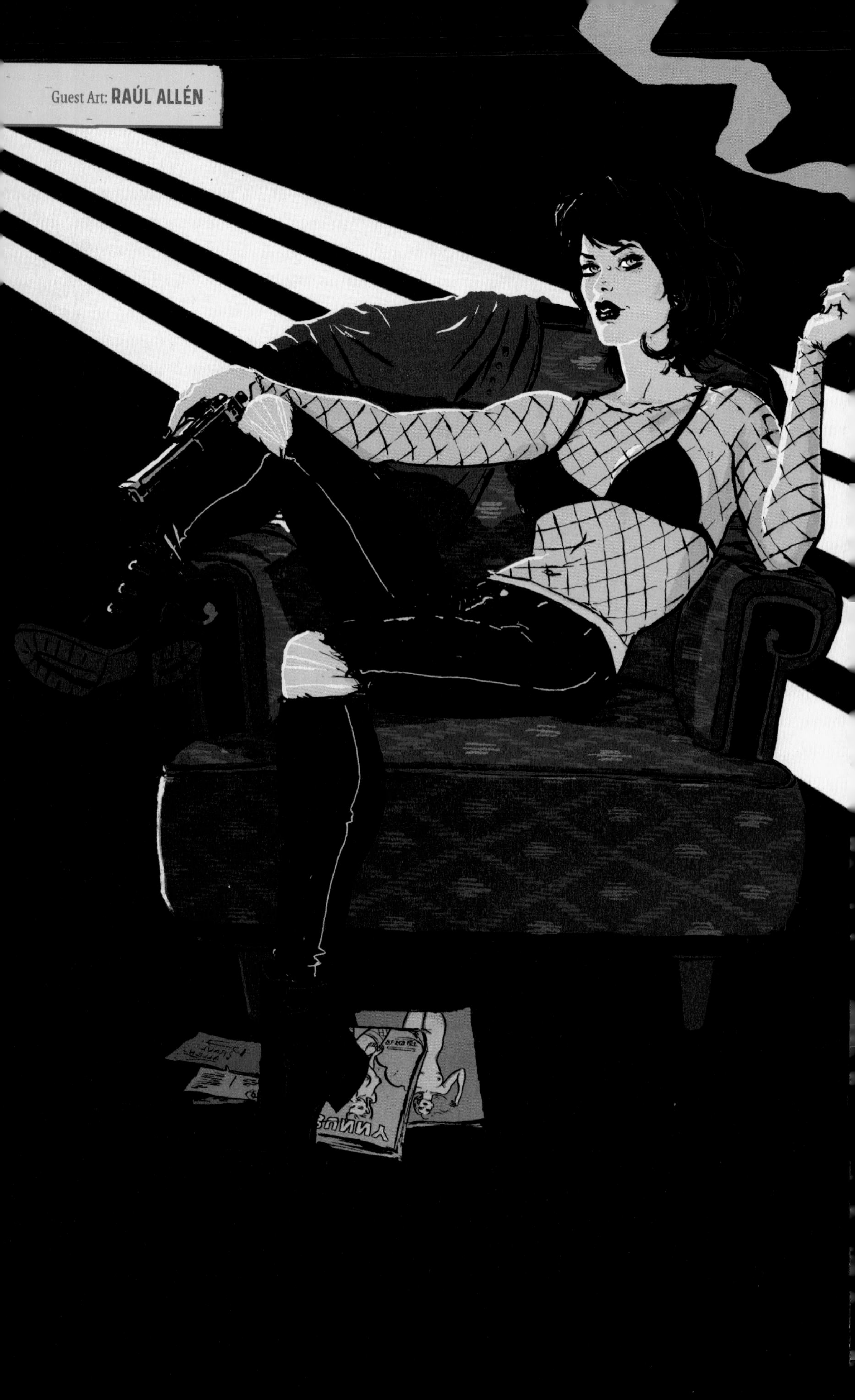
BUNNY

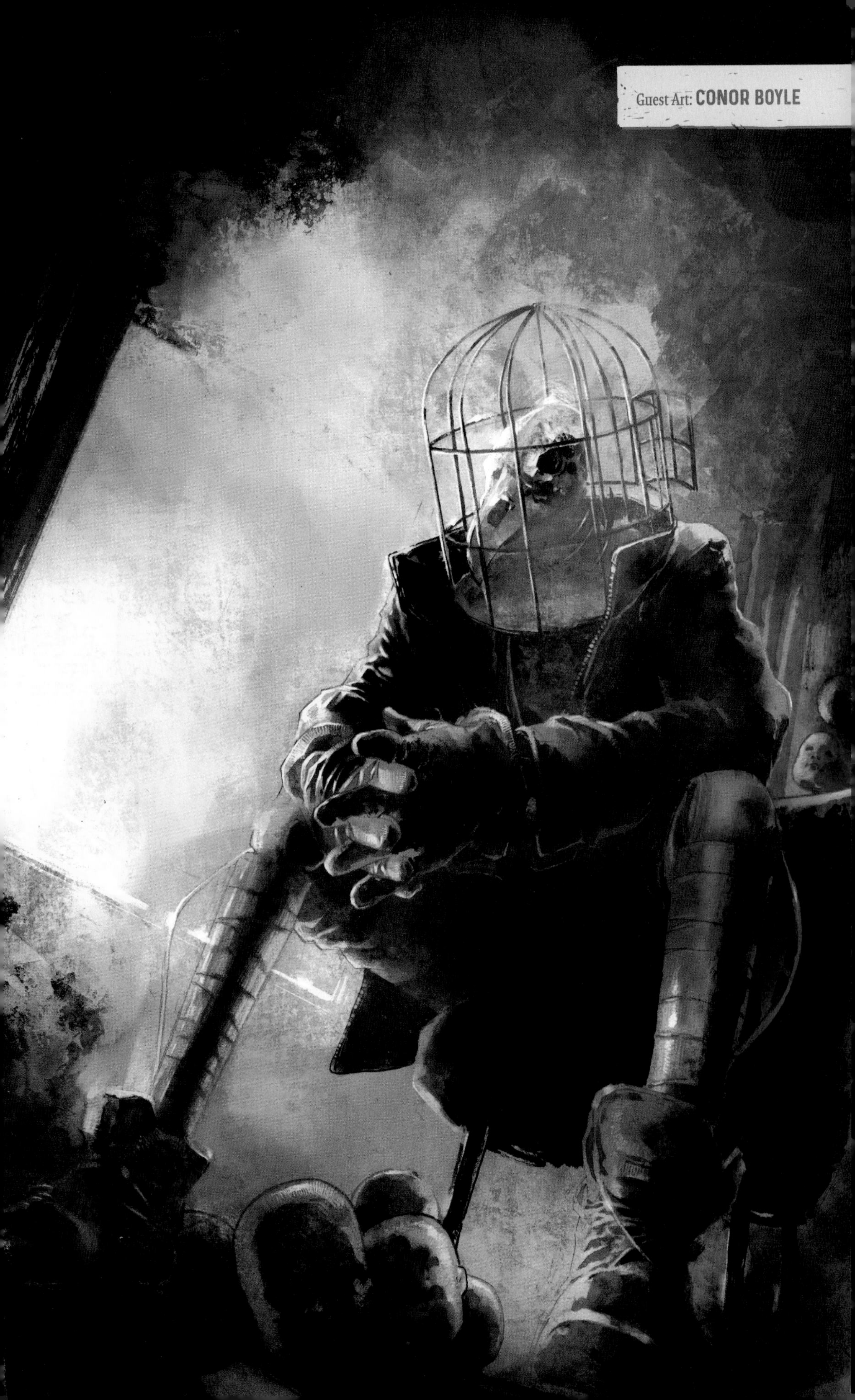
Guest Art: CONOR BOYLE

DAN

Dan Watters is a writer. He works on comic books such as *Lucifer* at Vertigo Comics, *The Picture of Everything Else* at Vault Comics, and HOME SICK PILOTS and LIMBO at Image Comics. He lives in West London with a vaguely ferocious cat, a partner, and far too many books for a West London apartment (or so he is told).

DANI

Dani was born in Athens, Greece in 1992 and studied sculpturing in Athens School of Fine Arts. She has worked for 2000AD, IDW, Vault Comics, Legion M, BOOM! Studios, DC Vertigo, and DC Hill House Comics. She loves her cats and travelling around the world.

BRAD

Brad Simpson's distinct color art has appeared in numerous titles including *The Amazing Spider-Man*, *30 Days of Night*, and in the current monthly series *Bloodborne*. He resides in Ashland, Oregon, with his wife, Sarah, and sons, Clive and Maddox. When he is not on a deadline, he enjoys anticipating future deadlines.

ADITYA

Aditya Bidikar is an award-winning letterer for comics like ISOLA, LITTLE BIRD, *These Savage Shores*, *Hellblazer*, and many more. He is also occasionally a writer and an editor. He lives in India surrounded by comics.

EMMA

Emma Price is a multidisciplinary graphic designer and illustrator. Her comics credits include Image Comics' SAVAGE TOWN and ANGELIC, Vertigo's *Motherlands*, and Aftershock Comics' *Stronghold*. She's also been the creative lead on digital campaigns for movies such as *Thor Ragnarok* and *Atomic Blonde*. But nothing compares to her latest creation: an 18 month old goblin.